CAR LAUNCH

The Human Side of Managing Change

THE LEARNING HISTORY LIBRARY

Series Editors

George Roth
Art Kleiner

CAR LAUNCH

The Human Side of Managing Change

George Roth

Art Kleiner

New York   Oxford
Oxford University Press
2000

Oxford University Press

Oxford   New York
Athens   Auckland   Bangkok   Bogotá   Buenos Aires
Calcutta   Cape Town   Chennai   Dar es Salaam   Delhi   Florence   Hong Kong
Istanbul   Karachi   Kuala Lumpur   Madrid   Melbourne   Mexico City   Mumbai   Nairobi
Paris   São Paulo   Singapore   Taipei   Tokyo   Toronto   Warsaw

and associated companies in
Berlin   Ibadan

Published by Oxford University Press, Inc.
198 Madison Avenue, New York, New York 10016
http://www.oup-usa.org

Library of Congress Cataloging-in-Publication Data
Roth, George, 1957–
Car Launch: the human side of managing change / George Roth, Art Kleiner
p. cm - - (The learning history library)
includes bibliographical references and index
ISBN 0-19-512946-6 (cloth)
1. Automobile industry and trade—Management Case studies.
2. Industrial project management Case studies. I. Kleiner, Art II. Title. III. Series.
HD9710.A2 R67 1999
629.2'068'4 -- dc21   99 - 23938
                                                                              CIP

9 8 7 6 5 4 3 2 1

Printed in the United States of America
on acid-free paper

CONTENTS

This section of Car Launch *introduces the executives and managers at AutoCo, a major automobile company, who decided to build on their interest in systems thinking and create a car launch that actually got the vehicle into the market without unnecessary stress and burnout.*

This section shows how the Epsilon car launch team gradually discovered themselves facing an unprecedented challenge. To achieve "hard" (high-quality technical) results, they would have to put into practice a "soft" conceptual approach, based on good communication, openness, honesty, trust, and superior relationships within the team.

Chapter 3: Setting an Example of Non-Authoritarian Leadership   41

The two senior-most managers within the Epsilon launch team were praised, repeatedly, for their change in behavior. They not only said they believed in openness and honesty, but acted in ways that showed they believed in the value of those principles. In this chapter, Epsilon team members described the impact this had on them, on the project, and on the managers themselves—and the devastating consequences of occasional slipbacks into old forms of heavy-handed management.

Chapter 4: Learning Labs: Teaching Techniques for Thinking Differently   53

In this chapter, participants in the learning labs conducted by MIT researchers describe their experiences. How much did the labs improve their capabilities, and how much did those improvements affect their work on the car? Finally, how much did they feel the learning lab techniques affected their attitudes about learning and work? The design and practice of the labs themselves is also covered in a way that can help any other team see the possibilities and some of the pitfalls.

Chapter 5: Combining Engineering Innovation with Human Relations: The Harmony Buck   73

An innovation developed by the Epsilon team, the harmony buck, has become standard practice at AutoCo. This is a new form of development prototype, in which engineers from different specialized component groups can fit and test their parts on a common model, early in the process and explore joint issues and problems. This chapter suggests that cross-functional innovations are possible because of two factors: a willingness to break established methods, and tangible opportunities to collaborate across functional lines.

Chapter 6: Partnerships

This chapter focuses on two outstanding efforts to develop close partnership relationships inside and outside the Epsilon team. These two innovations, a market research clinic and a collocation effort, show how physically changing the infrastructure is not sufficient in itself. It's also necessary to develop new habits and attitudes.

Chapter 7: Process Innovation in the Context of a Large Organization

As the Epsilon leaders came to feel isolated from the rest of the AutoCo culture, they dealt with conflicting and mixed signals from their AutoCo bosses. They opted for a strategy of shutting themselves away, hoping that results would speak for themselves. But in the end, the leaders were disappointed; they did not get the recognition and opportunities that many people felt they deserved and they left the company. This chapter explores why, and how, innovative teams and their executive leaders might develop more effective relationships.

COMMENTARIES

*In these chapters, leading management thinkers consider the
AutoCo Epsilon story from three critical theoretical perspectives.
From the standpoint of organizational learning, MIT lecturer
Peter Senge (author of* The Fifth Discipline*) describes the way
this story illuminates the natural cycle of growth for corporate
innovation. Rosabeth Moss Kanter of the Harvard Business School
offers a strategist's view of the opportunities and pitfalls that
faced the Epsilon team—and its lessons about sustaining feasible
change from the middle levels of a hierarchy. Finally, George
Roth of MIT and the University of New Hampshire draws upon
the insights of action science pioneer Chris Argyris to ask:
Where are the limits placed on innovation by management
defensiveness? And how can that defensiveness be broached?*

PREFACE

The document you are about to read was created to help teams of people learn from other teams' experiences. It's the first of a series of a new kind of case history—the "learning history," told by the people who directly took part in a critical organizational story.

Product launches are recurring situations in present-day corporations. Almost like an extended rite of passage, they involve dozens of people in feverishly creative, deeply collective work on a project with highly uncertain prospects. At AutoCo, the pseudonym of a major automobile manufacturer, the launch of a new car or truck brings together 200–300 full-time engineers (and almost 2,000 part-timers) for a single project. They work together intensively for three or four years, consumed with the need to create a vehicle together, wrangling over every technical detail. In her book *Car*, which is an anatomy of a car launch at the Ford Motor Company, Mary Walton describes the kinds of questions that launch engineers deal with:

> Would the metal "make," that is to say, would it bend into the shapes the designers wanted, rather than split or fall short? Metal stamping was a black art. It took years of experience to understand the mysteries of how metal flowed under pressure. . . . Would the engine fit under the hood? Were the doors thick enough to house the wiring and hardware for the power locks, power windows, and speakers, along with the new steel beam and foam padding required of all cars for 1997 for side impact protection? Could people get in and out without banging their heads? Would the body shape reduce wind noise?[1]

Most of these questions demand highly cross-functional solutions, in an environment so fragmented according to functional lines that AutoCo people routinely talk about being trapped in their "stovepipes" and "chimneys." On any typical car launch, electrical and fuel-handling system engineers must work hand-in-hand with body engineers, who, in turn, must work with the engineers responsible for the traction and handling of the car. All of them must keep closely in touch with the finance people, who track the costs of new components and their impact on the car's ultimate price. Yet despite their intimacy on the job, each of these functional groups reports to a different boss outside the project. Engineers report to engineering groups, finance people to finance groups, and human resource managers to the HR staff. Rarely are teams, anywhere, so deeply interconnected and yet so completely separated. It's as if the cocoon of the car launch contains not one but several dozen different caterpillars, each for a different kind of butterfly, which must all come together to create a composite, ultimate winged creature that will emerge and take flight.

The tension from the clash among functions helps explain why car launches are such painful processes. And it explains why one particular car launch at AutoCo, the Epsilon project, was significant. The story of Epsilon (also a pseudonym) began in the early 1990s when executives gave final approval for Epsilon's development budget. The styling, market positioning, and expenditures were already set. The program was already many weeks behind schedule. At the same time, "process improvement" as an endeavor was beginning to gain importance and attention at AutoCo. Making a great car wasn't enough; you also had to improve AutoCo's process capabilities.

The Epsilon leaders were veterans of previous, arduous "heroic" car launches. They resolved that this time, it would be different. Instead of undermining each other (and other parts of the car) in obvious and subtle ways, the cross-functional team would work together. When the deadline for the launch approached, they would not fall into the same old "heroic effort" frame of mind, when they worked prodigious hours, slept at the assembly plant, and spent large sums of money on the last-minute fixes. Most of all, this time there would not be the colossal wastes of time and money that occur from unnecessary rework; they would solve their problems early by being more open about them. And if they could accomplish all that, perhaps they would create a groundbreaking car, one that would galvanize the industry.

They accomplished many of their aspirations through a variety of innovative approaches. They integrated program management and training, so that all work on the car could involve systems thinking and collaboration. Early efforts were focused on bridging the barriers between functions: creating a shared vision of the new vehicle, collocating engineers in one large multi-functional building, and bringing design engineers in to the market research process at an early stage. As the team progressed, they caught up on their schedule. The Epsilon metrics, the generally accepted basis for success or failure at AutoCo before a car went to market, ascended from low initial levels to top-of-the-mark scores. Eventually, Epsilon set new company records for prototype-build parts availability and quality.

The Epsilon program completed its assignment at the end of 1994. The vehicle launch, which took place a week earlier than scheduled, was truly a "non-event," without the crisis atmosphere that normally leads to legions of engineers camping out at the manufacturing plant. However, the Epsilon results also included controversy. The launch coincided with organizational changes at AutoCo, in which Epsilon team leaders did not receive accolades for their accomplishments. As team members were assigned to new positions, some wondered if their efforts were valued or appreciated. Yes, they had broken performance records, but they had also broken some behavioral norms. For example, reports of problems had been deliberately brought to the surface earlier than usual. This had saved money and improved quality in the long run but had also led to the appearance that the Epsilon program was "out of control."

Moreover, when it reached the market, the Epsilon was not a groundbreaking car, at least not in the conventional sense. For one thing, it had been handicapped by its original mandate. The AutoCo Epsilon was to be an expensive luxury car, but it emerged into a market saturated by other luxury cars: Lexuses, Infinitis, Acuras, Mercedes, BMWs, Lincolns, New Yorkers, and Cadillacs were all crowding into the same growing, but still narrow, market. Some people at AutoCo still argue that the Epsilon never made much of a contribution or had much of an influence because it ultimately sold poorly. Others, at AutoCo and other companies, point to the Epsilon as the first car launch which—despite its lack of market success—visibly showed how much can be gained, not just from improving technological capability, but from improving human capability.

In other words, while they did not create a groundbreaking car, they arguably created a groundbreaking car launch process. They created a product launch with heart: fueled not just by car peoples' passion for the product, but by the managers' compassion and care for all the people involved. This meant not just developing new management techniques and a "systemic" understanding of their work, but recreating their relationships with one another and with the rest of the company.

It also meant developing a new partnership between automobile managers and academic researchers—in this case, from the Massachusetts Institute of Technology (MIT) Center for Organizational Learning. The project from which this learning history is drawn began in the summer of 1991, when senior managers from Epsilon and MIT researchers agreed to explore how Epsilon might incorporate tools for systems thinking, improving mental models and nurturing personal and shared vision into its product development process. The approach used by Epsilon to deepen and accelerate team learning is a synthesis of individual approaches that evolved from more than 20 years of research at MIT, Harvard, and elsewhere (and described in detail by Peter Senge in his book *The Fifth Discipline*). Elements had been applied within consulting practice, yet it had never been "tested" in a multi-year, practical work setting. The researchers envisioned creating "managerial practice fields" to enable people working together to periodically step back, reflect, talk together, and thereby deepen their understanding of the systemic nature of pressing problems. They hoped to establish practice fields that would serve Epsilon's managers' desire to improve cost, timing, and quality and allow them to study how practicing managers developed new collective learning capabilities.

The AutoCo learning history is one outcome of that study. Its purpose is to put episodes like the AutoCo Epsilon car launch in perspective, so other businesspeople can draw their own conclusions and develop more innovative approaches without having to reinvent some of the "wheels" that Epsilon's managers invented.

Learning histories are a new approach for transferring learning from innovative team efforts within and between organizations. The learning history work is part of a larger research effort on fostering collective learning—conducted at the MIT Sloan School of Management and the Society for Organizational Learning (SoL), an international multi-disciplinary consortium based in Cambridge, MA. (The learning history form was developed, in part, to help assess and evaluate projects like AutoCo Epsilon.) Learning history documents (and the group processes which have been developed for using these documents) have evolved, during the ensuing years, into a form of assessment that aims, in itself, to develop and strengthen collective learning capabilities during the process of evaluation, by helping people throughout an organization (and outside, in business schools) build the kind of judgment they need to assess and evaluate innovation for themselves.

From the beginning, you will see that this document does not resemble a conventional case study. For one thing, it is not just intended to be read by individuals. It is a tool for collective learning and for ongoing study and practice. The unusual two-column format allows for more in-depth group discussion by putting the "ground truth" of the story, as told by participants, side-by-side with key questions and perspectives. Reading the Epsilon story you will "hear" the team members reflect upon the impact of their innovations. Each will speak from his or her own perspective, telling his or her own part of the story. With access to these multiple voices and multiple perspectives, you don't have to accept any particular "moral" to the story; rather, you can come up with (and develop) your own understanding of the reasons why things happened this way and how they could affect your own endeavors.

The AutoCo Epsilon story, for example, contains a great deal of frustration and misunderstanding. Relationships between the senior Epsilon team leaders and their bosses, higher in the corporate hierarchy, start out uncomfortable and never evolve into unqualified mutual support. The team leaders never get the reputation that they hoped to achieve as innovators. The team's successes are questioned; its results are pooh-poohed. As readers, you can see this pattern unfold, you can recognize some of the reasons why it happened, and you can develop your own theory about building effective engagement between corporate management and innovative pilot teams.

That also explains why the company's name is disguised (AutoCo), why a fictionalized project name is used (Epsilon), and why all characters in the learning history are identified only by their titles. The company, program, and people are disguised to provide anonymity, protect AutoCo's need for confidentiality, minimize distraction, and help the reader to focus his or her attention on the universal themes herein.

Because they knew their anonymity would be respected, participants spoke freely; because the company is never formally identified, people can see this story for what it is: a typical example of corporate and organizational life. You can rest assured, however, that the story is true, that all statements were made by participants in the story, and that all quotes were rigorously validated—checked with the interviewees to ensure validity. Reading someone's account of an event, you might reasonably be skeptical that it actually happened that way; but you cannot dispute the fact that someone cared enough to describe the event a particular way and cared enough again to reaffirm their language when it was checked.

As a genre of business literature, the learning history rewards the intensive involvement of its readers. Organizations that commission learning histories do not merely assign them as reading; they establish working groups, like book reading groups, to consider the story's implications in light of the group members' own concerns.

"Here's a segment," a discussion group leader might say, "in which Epsilon developed an innovative new relationship with market research. What does this suggest about the subtle ramifications of our own company's market research?" As they talk about their own insights, and the differences in the assumptions and attitudes underlying them, the group members co-create their own collective understanding of their own situation, based on the narrative of the learning history.

If the Epsilon story is meaningful to you, you may find it valuable to establish a "book group" of your own—a group of people who meet several times, each time visiting a different part of the story in the context of your own issues and priorities. (We have found that it takes two or three hours, at minimum, for a group of six to eight people to consider any one of the themes in this document.) It will not necessarily be easy to meet this way. Collective learning is unexpectedly difficult. It requires ongoing study and practice, which requires a certain amount of time set aside for learning and a certain amount of support.[2] But it also yields unexpected rewards, by helping a group develop "actionable knowledge": knowledge embedded in the form of new skills, capabilities, and innovations.

Learning histories are designed around the premise that people learn not just by acquiring new techniques and information, but by understanding the context in which new techniques and information are effective. This type of context represents "reflectionable knowledge"—knowledge embedded in the form of inquiry, particularly inquiry into people's thought processes, assumptions, and perspectives.[3]

This is significant because it represents a way to deal with a perennial problem: that most "organizational learning" work does not lead to new results. As the work of Chris Argyris and Donald Schön has demonstrated, caring for people and good communication is not enough to sustain learning. People in professional and managerial situations often become defensive when asked to embrace new innovations or ideas.[4] Their existing ways of thinking and acting have been confronted, and it is difficult to suspend the attitudes that have led to past success and embrace new attitudes instead. Facing a learning history instead of an argument, however, you can consider new approaches on their own merits, in an atmosphere of reflection, with all the supporting information that you might need (such as "what they were thinking") to decide whether any new approach is worth embracing.

The process of reporting on an organization's change effort brings not just individual attitudes to the surface, but also the collective assumptions embedded in an organization's culture. As a reader of a learning history, you may find yourself embarking on a cultural journey, much like a tourist visiting a foreign country. Tourists often gain insight into their own culture by realizing, perhaps through painful embarrassment, that the tacit rules which governed behavior at home aren't universal. Foreign travel often reveals as much of one's own culture as of the culture being visited.

In the same way, hearing the stories of Epsilon's team members will help you as a reader begin to reflect on your own organizational experiences. You may start to think about the assumptions and attitudes that you take for granted in your organization or that you have never noticed before (until you became aware of the salient differences at AutoCo). You may recognize elements in the AutoCo story which are identical to aspects of your organization. And you may begin to wonder what it would be like to work on a team, like Epsilon's, that created conditions which fully engaged people in their tasks and developed an ethic of mutual learning—with and from one another.

Most of the material in the story was gathered through in-depth interviews—in which the learning historians made concerted efforts to detail how people were thinking as they applied different learning techniques. Participants were asked to tell their story of what happened and why; the learning historians then worked closely with the transcripts to develop the themes and narrative structure you see here. The resulting document builds on research traditions from oral history, action science, and qualitative social research. The Epsilon story, like all learning histories, is a "jointly told tale"—an anthropological term for a field study co-narrated by the anthropologists and the "subjects" of the study. Neither the outside "expert" learning historian, nor the people whose change process has been assessed, tell the story alone. Both groups tell the story together.

In preparing this book for publication, we have provided our readers with more than a historical account. We have included the complete Epsilon learning history as it was validated at AutoCo—and as it is used in AutoCo and other companies. The narrative is followed by analytical commentaries on the learning history written by Peter Senge, Rosabeth Moss Kanter, and George Roth. These commentaries provide insights into the case based on the authors' own research and experience in learning and change.

Why include several commentaries, instead of just one correct "explanation"? Because we recognize the complex and contextual nature of change in large corporate settings. There are no single responses or recommendations that will direct managers how to be successful in improving their own organizations.

Having multiple commentaries is meant to further encourage you, as a reader, to use the learning history in your own teams, to develop your own insights, and to apply them in your own settings. You may find yourselves disagreeing with the commentaries and with your fellow readers' assessments or conclusions. The spirited dialogue and debate that might follow are worthwhile; the idea of learning through open conversation lies at the heart of learning history methodology. In fact, we specifically suggest you avoid basing your thinking and sense-making process on the commentary of any of the "experts" (in this volume or elsewhere). Don't argue that one of the points raised in this volume is "right" or "wrong." When you find yourself making insightful statements, link them to their source—on what you read in the learning history. In what ways did you interpret it? How might others have seen it differently? Extend Epsilon's experiences to your own: How can your own everyday activities be considered in light of the AutoCo Epsilon team's experience? What actions would you and your team naturally take?

As you develop hypotheses, you can verbally test them by asking: How would your team have handled the events at AutoCo? How could your team have handled those events differently? Given the stories told by participants, what (in your view) should they do now? What issues should be considered in initiating, establishing, and sustaining an organizational learning process? What influences make it difficult to collectively learn in companies? What capabilities and factors sustain a team's learning as it interacts with the larger organizational system? How do we know when an investment in learning provides discernible business results?

By reading this learning history and discussing it as a team, we hope to help you and your organization develop new ways of seeing, thinking, and learning together. We encourage you to use the learning history to create a "transition time," a time for cultivating your judgment about past experiences, when your vision and your memory meet and you can collectively generate the possibilities for a new future. The narrative of the learning history is particularly well-suited for this, because as philosopher James Carse[5] has noted:

> Storytellers do not convert their listeners; they do not move them into the territory of a superior truth. Ignoring the issue of truth and falsehood altogether, they offer only a vision. Storytelling is therefore not combative; it does not succeed or fail. A story cannot be obeyed. Instead of placing one body of knowledge against another, storytellers invite us to return from knowledge to thinking, from a bounded way of looking to a horizontal way of seeing."

George Roth and Art Kleiner, editors

ACKNOWLEDGMENTS

As the first in a series, *Car Launch* has a great deal of precedent-setting to do. One precedent we'd like to set is appropriate acknowledgment for the people who helped this learning history process, this document, this series, and this volume become reality. In the crush of deadlines, someone important may be left out, and we hope they will excuse that oversight.

The managing editor for this volume, and for this series, is Nina Kruschwitz. She is the linchpin for the virtual organization which puts together these learning histories. An experienced learning historian in her own right and one of the developers of the form, she took on the role of production manager for this book. That meant overseeing the design and production from the authors' point of view, creating final diagrams and graphics, preparing and checking the various versions of manuscript, creating the layout of these complex pages, managing the interaction with Oxford University Press, and meeting a strict deadline. If this book shows evidence of coherence in detail and regard for readers, then Nina Kruschwitz deserves most of the credit.

Ken Macleod, academic editor at Oxford University Press, saw the potential in this series before anyone else in publishing did, and pushed with us to get it into final form. We are perennially grateful for his enthusiasm and jovial spirit, for his critical eye, and for his willingness to test the waters with a new form of case history. Others at Oxford University Press who deserve credit include Peter Ban and Roger Duthie (Ken's present and former assistants); Elyse Dubin (Manager of Editorial, Design, & Production, who focused some of her inimitable energy on the unique challenges of this new format); Production Editor Karen Shapiro (who helped us through the task of coordinating this book's unusual demands); and Oxford University Press marketers Scott Burns and Sally James.

Literary agent Joseph Spieler arranged the groundwork that made this series possible; we have been grateful for his interest, encouragement, and advice throughout. We also wish to thank Helen Basilesco of the Ford/MIT Collaboration, where George Roth is director; her day-to-day management made room for an occasional project like this to flourish on the periphery. Ben Florer and Maggie Piper provided some much-valued logistic support.

Ordinarily, we would effusively and gratefully acknowledge our colleagues at AutoCo by name—the people who helped initiate the learning history, who coauthored and coedited the document, who designed the workshops in which AutoCo people talked about it, who painstakingly helped it find funding, who championed it at all levels of the organization, and whose comments provided the substance from which we drew our intellectual understanding. We would also thank the AutoCo senior executives who recognized the value of this document, not just at AutoCo but elsewhere in the world, and who gave approval and support for its general release. We would especially acknowledge the Epsilon engineers and managers who permitted themselves to be interviewed and painstakingly made sure their quotes were accurate. They organized and implemented the Epsilon learning process described herein, working against significant odds to show AutoCo, the industry, and the rest of the world what is possible through learning.

Unfortunately, anonymity—and the agreement that allows us to make this story public—prevent us from mentioning any of these people by name. Nonetheless, we wish to offer them our heartfelt thanks and appreciation.

This learning history form, and the theories of organizational change and communication effectiveness which developed alongside it, have not come into being without challenge and colloquy. We are grateful for the support, contributions, help, and encouragement that we have received from several sources. Chief among them is the "earning historian's group," a series of workshops and critique sessions that took place under the auspices of the MIT Center for Organizational Learning. The participants in those sessions included: Ben Alexander, GS Technologies; Catalina Bajenaru, AT&T; Gary R. Becker, Federal Express; Linda Booth Sweeney,

Harvard University; Hilary Bradbury, Case Western Reserve University; Marty Castleberg; Brenda Cruz, Pacific Bell; Anthony DiBella; Janis Dutton, *The Fifth Discipline Education Fieldbook*; Faith Florer, New York University; Rik Glover, National Semiconductor; Toni Gregory, T.A. Gregory and Associates; Hugh Hodgins, Philips Display; Susan Hooker, Motorola University; Terry Johnson, National Semiconductor; Nina Kruschwitz; Kathleen Marshall; George Maxe; Dan Mlakar, Pacific Bell; Virginia O'Brien; Paul Peterson, Philips Display; Ruthann Prange, AT&T; Mary Scheetz, Orange Grove Middle School; Anne Starr, The Learning Circle; Ann Thomas; Jean Tully, Hewlett-Packard; Joe Tuttle, GS Technologies; Hugh Valleley, Harley Davidson; John Voyer, University of Maine; Diane McGinty Weston, Weston Consulting; Kenlin Wilder; and JoAnne Wyer.

The learning history form has been nurtured by the support and critical insight of a number of renowned organizational researchers, who have not hesitated to help us understand the opportunities and pitfalls that they saw in this form. All of the following people invested much-appreciated time and effort to help us move this form forward: Peter Senge, Edgar Schein, Chris Argryis, Robert Fritz, Hal Nelson, John van Maanen, John Carroll, Donald Schön, John Sterman and Karl Weick.

Our colleagues at the former MIT Center for Organizational Learning and at related organizations created an environment to try things that hadn't been tried before. We thank Daniel Kim, Bill Isaacs, Janet Gould, Ernst Diehl, Fred Kofman, Donald Seville, Robert Putnam, Louis van der Merwe, Joe Jaworski, Kaz Gozdz, and Otto Scharmer. We also wish to acknowledge the support and good cheer of the Society for Organizational Learning, the international consortium which grew out of the work of the MIT Learning Center. Stella Humphries, Sarita Chawla, Sheryl Erickson, and Judy Rodgers, have been particularly supportive and helpful. Administrators Steve Buckley, Angela Lipinski, Jane Punchard, Vicki Tweiten, and Jean Macdonald have all lent their support to the learning history process at one time or another.

There are some corporate and consulting practitioners whose conversations with us about organizational learning influenced and edified the learning history process. These include: Linda Pierce, Eric Siegel, Tim Savino, Vic Leo, Betsy Maxwell, Chuck Roe, April Flanagan, Iva Wilson, Tom Ryan, Argerie Vasilakes, Paul Monus, Judy Gilbert, Hans Houshower, Nancy Murphy, Napier Collyns, Colleen Lannon-Kim, Suzy

CAST OF CHARACTERS

ACKOFF, RUSSELL: His sessions at "AutoCo University" helped galvanize interest in systems thinking and organizational learning.

ASSEMBLY LAUNCH LEADER: A senior engineer with responsibility for the sub-team that coordinated the Epsilon effort with the external Assembly Launch Manager at the plant that would build the car.

ASSEMBLY LAUNCH MANAGER: Senior manager outside the Epsilon team responsible for the mass production of Epsilon (and other) vehicles at one of the AutoCo manufacturing plants; a longstanding AutoCo manager with strong influence over manufacturing.

AUTOCO UNIVERSITY MANAGER: A corporate staff manager responsible for sponsoring education sessions that introduced new concepts to AutoCo managers.

BODY ENGINEERING MANAGER: The manager responsible for integrating the Epsilon automobile body, he participated in some MIT sessions.

CHIEF ENGINEERING MANAGER: The manager responsible for overall engineering ("content") issues at Epsilon, he supported the learning initiative but did not play an active role in developing it.

CONTENT LEADERS: On the Epsilon team, work groups were organized around subsystems of the vehicle—electronic, interior/trim, powertrain, etc. Many of these subsystem development teams were assigned a "content leader," whose attention focused on engineering and technical concerns, and a "process leader" (see below). Several content leaders were interviewed for this learning history, which does not identify the particular subsystems in which they worked. On some subsystems, the "team leaders" had the same function as "content leaders" or as "content" and "process leaders" combined.

ENGINEERS, CAR PROGRAMS MANAGEMENT: Engineers who developed and managed the innovative "harmony buck" of Chapter 4.

ENGINEERS: More than 200 technical professionals worked on designing the components and overall construction of the Epsilon before its launch. Several of them were interviewed for this learning history. Unless it was needed for context, this document does not identify the particular subsystems in which they worked.

EPSILON PRODUCT MANAGERS AT KEY SUPPLIERS: Suppliers of critical components to the Epsilon assigned product managers to focus on this vehicle. Several of these product managers, each from a different supplier, were interviewed for this learning history.

FINANCE MANAGER: Assigned to Epsilon along with other teams, this individual supported the learning initiative and was an active, enthusiastic member of the "core team" in its initial conversations, but did not get deeply involved in the learning labs that followed.

INTERNAL CONSULTANTS: Active from the beginning, these two individuals felt increasingly responsible for the success of the learning initiative. Their job was to provide networking and coaching support for process improvement, for both "new" (organizational learning-oriented) and "old" (quality and continuous improvement) approaches.

LAUNCH MANAGER: "Second in command" of the Epsilon project, responsible for overall business planning; took a central role in designing and leading the learning initiative.

LEAD MIT RESEARCHER: Project leader from the MIT side, this researcher designed many of the learning lab initiatives, facilitated core team sessions, and conducted much of the training around system-thinking principles.

MARKET RESEARCH LIAISON: A member of AutoCo's Market Research function, this manager helped foster an in-depth relationship with AutoCo engineers.

MIT RESEARCHERS: These were research staff members (and, in some cases, graduate students) at MIT who visited AutoCo one or more times to facilitate sessions, interview people, or help lead learning labs.

PROCESS LEADERS: Epsilon subsystem teams were generally assigned a "process leader," whose attention focused on planning and coordination issues, along with a "content leader" (see above). Several process leaders were interviewed for this learning history, which does not identify the particular subsystems in which they worked.

PROGRAM MANAGER: With overall responsibility for AutoCo Epsilon, he set into motion the innovative approach, and his leadership challenges became a visible and central part of the learning initiative.

PROGRAM MANAGER'S BOSS: Outside the Epsilon team, he oversaw the program manager's work and reported to the Vice President. He was a consistent supporter of the learning initiative and expressed moderate advocacy for the new approach elsewhere in the AutoCo system.

PURCHASING MANAGER: A key member of the "core team" who supported the learning initiative and attended some MIT meetings.

SENGE, PETER: His sessions at "AutoCo University" sparked an interest in the "learning disciplines" of the MIT Center for Organizational Learning, which he directed. This led directly to the partnership between AutoCo managers and MIT researchers.

TEAM LEADERS: The engineering leaders responsible for a particular subsystem on the Epsilon vehicle—electronic, interior/trim, powertrain, etc. Team Leaders also often held the Content Leader role. Engineers in that subsystem reported to them, and they reported to a functional executive outside the Epsilon team.

VEHICLE DEVELOPMENT TEAM LEADER: Leader of a group of engineers responsible for scheduling and coordinating the ongoing engineering design of the Epsilon. He was not part of the Epsilon launch team and was critical of that new approach.

VICE PRESIDENT: Executive overseeing all vehicle launches and responsible for the Epsilon project's budget. He approved the learning initiative budget at critical points and expressed disapproval at other critical points.

Figure 1-0 *AutoCo Organization Chart*

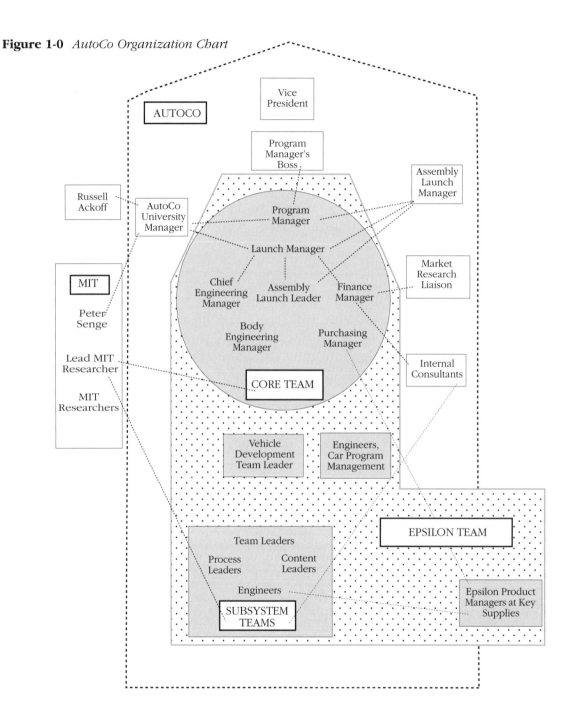

INTRODUCTION

CHAPTER 1

INTRODUCTION

◆ THEMES OF THE EPSILON LEARNING HISTORY

The AutoCo learning history is organized around six key themes. These themes cover the important issues that contributed to the Epsilon program's achievements and significant events.[1]

1. **Hard results, soft concerns:** When managers pay attention to human issues like openness and fostering trust, can teams produce better business results? In Epsilon, the focus on how managers think and interact started with nine months of intensive sessions in a cross-functional leadership team composed of most of the senior managers in the Epsilon program. These senior team managers developed systems models of recurring team problems, described their visions for themselves and their work, and talked openly about their own and each others' mental models of critical practical problems. Because the Epsilon car's senior team began the learning process long before the rest of the participants, they were the first to apply "soft skills" to the hard issues of scheduling and coordination.

2. **Setting an example of non-authoritarian leadership:** Many experts and consultants preach the need for a more non-authoritarian and participative approach to project leadership but can offer little help in how to develop and sustain such behavior. In Epsilon, new leadership styles became reality as project leaders found themselves compelled to use the tools and learning processes they were recommending for others. For these senior leaders, "walking the talk" was

not a trivial matter. It required concerted effort and mutual partnership. It fostered visible changes in their behavior. And it made a huge difference to other people on the team.

3. **Introductory "learning labs":** Teaching techniques for thinking differently. Eventually, a two-day "learning lab," taught by program managers and MIT staff, was created to introduce many members of the Epsilon team to the learning tools and methods with which the leadership team had been working. These "learning labs" included a variety of techniques, including computer simulation; in the end, people remembered them for their focus on candid conversation about key business-related issues in a risk-free setting.

4. **Combining engineering innovations with human relations:** The harmony buck. The "harmony buck" was an innovative prototype which allowed engineers from different functions to see their components placed online together. It speeded up the recognition of problems, and abetted quality design, by allowing people to come together and try out new engineering solutions. But it also required a growing environment of involvement and openness and, in turn, contributed to that environment. The result was an increased flow of information among team members testing their ideas together.

5. **Partnerships:** Functionally based people were drawn together in ways that bridged differences and focused on collaborative learning and action. Creating opportunities for experimentation across traditional boundaries led to benefits that the senior leaders did not predict or plan for.

6. **Process innovation in the context of a large organization:** The larger AutoCo organization responded to the Epsilon team in many ways, not always in ways Epsilon's members would have wished for. Innovative local line leaders recognized the tensions and hoped that, by proving that their innovations led to better business results, they could gain organization-wide credibility for their efforts. But this assumption proved faulty. Lacking senior management partners, Epsilon's managers lacked counsel on how to handle the larger system implications of their efforts, and the larger system lacked a coherent overview of the Epsilon innovations.

◆ How to read a learning history

A learning history is a new format for presenting the story of a project. The learning history report starts with an overview and then describes the origins of the Epsilon learning effort. (The "noticeable results," critical events, and observable measures which provide data on how the Epsilon program progressed are on page 9). The subsequent sections represent themes—key concepts that show the underlying significance of this project and thatemerged from a close reading and examination of the materials collected in our research. We present each of these themes in the form of a "jointly told tale," separating the researchers' comments from participants' narrative. There are four different types of material in these "jointly told tales," as illustrated in Figure 1-1.

This format is designed to portray the project as participants experienced it and to invite readers to draw their own conclusions. In this history we make the "sense-making process" visible—we report not just what people did, but how they interpreted events around them and what reasoning led to their decisions. To gather this information, we interviewed

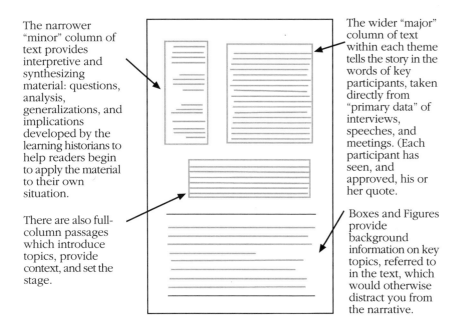

The narrower "minor" column of text provides interpretive and synthesizing material: questions, analysis, generalizations, and implications developed by the learning historians to help readers begin to apply the material to their own situation.

There are also full-column passages which introduce topics, provide context, and set the stage.

The wider "major" column of text within each theme tells the story in the words of key participants, taken directly from "primary data" of interviews, speeches, and meetings. (Each participant has seen, and approved, his or her quote.

Boxes and Figures provide background information on key topics, referred to in the text, which would otherwise distract you from the narrative.

Figure 1-1 *Learning History formats*

over 50 individuals. The interviewees included engineers, process leaders, content leaders (see page xxi), and managers at all levels and functions within the Epsilon team, along with suppliers, engineers from other functions, senior AutoCo management, and other key figures at AutoCo. We also reviewed transcripts of meetings, interviews, program documents, and speeches given by key participants during the program. People's perspectives and attitudes varied; we have made an explicit effort to include as wide a range of points of view as possible.[2]

The value of this document depends on the conversation it generates: How can AutoCo's Epsilon experience provide a useful example for your team or project? We thus ask readers, while reading the document in whole or in part, to suspend their assumptions—about automobile companies, management, engineering, and all other aspects of vehicle production—so that they can focus on what happened, how people described events, how they felt, and what their attributions were.

In reading the two-column format of the "jointly told" tale sections, you will find yourself having to make a choice. Which column do you read first? Do you skip back and forth, and when do you do so? There are no "rules" for reading a learning history; different people read segments in different orders.

As you make your way through the story, however, please pay attention to your own reactions. How credible do you find the story? How would you have dealt with the problems that faced the Epsilon team? How can their experience help inform the decisions that you (and your associates) have to make in the future? We recommend that you highlight and add your own notes, particularly in the minor (commentary) column, as the basis for further conversation. It is through the discussion and dialogue with colleagues, about the contents of this document, that we believe your own, your fellow course members', and your team's learning will best be served.

In 1996, the Epsilon learning history was distributed within AutoCo for use by managers and employees on other projects. To introduce that manuscript, and acknowledge the challenges AutoCo faced that were illustrated by Epsilon, one of the highest-level AutoCo executives wrote the following foreword:

◆ FOREWORD

The organizational learning history you are about to read emerges from a unique collaboration among practitioners, academicians, and product development professionals. It is an important document because it lays out the dilemmas, paradoxes, and human emotions associated with teamwork in today's complex organizations. Our future will most certainly depend on how well we learn to manage conflicting needs in large systems.

This study is more about learning how to learn than about the nuts and bolts associated with designing and building great automobiles. More often than not you'll conclude it's not about who is right or wrong, but about a world of perception and interpretation. For me, this is a human story because it reveals how different attitudes, beliefs, and assumptions rise to the surface and may rule the day.

What's especially revealing is how the product development function is demystified as an exact science of equations, engineering procedures, and computer-driven technology. Instead, you'll find dedicated people at all levels relentlessly seeking alignment, recognition, and assurances that the day's effort will yield value-added results over chaos and self-interest. This dedication also requires a balanced perspective. We can be extremely efficient by way of quality, cost, timing, and flexibility. But these objectives must be in service to the customer. Outstanding teams of the future will need to balance multiple initiatives more than ever before.

For me, this learning history is about a beginning, not an end. We are building on what we've learned with this first MIT effort by applying the methods and tools in two other vehicle programs. Additionally, there are many organizational learning projects going on in the company outside of product development. Perhaps this will enable us to see the connections among all these efforts and move to yet another new level of understanding.

— Senior Vice President
Product Development, AutoCo

FIGURE 1-2 *Chronology*

	1980s
	AutoCo's interest in systems thinking
MIT Project Engagement Clinic	
	1991
	MIT Project Engagement Clinic (9/91)
Three-day Offsite at Splendid Hotel (10/91)	
Team Collocation (10/91)	
	1992
	Core team meetings begin (1/92)
Market Research Clinic (4/92)	
	Core team system map (8/92)
	First Learning Lab (9.92)
	1993
Harmony buck completed (4/93)	
	Second Learning Lab (2/93)
Evaluation Prototype (EP) Build (4/93)	
	Third Learning Lab (5/93)
Change Requests (CRs) reach 500 (7/93)	
	Fourth Learning Lab (8/93)
Validation Prototype (VP) Build (10/93)	
	1994
CRs reduced from 350 to 50 (3/94)	
Accelerated 1st Production Prototype (PP) Build (6/94)	

LAUNCH BUILD (11/94)

◆ Epsilon's noticeable results, 1991-1994

This list of noticeable results was collected and amended through the learning history interviewing process. People were asked to comment on items, their significance, and if it was familiar, describe how it was accomplished and what if any role they and others they knew had in it. The items in this list are observable events or objective measures which provide data on Epsilon program progression.

- **Mechanical Prototype (MP) build (8/91):** The Mechanical Prototype is a production level prototype for the underbody and front end of the car. The Epsilon MP design represented a considerable stretch from the previous AutoCo vehicle; it incorporated multiplex wiring, all new suspension and accommodation for electronic navigation systems.

  In part as a result of earlier delays the MP drawings were sixteen weeks behind, but the first MP build was completed only four weeks behind the original schedule. The quality of the MP prototype build and maturity of its design allowed extensive testing to be done much earlier than is normally possible.

- **Team collocation[3] (10/91):** Although the Epsilon team had not been designated to be collocated, program management pushed for it. The Epsilon team collocated 37 months before vehicle launch (the date when production manufacturing was set to begin).

- **Market research clinic (4/92):** Forty engineers from the development teams participated in a market research clinic in California. This was said to be the first time engineers formally talked directly to customers this early in a vehicle program.

- **Harmony buck complete (1/93):** The harmony buck is a mechanism to review early designs and design changes prior to the periodic prototype builds. The harmony buck was an idea proposed by engineers on the Epsilon team. However, the $2 million cost to build a harmony buck was not covered in the Epsilon program's budget. Program management supported the concept and lobbied Vice Presidents to gain funding support. AutoCo now uses the harmony buck in other programs.

- **Evaluation Prototype (EP) build (4/93):** The EP brings all vehicle systems together, so that integrated testing can occur. The program team completed the first EP on April 1, 1993, making up for earlier delays and meeting the original program timing plan. Eighty-five percent of parts were available for the EP build (setting a company record; other car programs have had between forty and sixty percent of parts available at this point in their programs).

- **Change Requests (CRs) reach 500 (7/93):** Change Requests (CRs) are documents which engineers write to indicate the need for alterations in parts or technical specifications. CRs indicate that rework is needed; thus, senior management uses the count of CRs to evaluate program performance at any moment in time. Following the EP build, the Epsilon had 524 outstanding CRs, ordinarily a sign of very poor performance. (A more typical number would be 200.) Product development and manufacturing management said that they had never seen a program recover from such a high level of CRs.

- **Validation Prototype (VP) build (10/93):** Validation Prototype vehicles are built to test changes made after the EP build. The VP design was frozen in July of 1993—three weeks ahead of plan. Ninety-three percent of the VP parts were on time to the material requirement date. According to manufacturing management, the quality of the VP prototypes was the best any vehicle program had ever accomplished. The subsequent engineering release was completed in August of 1993, four weeks ahead of plan. Ninety-eight percent of the engineering release parts were delivered one month ahead of plan, with the other two percent known and accounted for. Four VP prototype vehicles were built on the regular assembly line at the Mission Hill manufacturing plant.

  The new owner vehicle assessment scores for VP were 96, compared to an average of 108 for other vehicle programs (lower scores mean higher quality ratings). The new owner vehicle assessment scores for the earlier build had been substantially worse than average; they were 145, compared to an AutoCo average of 105. Top AutoCo managers made what were described as uncharacteristic acknowledgments that the Epsilon program was performing well.

- **Accelerated first production prototype build (6/94):** The first production prototype build (which is the final prototype build done on the assembly line) began one week early. The team had 70 percent "production status" parts (normally 50 percent). The new owner vehicle assessment scores for the first production prototype were 28, a company record. The previous best new owner vehicle assessment score was 35, and the average score was 55 for other vehicle programs.

- **Launch accelerated by one week (11/94):** Production builds began one week ahead of the scheduled date. Starting production early was previously unheard of, and thought not feasible given the normal chaos that surrounds a car launch. The program was able to return an estimated $65 million of the $90 million budgeted for late changes to parts. Based on the comprehensive reports (eighteen pages of design and production statistics based on standardized measures) submitted at the end of product development, the Epsilon met or exceeded all forecasted goals (quality, weight, fuel economy, performance, functional image, customer satisfaction, variable costs, investment, and vehicle profitability).

- **Final quality results:** The final new owner vehicle assessment score for the Epsilon was 5.8—significantly lower (better) than the average new owner vehicle assessment score for the last six recent launches (which averaged a score of 9). Subsequent quality rating by an independent market research organizations (Competitive New Vehicle Quality) showed a 30% improvement in quality as measured by things gone wrong, rating AutoCo's Epsilon in second place for automobiles in initial customer quality.

The noticeable results are measurable and provide firm indication of the Epsilon program's achievements. These noticeable results were used to focus description and evaluation in interviews.

◆ ORIGINS OF EPSILON'S LEARNING PROJECT

AutoCo's interest in systems thinking (which later included organizational learning) began in 1989, when Peter Senge (who was developing a Center for Organizational Learning based at MIT) and Russell Ackoff (professor emeritus at the University of Pennsylvania's Wharton School) started giving monthly presentations in AutoCo's Executive Development seminars. A manager at AutoCo University [AutoCo University Manager], who sponsored the monthly training sessions, was interested in testing the concepts of systems thinking in one or more live business settings at AutoCo.

At the time, like most American automobile companies, AutoCo had spent several years adopting statistical process control and many managers had been exposed to the total quality movement (TQM) in general and the ideas of Dr. W. Edwards Deming in particular. In his seminars and speeches, Deming had often noted that "management's job is to optimize the entire system," instead of aiming for results that benefited only one department or function.[4]

The concept of "systems thinking" carried this one step further; Senge (using Jay Forrester's system dynamics modeling techniques) and Ackoff (using a set of techniques and methods derived from his work in planning for corporate development) both suggested ways to map and articulate the interrelationships among components of a system and to look for leverage in changing those interrelationships effectively. Senge's work, in particular, provided entry-level ways to begin thinking about organizational systems in terms of archetypal "generic structures" that might appear in a large variety of systems, from an ecological niche to a political party to a climate system . . . to an organization like AutoCo.[5]

Note how seeds were sown for some time before a project opportunity emerged at AutoCo. The company "pulled" the effort in, rather than being "sold" a bill of goods. As at other large companies, AutoCo internal "change agents" had to consciously decide between a "bottom-up" or "top-down" approach in any given initiative. From the beginning, this effort took the "bottom-up" approach. This meant it would be easier to implement, but harder to expand to fit the larger AutoCo system.

This learning effort begins (as Peter Senge suggests in The Fifth Discipline Fieldbook) *by drawing forth a core set of "guiding ideas".[6] Globalization, thinking differently, and leadership.*

AUTOCO UNIVERSITY MANAGER: We had just finished our first executive education program for the top 2000 people worldwide. It was a gathering from the four corners of the world, and it was quite a happening. The question was, what should be in the second round?

We decided on a "bubble-up" rather than "top-down" model. We went around the world and interviewed executives and asked them what was on their minds. What would be of the greatest interest to them? Three issues surfaced: globalization, thinking differently, and leadership.

Underlying the first two issues was the pervasive issue of change. We then went about exploring what would be a senior executive program built around these three themes. There was controversy in presenting them to the top of the house because the top felt they might not be ready to get into all this subject matter. Nevertheless, they said, "press forward."

In the arena of "thinking differently," we came across two outstanding voices: Peter Senge and Russ Ackoff. The more we dug into the area, the more we found a very significant message coming out of Senge's and Ackoff's world views.

By late 1989, early 1990, we had both Senge and Ackoff doing a program at our center every other week. In our analysis of participants' reactions, there was a large voice saying, "The ideas are intriguing, but I don't see how I would play them out in my ballpark—on Monday morning!"

In all fairness, we had asked both Senge and Ackoff to take us on a broad journey, and not to focus specifically on application. It's not surprising that participants were intrigued with it, and saw its depth, but they were right in feeling that there needed to be an ability to see further down that chain of, "What happens next?"

That's when I formulated the challenge for myself and AutoCo University to continue to pursue this subject area. I had the good fortune to be able to sit in on numerous sessions with Peter and Russ, and in the fifth or sixth session, the ball bearings started to rotate in unison.

I asked Ackoff publicly, "Russ, I've been sitting here for several sessions, it's an outstanding message, but I'm still having trouble digesting it and its implications."

Russ turned to me and said, "Well, that's because you'll never get it."

I turned beet red. Here I was standing in front of 50 executives, and the room was dead silent. Then Russ let me off the hook. He turned to the group, and said, "And you won't get it, either. We have built up over 400 years of methodology of 'reductionist' thinking. It is so powerful, so pervasive, that probably your children and their children will have a much easier time. For you folks, it's going to be tough grind."

Down to my socks, I understood that you can say you understand it, and still not understand it. The implications were absolutely profound. Organizational learning didn't mean letting go of analytical processes. It meant complementing and supplementing them with synthesis or sys-

But do abstsract concepts like "thinking differently" mean the same thing to different AutoCo managers and executives? If not, does that matter?

Senge and Ackoff both proposed that an organization's work could not be understood in fragments. AutoCo's managers responded to this message with approval because it helped clarify the perennial problem of miscommunication and conflict between functions. But as this comment shows, it wasn't obvious how to implement a change based on that idea—not without reconfiguring AutoCo's governance structure, which couldn't be done from the "bottom up."

The AutoCo University Manager took the reponse of senior executives as a challenge to find a way to operationalize systems thinking throughout AutoCo.

Is it possible for executives who have spent their lives thinking in a particular way to change their thinking?

tems thinking. It's not such a clean thing—"Just throw out all the traditional tools, my past life—and switch into new formulas." It means learning something in addition: the "and," not the "or."

AutoCo's introduction to systems thinking thus represented a challenge: How could the organization make use of systems thinking in a business context?

In 1991 a diverse group of AutoCo managers attended a series of five two-day training sessions on the core competencies of a learning organization. These sessions were run by faculty and staff from the MIT Center for Organizational Learning. To the surprise of the AutoCo University manager, given the abstract nature of the materials, the first AutoCo audience members were enthusiastic and wanted more exposure to the approach. This audience was composed, in part, of managers from product development. In particular, the Epsilon Program Launch Manager expressed keen interest. He was responsible for the vehicle development program to design and build the next model of the Epsilon luxury car. Past experiences in developing cars at AutoCo had been frustrating, wasteful experiences for many people, but there was no consensus in the organization about why. Here, the Launch Manager shows that he had, independently, internalized his own view of the reasons.

How many different views might exist in a company this size? Although good quality and timely delivery are held up as critical, achieving them does not make cost overruns acceptable at AutoCo. Does that imply a lack of endorsement "in use" for the idea that improving quality will reduce cost in itself?

This is not the only example where team dynamics was not accepted as a convincing explanation for good performance or where technical innovation was assumed to be the primary key factor.

LAUNCH MANAGER: I had worked on the Delta program [another vehicle program] for several years as the Business Planner and Launch Manager. We had discovered, a year before Job One, that the program was 17 months behind schedule. So we quickly organized a 100-person launch team and we put the program back on schedule, with quality that was better than the first car. We met all of our program objectives except cost, which we knew from the beginning we could not meet.

I remember a meeting where a Vice President listened to us present the reasons for our success [on the Delta program]: team leadership, and the fact that everyone had the same goals and knew that they depended on each other. "That sounds really great," he said, "but what did you do?" He finally said it must have been a fluke, and that was the end of it.

There was no learning from the experience. It bothered me a great deal. AutoCo is in love with managing by crisis; without a crisis, we don't know what to do. I resolved to learn how to produce a car launch without a crisis.

Why would task-oriented explanations be easier for management to accept in this (or another) company?

In July 1991, the AutoCo University Manager and an internal consultant working with the Launch Manager, wrote a letter to Peter Senge, director of the MIT Center for Organizational Learning. They requested an active relationship between MIT researchers and the Epsilon Program.

Project Engagement Clinic

The formal partnership between the two organizations started with a project "engagement" clinic in September 1991. The goal of this clinic was to engage one another: asking difficult questions about AutoCo Epsilon's readiness for learning and MIT's ability to help. Both sides hoped to create the rare kind of corporate-university partnership that might simultaneously produce business improvements and research results. Attending the meeting were the key AutoCo people in the Epsilon project at that time—the Program Manager, Launch Manager, and Body Engineering Manager for the Epsilon Program, two internal consultants on process improvement (who were to integrate systems thinking at AutoCo)—along with five researchers associated with the MIT Center for Organizational Learning. One researcher had visited AutoCo and conducted interviews in advance.

These interviews were summarized in a report that singled out several key issues:

- The Launch Manager wanted the partnership to focus on improvements in the Evaluation Prototype (EP). If the EP could be made to "work" as it should, the car would be successful, he said. He also wanted to create a climate within the team which reinforced more effective cross-functional communication, more responsibility for objectives, and less "games-playing."

- The Epsilon Program Manager (the Launch Manager's boss, with overall responsibility for the Epsilon project) believed that concentrating on one prototype, like the EP, was too narrow. He felt the need to look at AutoCo's overall product development paradigm. Present product development management practices controlled resources ineffectively, treated suppliers with indifference or hostility, and had a history of not achieving quality, cost, and time objectives. The Program Manager mentioned the inability of a program to reach a point where management could say, "Enough changes this time," put a halt to unnecessary rework and redesign, and move rapidly and smoothly toward completion.

- AutoCo's vehicle program management needed to see tangible improvement. The new product development program officially involved a 48-month time period, but this had been compressed to 42 months and involved very ambitious deadlines. Chronic dependency on "heroic" efforts took key people away from the general product development process so they could fix more urgent problems. Some people felt certain that it was just a question of time before a real crisis further weakened the effort.

- MIT's researchers wanted the project to further spur forward the investigations being done in the Center for Organizational Learning. Supporting research would require more than a relationship where MIT played the role of expert consultant and AutoCo took the role of client. Instead, both organizations would have to collaborate in a systemic approach to improving the product development management practices and understanding the results that were achieved. Measurement would be important in determining if improvements occurred over time.

As they talked during the project definition clinic, participants identified a set of critical issues affecting the management of product development within AutoCo.

- Limits and constraints in the established AutoCo system: Program managers were reluctant to talk about learning efforts or process improvements higher in their chain of command without being able to show "results" first.

- Secrecy and mistrust: Few engineers were willing to be the first to report a problem or "failure," so they delayed reporting problems.

People who reported problems were given performance reviews that reflected failure, attributing the creation of the problem to them. By the time problems were reported, it was often too late to do much about them without incurring program delays. Information about delays and recurring problems did not reach people in charge until it was too late, and then everyone reacted in an exhausting "heroic" mode to solve the crisis.

• The desire to build a sense of personal, emotional commitment in the team: The program manager wanted to move people from a frame of mind in which their interactions were based solely on individual competence, to a sense of mutual concern and willingness to find common solutions.

• Room for experimentation and failure: Team leaders expressed concern about being "put under a microscope" if their efforts attracted top management attention.

Following the project engagement clinic, several meetings were held to determine the project focus and how MIT researchers would work with the Epsilon team. In January of 1992, a core "learning team" of managers from the Epsilon program began meeting regularly, at one- or two-month intervals.

The core "learning team" consisted of eight Epsilon managers (including the Program Manager, Launch Manager, Assembly Manager, Finance Manager, Body Engineering Manager, Purchasing Manager, and two internal consultants). The lead MIT Researcher was present as a facilitator. These meetings provided opportunities to plan, learn techniques and tools that facilitated learning, and practice using those techniques between meetings. The meetings of the core learning team ushered in the first intensive phase of Epsilon's learning initiative.

CAR LAUNCH

CHAPTER 2

HARD RESULTS, SOFT CONCERNS

The Program Manager expressed a twofold ambition: to create an excellent vehicle *and* to develop a process which valued and inspired people on the team.

This section describes the challenge that Epsilon's leaders gradually realized was confronting them: the difficulties of achieving "hard" results (producing high-quality technical parts, sub-assemblies, and a complete vehicle efficiently) through an emphasis on concepts that many people termed "soft" (good communication, openness, honesty and trust.)

◆ LEARNING IN THE CORE TEAM (JAN. 1992–SEPT. 1992)

The core "learning" team began with an awareness that Epsilon faced (as one team member put it) "real internal conflicts." The Epsilon program was unofficially expected to be a "Lexus-fighter at the price of an [American economy car]," although as a front-wheel drive car with its planned variable costs, it would be difficult to compete with rear-wheel drive luxury sedans like Lexus.

The core team members all felt a high level of frustration and a sense of urgency, since the program was already late. They recognized the dilemma of being a pilot learning project; they could already see that their effort might mean "taking on" issues in AutoCo's overarching management culture. This culture included a strong reliance on hierarchy and functional authority—an expectation that the boss is on top of technical details and makes decisions. On top of that, the core team members had difficulty communicating with each other. "I couldn't talk to [the Finance Manager] at first," the Program Manager noted, "in less than a high-decibel range."

At the beginning of 1992, the core team met every one or two months, working with a variety of communication and conceptualization techniques such as the ladder of inference, the left-hand column, role-playing, and system mapping (see Boxes 2-1 and 2-2). Their ability to communicate improved, and they began to focus on their most serious problems.

To give them a broader perspective, several members of the core team interviewed a dozen people from the rest of the Epsilon project, asking:

Box 2-1

WHAT ARE SYSTEMS ARCHETYPES?

The systems thinking process involves building new collaborative understandings of the interplay of forces at work. To accomplish this, participants use "archetypes": images of common systemic situations. Each of these patterns occurs in a wide variety of domains, from ecology to economics to manufacturing; each offers its own strategic insights and gives people a better picture of how the forces of the system may trap them.

System dynamics researchers have published descriptions of about a dozen archetypes. They include "Limits to Growth," in which a seemingly boundless growth pattern runs up against unexpected limiting forces. (Total quality campaigns, for example, run up against institutional disappointment after the "low-hanging fruit" is picked.) In another archetype, "Shifting the Burden," a more immediately inviting, short-term solution to a problem is chosen instead of a sollution that would solve the system's fundamental issues. This choice weakens the system's ability to develop a more fundamental, but slower, approach later.

Another archetype, the "Tragedy of the Commons," describes how competing individuals can unwittingly collaborate to destroy limited resources without replensihing them. This became the basis for the Epsilon team's "Tragedy of the Power Supply" (described later).

Compared to computer models of systems, archetypes are simplistic; they have been compared to "training wheels." But in well-designed group workshops, they can lead to very sophisticated collective understandings of common problems. Because archetypes imply counter-intuitive, but effective, alternatives for action, they are generally very useful strategic tools.[1]

What did people feel their greatest challenges and strengths to be? The team returned for a working session in March of 1992, ready to pick two or three problems and start fixing them immediately.

Around this time, the lead MIT Researcher reported his impressions of the core team: They were "bright" people, burdened with frustration and puzzlement but not resignation. He, too, noted the seemingly innate tendency to conflict among the various functional leaders on the team.

LEAD MIT RESEARCHER: The participants had locked horns and couldn't get anywhere. [The Launch Manager] told me much later in the process that [the Program Manager] was ready to hang it up after a few months. But he saw enough value to keep him going. In one critical incident, early in the sessions, we used a ladder of inference and left-hand/right-hand column exercise to begin to look at the ways in which finance and program management couldn't communicate.

The conflict that the researcher describes here was noted by several observers as generally typical of the relationships among managers from different functional areas at AutoCo.

The exercises opened things up so that they could really look at their assumptions. Program management revealed how they assumed that the finance people "want to hold us to [American automobile] costs." Essentially, program management thought that finance didn't have a clue (and didn't care) about what it took to build a car. "They just want to meet the numbers."

The finance people showed their assumptions about the program managers: "These program guys don't care about costs. They don't want to work to get to the kind of car that we said we would. They won't control costs."

I said, "Look, we're here to do something different from the way you continually do things." Instead of having a normal "let's-solve-it" style consulting project, I suggested that we "try to understand our own assessments of the problem. We are blind to the limitations of our assessments, and thus we can never see what is really happening. Yet we design solutions based on our own individual assessments." The core team members understood that argument, and went along with another round of experimentation.

The core team's experience suggests further attention to the use of "reflection and inquiry" tools as a way to help people understand one another's positions. These seemingly simple conversational devices are often credited as the most immediately powerful of the learning organization tools. They are based upon the premise that openness of communications, and the willingness to address assumptions, would lead to workplace efficiencies and effectiveness.

Box 2-2

WHAT ARE THE "LADDER OF INFERENCE" AND

"LEFT-HAND COLUMN"?

These "action science" devices are designed to build skills of "reflection and inquiry:" ways of holding conversation that lead to greater understanding of both process and content. The tools are simple exercises and metaphors that help people unlearn their own defensive, counter-productive conversational habits. For example, in many work situations it's more effective to systematically inquire into why other people feel the way they do, instead of trying to hammer your own point home as dramatically as possible.

The "ladder of inference"[2]—a term coined by Harvard Business School Professor Chris Argyris—is a metaphor that shows how rapidly we can leap to knee-jerk con-

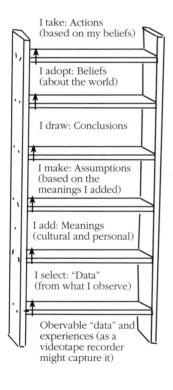

I take: Actions
(based on my beliefs)

I adopt: Beliefs
(about the world)

I draw: Conclusions

I make: Assumptions
(based on the
meanings I added)

I add: Meanings
(cultural and personal)

I select: "Data"
(from what I observe)

Obervable "data" and
experiences (as a
videotape recorder
might capture it)

clusions with little data and no intermediate thought process, as if rapidly climbing up a ladder in our minds. You start at the bottom with the observable data, which is so self-evident that it would show up on a videotape recorder ("Larry has yawned at a meeting"), and within a few seconds, leap up to assumptions ("Larry is bored"), to more generic conclusions ("Larry doesn't care about this project"). Since most of these conclusions are never discussed openly, there is no way to check them.

Incorporating the "ladder" into everyday conversation has proven to be a pivotal component of learning organization work. It gives people a safe way to raise and check their varied interpretations of events.

In the left-hand column exercise,[3] people select a difficult situation and reconstruct a pivotal conversation. In the right-hand column, they write down what was said. In the left, they articulate what they were thinking and feeling, but not saying. The case becomes an artifact through which people can examine their own thinking, as well as the systemic problems which underlie the impasse.

I had them break up into two groups (because there were so many of us) and each group did a "K.J." We used the technique to sort through the information gathered from interviewing Epsilon team members. "Listen to what you think people are trying to say," I said. "Get away from thinking only rationally about the comments. How do they feel to you?" We went through a "scrubbing" process [rewriting the statements to be clear], then grouped them intuitively. This is usually a very frustrating and bewildering process, especially for an engineering or action-oriented group, because everything is interconnected and diffuse.

See Box 2-3. The "K.J. diagram" combines the intellectual-rational thought process with intuitive-emotional feeling data. It is generally used to process a group's own thoughts and observations; here, they used it to make sense of their interviews. Because it is based on data from interviews, it incorporates multiple perspectives and gives different voices equal weight.

Our theme question was, "What is the biggest weakness with our product development process?" And the overarching answer that emerged had to do with lack of trust and openness. This was unspoken before this point, and I think it wouldn't have been captured otherwise.

The K.J. diagram appeared to have brought to the surface an interrelated and interdependent set of problems.

Now they couldn't accuse me of "making them" pay attention to this trust issue. They had seen firsthand how it was at the core of their own problems. This incident made a lasting impression on [the Program Manager], and changed the dynamics of the relationship with Finance, which was very important.

The MIT researcher focused on problem articulation rather than problem solution (see Box 2-3).

PROGRAM MANAGER: There were really only a few core issues. The rest of the problems all generated from those.

- Fear and the consequences of being wrong led to people not sharing information;
- The boss's need to control came at the expense of drawing forth individual capabilities on the team;
- Other people weren't trusted to help you; they tended to one-up whatever you did.

Are these three key issues important on any product launch? Are they endemic to the product development process? Do they stem from AutoCo culture? Are they worth taking time to deal with?

By this point, we had been working together eight months. We had learned to generate trust in our own core team, so we could look at these issues and agree: "Yeah that's really what's going on."

◆ THE SYSTEM MAP (LEARNING TEAM MEETING, AUGUST 1992)

Now the "core learning team" engaged in a "systems mapping" process, to connect the concerns of trust and openness that had surfaced in the K.J. diagram with other symptoms in product development, such as the chronic critical problem of late parts (see Box 2-5).

Focusing on one key problem—in this case lateness of parts—again showed the interrelatedness and interdependencies of all the problems facing the team.

PROGRAM MANAGER: We weren't sure what to do next. We didn't know how to "change" fear or mistrust. So we started to look at a key problem: Why we were always late no matter what we did, not matter how we approached the problem, parts were chronically behind schedule. We began to share our views about why. Over the course of a day, we built up a diagram of the system.

When one engineer changes parts, that part usually affects somebody else. The "A" engineers can't start part

---

BOX 2-3

WHAT ARE "AFFINITY DIAGRAMS (K.J.s)"?

Affinity diagrams ("K.J.s"), named for their inventor Jiro Kawakita, emerged from the quality movement in Japan. This group process is used to collectively think through the ambiguities and multiple perspectives that people bring to a complex decision they must make together. In a typical K.J. process, a team of 5–10 people considers a mass of issues, posts statements related to a main question on a wall, and repeatedly groups and rephrases them, adding title cards as needed. Over the course of several hours, a final pattern emerges: This is generally a coherent set of themes that reveal key underlying issues.

The illustration opposite shows half of the Epsilon team's final K.J. arrangement. Each one of the groupings represents a key theme; the arrows show how (the team felt) one theme influenced another. The diagram may look carefully considered and well-organized, but this final snapshot does not show the hours of "messy," unfocused, frustrating deliberations that went into it. First by conducting interviews, and then by using the "K.J." process to sort and analyze that data, the core team discovered a critical issue: the extent to which engineers trusted managers and felt free to speak openly.

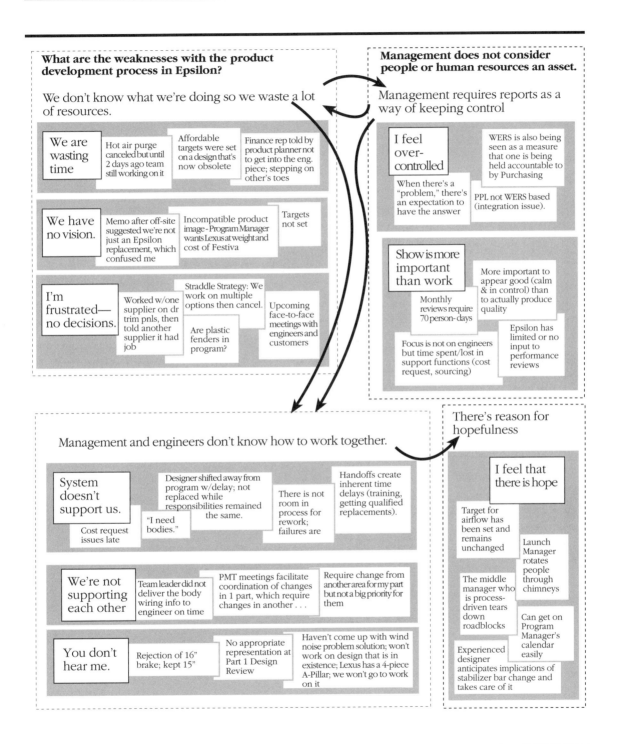

What are the weaknesses with the product development process in Epsilon?

We don't know what we're doing so we waste a lot of resources.

We are wasting time

Hot air purge canceled but until 2 days ago team still working on it

Affordable targets were set on a design that's now obsolete

Finance rep told by product planner not to get into the eng. piece; stepping on other's toes

We have no vision.

Memo after off-site suggested we're not just an Epsilon replacement, which confused me

Incompatible product image - Program Manager wants Lexus at weight and cost of Festiva

Targets not set

I'm frustrated— no decisions.

Worked w/one supplier on dr trim pnls, then told another supplier it had job

Straddle Strategy: We work on multiple options then cancel.

Are plastic fenders in program?

Upcoming face-to-face meetings with engineers and customers

Management does not consider people or human resources an asset.

Management requires reports as a way of keeping control

I feel over-controlled

When there's a "problem," there's an expectation to have the answer

WERS is also being seen as a measure that one is being held accountable to by Purchasing

PPL not WERS based (integration issue).

Show is more important than work

Monthly reviews require 70 person-days

More important to appear good (calm & in control) than to actually produce quality

Focus is not on engineers but time spent/lost in support functions (cost request, sourcing)

Epsilon has limited or no input to performance reviews

Management and engineers don't know how to work together.

System doesn't support us.

Cost request issues late

"I need bodies."

Designer shifted away from program w/delay; not replaced while responsibilities remained the same.

There is not room in process for rework; failures are

Handoffs create inherent time delays (training, getting qualified replacements).

We're not supporting each other

Team leader did not deliver the body wiring info to engineer on time

PMT meetings facilitate coordination of changes in 1 part, which require changes in another . . .

Require change from another area for my part but not a big priority for them

You don't hear me.

Rejection of 16" brake; kept 15"

No appropriate representation at Part 1 Design Review

Haven't come up with wind noise problem solution; won't work on design that is in existence; Lexus has a 4-piece A-Pillar; we won't go to work on it

There's reason for hopefulness

I feel that there is hope

Target for airflow has been set and remains unchanged

The middle manager who is process-driven tears down roadblocks

Experienced designer anticipates implications of stabilizer bar change and takes care of it

Launch Manager rotates people through chimneys

Can get on Program Manager's calendar easily

The K.J. and causal loop diagrams appear to have influenced not only how people thought about the problems, but also their perception of problem symptoms.

How can a team effectively build a group understanding of a systemic issue so all members "own" that understanding?

This story of the finance manager's role was often repeated to illustrate how the system dynamics work is valuable to a cross-functional team. Finance people typically don't get involved in engineering change processes; here, that involvement helped build a deeper understanding of systemic issues.

The systems map was described by most people as enormously useful. When a group "sees the same picture, and comes to the same conclusion," is it the visual (like the system map) that helps them focus on issues systematically? Or are some other phenomena, such as the experience of developing the image together, operating?

of their work until the "B" engineers solve their problem. Parts get late. This leads to pressure to get back on schedule, so we compress the supplier time. But then something else would become late, because we would be putting all our resources on the part that was late. When parts get so late that we can't recover, we revise the build schedule. Then people feel they have more time, so more parts get late. Worse still, the next time you have a build, people will assume you're just going to revise the schedule again, so they don't even try to meet the dates.

We eventually got all this into a complex chart. We all understood the whole system as it related to us, and we had all contributed to this map.

The map became critical. And the person who pointed the key leverage point wasn't an engineer, a development manager, or a planning manager. It was the finance manager. She pointed out that just before the "reporting of lateness," there's usually a delay. The reason for the delay is: people are afraid to be criticized. There is a basic cultural commandment in engineering—don't tell someone you have a problem unless you have the solution. You're supposed to solve it—and then tell them. But during that delay, nobody knows about the problem, and nobody can react. That delay automatically compounds delays in other loops going on through the system.

PROGRAM MANAGER: We all saw the same picture, and we all came to the same conclusion: This was a leverage point for us. We began to look at how we could structure the project to ease that delay, and we concluded that our real leverage was in improving the communication process, improving honesty, and improving trust.

We had begun to build these in the core team, but they didn't exist between the functional groups in the rest of the team. But we knew that building trust was possible, because, after all, if we hadn't shared our views of the system honestly, we would never have gotten to this point.

PROGRAM MANAGER: Only a small [percentage] of the members of the team actually worked for me, where I could promote them and give them their performance reviews. Most of them worked for other functional organizations—finance, assembly, body engineering, climate control, plastics. If I just pulled the team together the normal way I would get what we always get. People would protect the objectives of their organization. They would work on the product, but their organization would come first. My greatest leverage was to make them view the other members of the team as people with whom they had a personal relationship. If I could make them feel that they depended on each other, and that they wanted to help each other as people, that would counterbalance the material reward from their functional organization.

We had been talking about open, honest communication around this company for as long as I've been here and I've been here 29 years now. We don't know how to do it. This was the first time I thought it might really work.

Another factor accelerating the decision to promote open communication was the increasing complexity of automotive technology, particularly with fast-changing subsystems such as the electrical system. The better the team became at working together, the better it would deal with intricate components which cut across two or more functional roles.

Was the statement that "we don't know how to make open communication work" a self-fulfilling belief which kept people from trying to be more open?

◆ THE TRANSITION TO OPENNESS

Now the core team members had given themselves a mandate: to implement an atmosphere of honesty and trust in the Epsilon team as a whole. This would be an ongoing process, with many setbacks, continuing throughout the 42-month program.

LAUNCH MANAGER: In one of our earliest design reviews in February, 1991, folks were standing around saying, "What do you want us to do?"

I said, "Wait a second. You're the engineer. What do you think is the right thing to do for the customer and for the company? What is your recommendation?"

They couldn't answer that question. I realized then that this team needed a lot of help. They were accustomed to putting all the alternatives together and the

A premise of a learning orientation is that the boss isn't the one with the answers. Bosses are teachers and coaches who help others learn and apply their learning.

To the program manager and the launch manager, "empowerment" meant the recognition that engineers

(and others on the team) needed to make decisions and feel responsible for those decisions.

planning manager or Program Manager would decide. I knew I had the prerogative, based on my experience and knowledge, to tell people what should be done. But I told them I would reserve that prerogative for when I was willing to challenge them. I didn't want to make decisions that they should be making.

Box 2-4

PROBLEM SOLUTIONS VERSUS PROBLEM ARTICULATION

Under conditions often referred to as "fire, ready, aim," most managers can't easily (and aren't expected to) consider multiple causes of their problems and the unintended consequences of their proposed actions. Solutions are often developed and implemented before the full ramifications of the situation are understood.

Technical problems, involving physical machines, can often be solved quickly through the conventional rational problem solving approaches. As systems get more complex, however, delays between problem and solution mean that it is increasingly difficult to see the unintended consequences of new "solutions." Decision-making researchers March and Olsen[4] have established the existence of a the delayed feedback between hastily articulated solutions and new problems at individual and organizational levels.

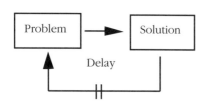

A "problem solving treadmill"[5] is created by problem solving in this manner over time—solving one problem will lead, after a delay, to new problems. The "problem of problem-solving" is exacerbated by the fact that a problem's identification depends, at least in the short term, upon a person's position and perspective.

This manifests commonly in the way that problems are framed—as preordained solutions. Consider commonly heard statements: The problem is . . . "we need a better management information system," "the reward system needs to be revamped," "our

I realized over a period of time that AutoCo wanted to "empower" its teams, but on this team, people didn't feel empowered to do anything. That was our first realization that this was a dysfunctional group, probably very typical of most groups.

The launch manager saw the group's behavior as "dysfunctional." But how "functional" was it within the context of the larger AutoCo culture?

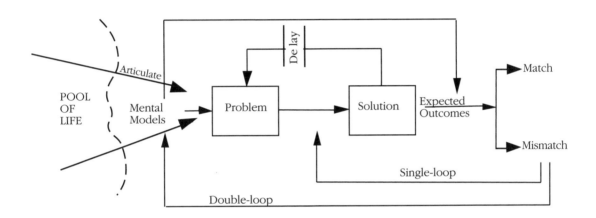

costs are too high," "our management philosophy is outdated," or "we need a learning orientation." In reality, there may be no need for a management information system at all, the reward system may be fine, costs may be too low (given the need for new investment), and neither management philosophy nor learning orientation may be flawed. But stating the problems as solutions precludes reflection on other solutions And, when new problems emerge related in part to previous solutions, people fail to make the connection. The problem solving treadmill leads organizations to attempt the same "fix" over and over and expecting different results!

Systems thinking provides an alternative to the problem solving treadmill. By considering problems and solutions as linked, solutions are also evaluated on the basis of potential unintended consequences. Rather than moving to action, the systems thinking approach focuses on the assumptions, or mental models, from which the problems were articulated in the first place.

BOX 2-5

THE CORE TEAM'S VIEW OF "PARTS BEHIND SCHEDULE"

This picture is a simplified version of a causal loop diagram produced by the Epsilon core team. The key problem is the central concern, "parts behind schedule." At the left are a series of forces (many involving exponential growth) that contribute to increasing numbers of part changes and late decisions. At the right are many of the "fixes" that the conventional system uses to "solve" the parts behind schedule problem, and the unintended consequences of those fixes (staffing shortfalls, the taking up of supplier time to help engineering) that actually make the problem worse.[6]

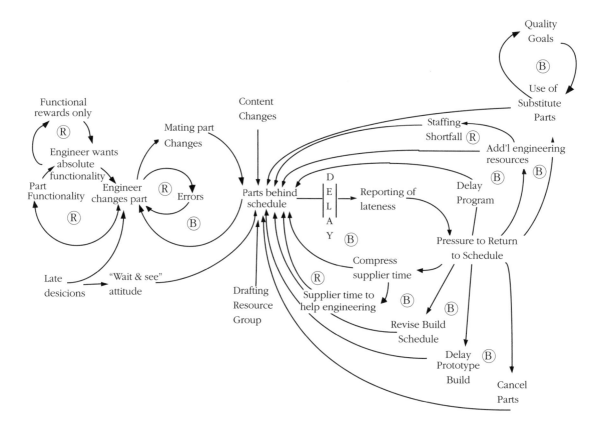

CONTENT LEADER: Every once in a while we bosses have to grit our teeth and swallow a decision that the team made, even if we personally think, "Well I'd rather not go on that path." If their thinking is reasonable enough, and they haven't missed any obvious issues, then my objection is just a matter of: "I would go the other way."

Involving people in making decisions suggests that leaders must make their own reasoning process explicit or, as in this case, justify it as "reasonable."

LAUNCH MANAGER: A new project manager, after sitting on a very typical discussion, ran up to one of my team leaders and said, "My God, your program is a disaster. You're not going to make it."

The team leader said, "No, this is the way we always talk. Everything that we know is thrown on the table. We thrash about, and issues sound a lot worse than they really are. This is our way of sharing what's going on."

The behaviors associated with letting people make their own decisions can appear messy to outsiders, as they did here.

The project manager said, "You've got to be kidding me. If anybody had said anything remotely like that on [my previous program], he would've been killed. Problems would have to reach a level of disaster before people would ever talk candidly."

Does there have to be a level of disaster before people will talk candidly?

ENGINEER: Every day someone comes in and says, "That was a really stupid thing you said in that meeting the other day. We all talked about it and we think this . . ." I may say, "Yeah, you guys are right," or maybe I don't agree. But at least nobody has any problem coming in and saying, "I don't agree with what you said," or "Other people think this," or "You didn't think about that." And it helps.

ENGINEER: When an engineer goes on vacation we cover for him. We all work as one, which I think would be pretty unusual in most other jobs.

These comments are typical of the remarks made by engineers about trust and openness; they were gathered throughout the stages of the car project.

ENGINEER: You don't hear dialog like, "People from body engineering are dragging their feet," or "Those hard noses from Assembly." We got that out of the way up front. Now we can get together and do the job.

◆ CREATING THE ATMOSPHERE OF TRUST AND COOPERATION

Based on interview data, the following factors appear to be important in creating an atmosphere which leads to trust and cooperation. These factors related to behaviors the core team sought to practice throughout the program. Each point is described and illustrated in a section which follows.

- A mandate that "bearing bad tidings" would be safe

- Ongoing sharing of information and perspective

- A culture of greater inclusiveness

- Deliberate encouragement of informality and friendship

- A mindset that "no one has all the answers"

Factors described elsewhere in the learning history also seem important:

- Leaders who modeled the desired behavior (see page 41)

- The conversational tools of the learning lab (see page 53)

- Collocation[7] (see page 87)

A mandate that "bearing bad tidings" would be safe

The Epsilon leaders had to start by mandating that candor, bringing in bad news, or raising uncomfortable questions would not be punished.

How can a team effectively change its culture from one that expects everyone to "have the answers" to one that encourages people to experiment and raise issues before the answers are certain? This comment was one of many illustrating how engineers came up with and contributed new ideas because they felt they would be heard.

What does it convey to subordinates when the boss admits he or she "doesn't have oo the answers"?

CONTENT LEADER: If people know they're not going to get punished (for taking risks), they'll try harder. We had all kinds of ideas coming out of the woodwork that people had been keeping in their hip pockets. The net we use for umbrella storage was an idea of one of the engineer's.

Engineers [on other projects] don't generate ideas like that; they wait for you to tell them what to do, so if it screws up they can say it wasn't their idea.

TEAM LEADER: [The Program Manager] always gave us a strong feeling that he wouldn't treat you like you were an idiot if you didn't know the answer. Or if you came to him for help, he would try to help.

Ongoing sharing of information and perspective

Sharing information from different aspects of the devel-opment process with a broad range of people appears to have helped create a greater awareness of program issues as a whole. Efforts were made to help people become aware of everyone's role in light of the overall program goals.

FINANCE MANAGER: We had a better understanding of why each of us does what we do. This understanding was helpful in the long term, because it gave us a base of trust and understanding. I think it started to reduce people's sensitivities a little bit. You understand why something happened. If it wasn't necessarily what you liked to hap-pen, at least you understood why.

INTERNAL CONSULTANT: When a supplier has a good rela-tionship with the engineers, the supplier will say things like [for example], "You didn't hear it from me, but some-thing is going to be late and somebody's lying to you. Don't tell anyone I told you."

One of the questions the managers considered was whether the extra time spent sharing information broadly could be made up by improvements in people's work effectiveness.

As managers shared information more openly, what new types of fear and anxiety might emerge? What message would information-sharing send to those who had kept information hidden?

A culture of greater inclusiveness

Including people, not just on the basis of who needs to know to do their job, appears to have created an atmosphere where people were more aware of the whole of what they were trying to achieve.

CONTENT LEADER: I think if you talk to any [Epsilon team member], they'll say, "Oh yeah, we've got fantastic team work." Well, every program's got team work.

On this program, [the Program Manager] provided a strong network for team work. He allowed it to happen easily. It's more than just collocation or expertise.

For instance, take the EP prototype build; chassis engi-neering was given credit for having 100% of their parts there, and that was the first time something like that has been accomplished. That says a lot about the strength of the engi-neering community as well as others who helped. It's like every day you're putting on your Epsilon suit and you're going in there and you're going to make a difference.

Team work was a much talked about concept at AutoCo. However, there were no common standards or definitions of team work, and managers often disagreed about which teams were more effective.

What difference is made by opening new channels of communication, such as including suppliers in internal meetings?

[The Program Manager] made the program very, very inclusive. He was adamant about having suppliers in there for [internal prototype meetings]. The meetings up front were pretty boring but Epsilon seemed to achieve their success because of the meetings.

Deliberate encouragement of informality and friendship

In the early stages of the car launch, some attributed the quality of the Epsilon team process to collocation (putting most of the Epsilon engineers in one building). Some attributed it to the people who had been chosen for the team and the quality of the engineers. Others argued that the team appointment process was random; indeed, Epsilon probably didn't get the "best" engineers, who would have gone to a higher-visibility automobile.

No matter the cause, there was an atmosphere of informality and friendliness which promoted good working relationships among team members. Managers invested in and sought to actively encourage the development of a climate which allowed people to work more informally with one another.

Offsite meetings where people were in residence were typically frowned upon at AutoCo because of cost implications.

The time and effort the core team put into developing relationship and open communication was not valued by all team members.

How important is it to develop a focus on the personal as well as the professional relationship?

Was knowing people beyond their role something that would help team members through more challenging and ambiguous situations?

ENGINEER: There was a three-day off-site [Oct. 1991], where you basically had to walk away from your desk, designs, and drawings. A lot of the team thought it was a waste of time; I think a lot of people walked away still not exactly sure what [the Launch Manager] and [the Program Manager] were trying to do. To me, the most critical thing that happened there was it really glued the team together. It was the first time everybody looked around and really realized they were all in this boat together. It was powerful.

Some of the dynamics and camaraderie and friendship came from living together at the hotel for three days, eating together, working together, and going and having a beer together. There's something about friendship outside of the work place that I think really helps build trust. If you met new people and had a beer with them or whatever, then two months later if you had a problem with an issue on the job you felt a little bit more comfortable approaching them. And I think it's human nature that if you get an opportunity to know a little bit more about a person's family and their interests outside of work, you trust them more than a total stranger. At the offsite we started talking about visions, and what the car was going to be, and everybody's roles and I think it created the bond. It was a reality check: This group of people was going to build this car and either make it a success or not.

A mindset that "no one has all the answers"

The managers told people that they didn't know the solutions to many problems or the answers to every question. They needed to learn too, and they needed to create the conditions where their teams could learn. This statement supporting "not knowing" ran counter to the expectations most managers and engineers held—of one another, their system, and themselves.

VEHICLE DEVELOPMENT TEAM LEADER: This was foreign to a certain degree; it was uncomfortable that the boss was learning with us. He didn't have the answers. We were going to do this together. As uncomfortable as it was on one hand, it was exciting on the other, because all of a sudden we felt like we were paving new ground. We weren't just being fed "the right thing to do in a corporate environment today."

How can business culture learn to acknowledge and accept mistakes in a constructive way?

Some of the appeal may have to do with the word "failure." If you stumbled, it wasn't perceived by [the Program Manager] as a failure. Instead, the reaction was: "It was a good honest effort, I appreciate your energies, and what have we learned from this?"

◆ BEHAVIORAL VERSUS TECHNICAL: A ZERO-SUM GAME?

As the Epsilon program developed, the core team placed strong emphasis on what they called "process" issues—explicitly learning to improve human communication skills, decision making methods, and understanding of each others' points of view. This emphasis on behavioral considerations—people and process—was neither familiar nor wellunderstood in AutoCo, which has a heritage of strong technical and engineering achievement.

In the larger company culture, most people felt that time was scarce and thus needed to be invested, as much as possible, in technology and engineering. These thoughts about time were based on an implicit assumption that behavioral and technical skills were caught in a zero-sum game; one could only be improved at the expense of the other. In contrast, the Epsilon team leaders believed that a well-designed learning process would result in engineering and people skills reinforcing each other. Technological capabilities could be more easily applied, and have greater impact, as engineers' people skills improved and they developed the capacity to handle systemic and interrelated issues.

The comments here were echoed by many people at AutoCo: "First handle the technical and then, if you have time left, you can work on the behavioral."

Do "process people" sometimes assume that their work is denigrated by the larger culture, when in fact it is not? Do they falsely assume process work is valued more than it actually is?

An implicit assumption, which came out clearly in other interviews, was that "if you can't measure it, you can't manage it." Process skills are difficult to measure, and their impacts are not easily assessed from the outside. How, then, can process work be evaluated?

VICE PRESIDENT: The first thing we have to do is make sure that people really understand the engineering processes —design verification, quality operating systems, prototype process, change control, the timing discipline, and so forth. If you asked me, "Do I do that before I do any teamwork and team building?"—the answer would be an unequivocal yes. I think if you don't have a fundamentally strong engineering framework, then no amount of team building or team process will ever overcome that weak system. You'll fail. The team will thrash about with all kinds of good intentions.

Now, the converse, I guess, is—assuming you have a fundamentally solid engineering process— as you encounter difficulties or fall behind in one area, team building and the human side of teamwork come into play. A team can rally, help each other overcome difficulties, and move on.

As I understand organizational learning, it preaches an appreciation for the other person's point of view. If you, as a team person, understand that your action or non-action causes another person a problem, then you will try hard to make that not happen. That understanding comes from team building experiences. The team is a very large family that's working together. How you measure that understanding, I don't know.

PROGRAM MANAGER'S BOSS: I could tell that the Vice President was really interested in getting this car program implemented. I think there were times when he was concerned that the team was spending too much time on the soft stuff and that could get in the way of hard results.

I have been very supportive of this work, but at the same time continued to stress to [the Program Manager] that he had to get results.

◆ THE DILEMMA OF INTEGRATING PROCESS AND ENGINEERING KNOWLEDGE

Despite the team leaders' intentions to have process knowledge and engineering knowledge reinforce each other, the synthesis was imperfect in practice. In at least one case, there were complaints that the engineering knowledge was short-changed. This had to do with the team's change of structure—bringing engineering and process authority together, assigned to work as one group of people—without looking closely at the assumptions that these people would hold about one another.

CONTENT LEADER: But when it came to dealing with some of the particularly difficult engineering issues, we were left out in left field, and we had no one to go to. I don't think it was [the Program Manager's] problem to get involved with these issues, because he doesn't know about engineering. But we should have been able to discuss the problem [that engineers felt unsupported.] I think after a while we recognized it and we avoided [dicussing it].

The fact that Launch and Program Managers were not engineers meant that they didn't jump into difficult engineering problems and participate in resolving them. Instead, they put them back on the team. As the comment shows, some engineers did not feel free to raise this problem.

Bringing the process leaders and the content leaders together on a team, it was thought, would allow them to recognize one another's blind spots and develop an appreciation for how the other side saw things. This, however, did not always happen.

CONTENT LEADER: There were some rough roads on this program. There used to be a conventional breakdown of car program management. You'd have separate managers for business planning, vehicle engineering, launch, and vehicle development.

On Epsilon, they tried to combine all those skills into one person. This was the first time they tried that man

The contrast between process knowledge and engineering knowledge was prominent within the Epsilon team as well as in the larger organization. People seemed to be experts at one or the other, but not both.

*Communication was not strong
between the two groups of experts
and some issues may have been overlooked.*

*How can we design learning so that
technical and process knowledge
reinforce each other?*

*Could members of both groups be
empowered simultaneously?*

agement system and the way they implemented it didn't work very well. It worked in fits and starts.

The real engineers all ended up reporting to the Chief Engineer, and the planning types ended up reporting to [the Launch Manager]. [The Launch Manager] is not an engineer by background. The planning people worked with the Design Center effectively, and knew how to talk about the features of the car, but they didn't have the background to say, "OK, now we need A and B completedby this time and we always have problems with B, so let's concentrate our efforts there."

We found out after a three-month delay, for example, that some engineering issues affecting the audio system were not being elevated to the Chief Engineer's level of discussion. Some of the vehicle leaders didn't seem to know enough to bring up the right questions. They should have had much more deliberate communication between the groups from the beginning.

CHAPTER 3

SETTING AN EXAMPLE OF NON-AUTHORITARIAN LEADERSHIP

Many Epsilon team members commented on the Launch Manager and the Program Manager's attitudes. Like many managers, the two Epsilon leaders said that they believed in openness and honesty. These two leaders were credited, however, with acting in ways that showed they believed in the values they were espousing. This was all the more striking because it was in contrast to the conventional approaches to management at AutoCo, and specifically to the ways these managers themselves had behaved in the past.

◆ LEADERSHIP ROLES: MODELING NEW BEHAVIOR

People throughout the Epsilon team, when asked what factors provided them with the greatest opportunity to learn and change, singled out the examples set by the Program Managers' "walking their talk."

CONTENT LEADER: I've known [the Program Manager] for 25 years. He was a typical senior program director when he came aboard—very autocratic and power-based, and always had been. But I've seen [the Program Manager] do a 180-degree turn in the last two years. It wasn't sudden; there were a lot of very subtle bends in the road over

Several people who had known the Program Manager for years remarked upon about his changed behavior. He had changed from having a punishing, frustrated, angry

style to being relaxed, approachable, and willing to ask questions, listen, and learn.

This seemed to make everyone more willing to raise questions and problems—not just directly with the Program Manager, but with the entire team.

Was this influence a result of the Program Manager's new approach in itself or a result of the visible contrast that people could see between the "new" and "old" Program Manager?

The managers created an atmosphere which helped people feel safe and valued. They worried, however, about whether the same nonconfrontational, open-minded style was viable in the larger AutoCo organization.

time. But he has gone through a complete change in management style. [The Launch Manager] deserves a lot of the credit for turning [the Program Manager] around, but as [the Program Manager] began to see the value in the learning labs, he became more supportive and he initiated a lot of the new approach.

I enjoyed it because it was the first time in 30 years at AutoCo that I, as an individual, felt valued by management. I felt that they had an absolute trust in me and in the team—not initially, not midway through the program, but by the end of the program. They provided the vision and they gave us the guidance from a total car point of view, but they put absolute trust in us. They would ask, "What do you guys think is the best for the car? Here is your objective. How do you think you'll do it? Tell me."

I think we responded very positively. Because I had trust from them, I put a lot of trust in my team. On other programs, I was constantly double-checking and telling people what to do—not asking them, "What do you think we should do?" I think we felt the weight of the responsibility we were given, and we tried to do a much better job because of that. I think we succeeded. It's enthused a lot of people who had not been enthused at AutoCo for 20 years. And it depended on the program leader's managing style.

To be honest with you, I'm spoiled. I'm worried. Who am I going to work for next, and can I adapt to that old AutoCo style again?

Episodes involving senior managers became part of the team's collective "mythology." Three people, for example, mentioned a meeting over a microphone package, in which the Launch Manager confronted an engineer in a way that people weren't used to, especially in front of other AutoCo managers. After a pause, the Launch Manager explained the reasoning behind his disappointment and inquired into the engineer's circumstances.

LAUNCH MANAGER (at the microphone package meeting): You know, I am very disappointed with what you've done. I just want you to know that. I don't understand why you did it. I need you to help me understand and I think we all need to understand what our roles are here.

ENGINEER, AN ATTENDEE AT THE MEETING: I had never seen that honesty and openness from a man at his level before.

ANOTHER ENGINEER: There's so little paper work on this team compared to other teams. We didn't have to prove everything to the last detail to [the Program Manager]. Other program managers spend so much time on studies. Say, for example, that a program manager wanted you to put the speedometer in the A pillar. An engineer would say, "I don't know how to tell you, but you can't do it."

"I don't care," the manager would say. "I want you to come back and tell me why." So you go out and do all these wiring studies. You pull a designer in to get the drawings done. You talk to your division manager. You get a nice document pulled together, showing every tic mark why you can't do this, and you call everyone together into his office and run through all the points. And he would say, "OK," as you've known all along he would, because the answer is implicit. But [the Program Manager] didn't have to do that.

We didn't make blind recommendations. The team did their homework every time. But we did not have to spend hours at the computer getting our reports to look just perfect.

EPSILON PRODUCT MANAGER AT A KEY SUPPLIER: Here's the famous quote from [the Program Manager]. We were sitting in a meeting one time looking at this floor console and he was playing with some of the features on it. He looked at us and said: "You guys really do good work." Then he played with the floor console some more and said, "You guys are really expensive."

He didn't yell at the cost. He made a statement about value versus cost. He liked the floor console, but he thought it cost a lot. Certainly, cost is important; but others

The Launch Manager's general level of honesty and directness was considered much higher than the AutoCo norm.

Engineers knew they were trusted because they were not required to complete the paper trail that documented "who did what, and when." This approach saved time and freed people to concentrate on the tasks at hand.

The change in managers' behavior extended to people outside AutoCo. Suppliers, vital producers of the parts that make up the new cars, also commented on the treatment they noticed from Epsilon program managers.

Even a small amount of positive reinforcement seemed to carry a lot of weight with suppliers. Those interviewed for this learning history sometimes commented that they were "used to being beat up" elsewhere in the auto industry, and thus appreciated their treatment here.

at AutoCo would have said, "You've got to cut the price," without regard to the value being delivered to the customer.

I was walking down the hall here with a young engineer from [my company], and [the Program Manager] saw us and stopped to chat. "You know," he said, "I really like it when I see you guys walking through here like this. It lets me know that you think this program is important to you." He didn't have to say that. Tactically, I don't know the degree to which he meant it. But it had a positive effect. The young engineer went back to our supply company office and said, "You ought to hear [the Program

Manager]. He said he likes the way we support the program." That got translated into a whole host of things that were all positive for our work on the car. And that was just a side comment going down the hall.

◆   WHAT MADE IT POSSIBLE FOR LEADERS TO CHANGE THEIR BEHAVIOR EFFECTIVELY?

We examined this question, directly and indirectly, in the interviews. The responses clustered into several ways in which new behaviors were demonstrated.

The core team meetings "trickled down"

These meetings, limited to the senior-most managers on the Epsilon team, became a concerted effort to improve communication among the Epsilon senior leadership. That improvement, in turn, influenced the behavior of senior managers in ways that were noticed by engineers on the program.

How do people begin to unlearn behaviors that have rewarded them up until now?

TEAM LEADER: Some people are natural-born team leaders. I don't think [the Program Manager] was one, but I think he has become a dynamic leader now. I don't think he would have changed without the core team learning effort.

LAUNCH MANAGER: It took the bosses literally eight months to learn how to quit being bosses. When we started Epsilon, we knew all the answers. That's why we were bosses. At least one of us always knew that our answer to the problem was the right answer; and boy did we defend our positions! We had conflict, mistrust, gamesmanship: all the dysfunctional stuff you hear about.

But, as we began to use the tools, and practice with them, [we started to listen to the rest of the Epsilon team members]. Can you imagine the bosses listening? We quit telling them what to do. We started to inquire. We started to challenge their perceptions.

One of the greatest struggles that educators have is getting students to unlearn the old so that they can absorb something new. What kinds of "unlearning" are appropriate to expect, or possible, in a business setting? How much "unlearning" is necessary to improve performance?

Is the team environment a necessary factor in changing individual behaviors?

Program management demonstrated commitment by taking part in every learning lab

Managers did more than talk about their behaviors. They participated in learning events, exhibiting their willingness to "try on" new types of behavior and demonstrating their support for the learning initiative to team members. As the leaders continued to increase their own capability to understand changes in themselves and others, the rest of the team began to notice.

LAUNCH MANAGER: My fundamental role [in the learning lab] was not so much to teach a new insight as it was to participate with them in creating a psychological safety net . . . [to show them] I was willing to make mistakes with them and share my own frustrations, and that it was okay to discuss these issues.

MIT RESEARCHER: I saw the changes in [the Program Manager]. Earlier in the program, I saw how intimidating he could be, sitting in that chair and grilling people. He could be very accusing: "I will not accept that." And I could see why he acted that way; in the AutoCo culture that is the only way to have credibility, to get heard, and to get things done. [The Program Manager] lamented that he got screwed unless he acted autocratically. We had one meeting where he talked about a dilemma where he was unsatisfied with one person's priorities. He felt he had to go back and make that person's life more miserable than anybody else's. That was his standing strategy up to that point.

I asked [the Program Manager] if he could share the dilemma with the person involved. Perhaps he could say something like, "Look, I'd rather not make your life difficult, but I have found that if I don't do this, I get screwed. Can we work together differently or is this the only option that I have?"

He said that he hadn't thought about doing that, and it couldn't hurt, because he always had the other option. I don't know if he ever did that . . .

PROGRAM MANAGER: I was really upset and I said, "We're going to miss this [deadline] . . ." I really gave them a hard time and they sat there and listened.

Then one team leader looked at me and said, "I can see why you would feel that way from what you've heard. Let me give you a different perspective on what's going on." He just stopped me cold and told me what was happening from his perspective. Then we talked about what we might do differently.

When he left, I had an entirely different feeling about what he had done, what he was trying to accomplish, and how he was doing it. He had a better understanding about what I was after. I didn't do that. He did that.

The changed behavior of the two top managers now began to filter down to influence other key leaders on the Epsilon team. Sometimes, this was the result of deliberate interventions by the top managers.

LAUNCH MANAGER: I called in [a problem supervisor] and said, "Let me tell you what I'm hearing in the halls about you. I don't know whether it's true. . . ." I repeated complaints I had heard and he defended himself. I said, "What do you think we should do about it?" He said he didn't know.

I suggested, "Why don't you go and ask people what they think about you? Why don't you do an interview about yourself?"

He did that over the next two months, then came back and said, "My God, [Launch Manager], I couldn't believe what they were telling me, although I had to practically beat it out of them. I've really been a horrible person. I learned a lot about myself and I don't like what I've learned."

And I just left it alone. Four years ago, I would have said, "You've got to stop being a tyrant" and told him to go to the Carnegie School of Whatever-it-is. And he would have just defended himself against my criticism. But if he heard it from the people that worked with him, he couldn't ignore it. He has made a lot of progress since then.

Partnership: Having the two leaders learning in tandem provided necessary support for one another

Several people (including the Program Manager and Launch Manager) explicitly pointed out how important the two men were to each other's success. They needed each other for perspective as "mirrors" to each other. They also needed each other's advice and encouragement.

LAUNCH MANAGER: Without [the Program Manager's] acceptance of the process changes; without [the Program Manager's] encouragement for us to learn; without [the Program Manager's] coaching in the difficult situations, this would not have been possible.

If there had only been one leader committed to fostering this learning effort, would the same level of innovation have occurred?

Relevance to results: Building a better car

Throughout all the interviews, the Program Manager never said, "I set out to change my personality—to become the kind of guy of whom people say, 'He really listens.'" He explicitly stated, instead, that his intent, from the beginning, was more capable collaboration across functional chimneys. He modeled a new way of acting on the job as a means to that end. He didn't try to act in new ways for the purpose of his own personal development.

Epsilon leaders faced a dilemma when they tried to explain their success to other AutoCo managers. On one hand, they were reluctant to emphasize their own personal change because that carried an implicit message that, "you [other AutoCo managers] must change your behavior as well." On the other hand, if they left out their personal change, a key element of the story (and a fundamental reason for their success) was lost.

◆ MODELING NEW BEHAVIOR: "I DON'T TRUST YOU"

The learning labs created further opportunities for Epsilon leaders and team members to address deeper issues together. Many of the critical issues involved trust and vulnerability, with both upper and lower levels of the hierarchy (within the Epsilon team) feeling the pressures of AutoCo's longstanding, prevalent habits of micromanagement.

CONTENT LEADER "X": Another content leader ("Y") and I were down at the learning lab and we were going through this struggle [with the Launch Manager] about managing change control. My biggest pet peeve is that we were wasting our time in sometimes four and five change control meetings a week. This is not unique to Epsilon; this was going on for years at AutoCo.

But [the Program Manager] and [the Launch Manager] would go after the little [change issues], rather than letting us manage them ourselves.

LAUNCH MANAGER: "Look [Launch Manager]!" they finally said, "You're making our lives miserable. You're making our jobs difficult because you're trying to control us. I can't get anything approved without coming to you and getting permission from you to get it approved. Why do we need a system that is so cumbersome?"

Lo and behold, I said: "Because I don't trust you."

INTERNAL CONSULTANT: When [the Launch Manager] said that (and, actually, he shouted it), there was an uncomfortable silence in the room. What went through our minds was: We always suspected [the Launch Manager] didn't trust us,

Managers, having promoted a climate of openness, heard directly about the impact they had on engineers.

Which required them to answer honestly . . .

. . . and that, in turn, allowed people to speak much more truthfully about underlying issues.

and now he's telling us as much. Then [the Launch Manager] proceeded to say, "And let me tell you why I don't trust you. If I did nothing to pressure you, you wouldn't meet your deadlines."

LAUNCH MANAGER: I would have had a difficult time saying that in the past. It would have cut the cord of communication and any hope for trust.

What personal qualities does it take, under these circumstances, to keep from feeling threatened or attacked?

But what happened next was amazing. I hadn't insulted them. They didn't get mad at me. They simply accepted that it was my position: I thought they would disrupt the system. And I accepted their position: that they were upset with the way I was acting with them. All of a sudden the truth came out. We finally got down to the nitty gritty—a meaningful discussion about how to dispel the problem.

CONTENT LEADER "X": In that discussion, [the Launch Manager] said he would help us. He did write a nice strong letter. As it turned out, our solution didn't matter, because within a week, it was all turned around. We were forced to start daily "pink" meetings [named for the color of change request forms], and that was it. So it didn't work.

An episode that made a strong impression on the leaders didn't necessarily have the same impact on other participants . . .

ANOTHER CONTENT LEADER [interviewed 8/93]: I'm one of the people "X" and "Y" had fought with in the past. I've noticed already that they handle issues differently than they did six months ago. They try to listen. They understand that it comes back around to them in the end a lot of times, because you can stonewall something only for so long.

. . . except where people perceived a more delayed, dispersed effect.

Recently "X" made a change that I was pretty upset about. I called him up and said, "You SOB," and started talking through with him the technical effects of that change on my part of the car.

And he actually apologized to me. He said, "You know, I'm sorry. We didn't know we were doing it to you."

I called "Y" up not long ago and said, "Your engineer rejected this change, but we really need it." I assumed that he was going to refuse to help me, and I would have had to force the issue with [the Program Manager]. Instead, he said, "We did that for a good reason. Why don't you and I meet and talk about it?"

We met and brainstormed together yesterday morning, and came up with a couple of ideas. That would have been unheard of in the past; he would have simply said, "I'm not helping you."

I realized that I've got to be retrained too, because I still don't trust them.

◆   DAMAGE FROM BACKSLIDING

The Epsilon leaders occasionally "fell off the wagon"—they slipped back to the authoritarian management style. Stories of lost temper, or accusations of "playing favorites," seem to linger for years in the folklore of a corporate change effort. Epsilon was no different. Several stories of backsliding were told in our interviews—particularly about the damage done when a leader did not rein in his temper. This story is typical:

Do people expect more from managers who espouse openness and cooperation?

TEAM LEADER: In January 1992 we were having a lot of problems on our team. At an offsite meeting, which was supposed to be a group team-building session, [the Program Manager] blew up. He told us that everybody was finding excuses for why our division screwed up. That was the low point of our morale as a team.

He apologized, but it happened repeatedly. He would fixate on us as a scapegoat, and a week later he'd apologize one more time. After about three times, I made a joke in front of everybody. I said, "When am I going to start believing you, [Program Manager]?"

What shift in assumptions drive a leader to move from a command-and-control style to a more collaborative approach?

But in the last year and a half, after he started to espouse the learning methods, he's changed quite a bit. Now, when he asked for a last-minute change that we would consider an unfair request on his part—say, a minor change in nomenclature which nonetheless affects our software and other technical considerations—he called in the design supervisor and me and personally explained why the name change was so important to marketing the vehicle. He took the time to personally ask our support. That was a big difference from the way he used to dictate from above.

Other interviewees described episodes of backsliding which did not have this "all's well that ends well" quality. In general, the Program Manager was seen as having "genuinely changed his stripes," but either people carried grudges from the time before the change, or they still perceived the Program Manager as harsh. Significantly, at least one person opted not to include a harsh comment about the Program Manager from their interview in this learning history—because he did not feel it was fair? or because he feared exposure as the author of the comment? or both?

CHAPTER 4

LEARNING LABS: TEACHING TECHNIQUES FOR THINKING DIFFERENTLY

What exactly did the Epsilon engineers feel they experienced in the learning labs conducted by the MIT researchers? How much did the labs improve their capabilities, and how much did those improvements affect their work on the car? Finally, how much did they feel the learning lab techniques affected their attitudes about learning?

Some of the participants we interviewed were indifferent to the labs, while others found them surprisingly relevant.

PROGRAM MANAGER: The MIT stuff is not new. I don't think there's a single technique that hasn't been talked about for 20 or 30 years. But they have put it together in a powerful way that lets people understand it quickly, implement it, and really do something with it.

Although the learning techniques and tools were not new individually (many simply represented common sense), their integration and use in a seminar seemed powerful.

◆ DESIGNING THE LEARNING LABS

MIT RESEARCHER: A group of us at MIT had created a learning laboratory at Hanover Insurance, using a computer-based management simulator. There, we had learned how

For the adaptation of the "simulation" approach to the Epsilon environment, see page 66.

effective it was to tell people about mental models and surfacing assumptions. I had that framework and flow in mind when we began to set up the learning labs at Epsilon.

The core team thought that our work with them, including the system dynamics and mental models tools, was valuable. They wanted to include more people in the conversation. We decided to develop the lab as a "practice field"—a safe place to talk about and work with the issues that participants would be wrestling with.

Box 4-1

WHAT ARE LEARNING LABORATORIES?

"Learning laboratory" is a term used originally by the MIT Center for Organizational Learning (and subsequently by the Society for Organizational Learning) for a work-shop, often also called a "managerial practice field," where people come to develop new skills, cycling back and forth between study and practice. As this Figure 4-1 sug-gests, the practice field (or learning lab) seems separate at first from the work envi-ronment, but gradually its concepts and values become integrated into regular work issues and the day-to-day job setting. This makes learning labs different from most training sessions, which take place off-site and "teach" techniques that rarely get put into practice on the job.

One model for the learning laboratory is the "practice sessions" held regularly in sports, the arts, and the military. Teams, simulate real events where members learn from mistakes and each others' examples. Similarly, learning labs simulate normal business set-tings, providing an opportunity for management teams to practice together and make mistakes without penalty or the pressures of performance. Participants learn new tools by applying them to the issues they face in their day-to-day jobs. The MIT-COL learn-ing labs at AutoCo focused on skills of conversation, reflection, and systems thinking.

The two-day learning labs at AutoCo were designed and facilitated by the Lead Researcher from the Center for Organizational Learning and selected managers from the Epsilon program team. The Launch Manager was the first AutoCo facilitator, and he was directly involved in all the learning labs.

The designs were based on the experiences of the first core team, and modified after each session in light of the experience of new labs, the makeup of participants, and new issues faced by the program. Some participants in early labs became facilitators of later labs. Four learning labs were run during the program. Over 100 people—more than a third of the full-time, dedicated engineers on the program—attended.

The learning labs at AutoCo[1] alternated between conceptual sessions for learning new tools (of conversation and systemic thinking) and exercises for practicing their use. These exercises were deliberately designed so that people could consider their own work issues with perspective that came from the deliberate telescoping of time and space. For example, a computer-based "management flight simulator" (see page 64 for more details) allowed participants to spend an afternoon working together through a product development process that would normally have required three to four years.

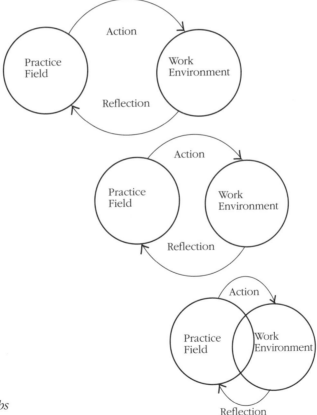

Figure 4-1 *Learning Labs*

Box 4-2

AGENDA FOR A LEARNING LAB

The Epsilon learning labs were two day sessions where participants were away from their work as they learned new tools and used them to reflect on their own issues. A typical learning lab had the following flow and content:

Day 1	Day 2
Introductions and Objectives	**Creative Orientation**
• teach techniques for thinking & learning • reinforce learning as a part of work • achieve commitment to use new tools in work	• creating shared visions • stories of successful team experiences • creative tension structure • personal visions exercise • barriers and enablers to car vision exercise
Center for Organizational Learning and its Work	**Systems Perspective**
Overview of Learning Lab	• levels of explanation • new ways of thinking and perceiving • changing ourselves versus changing "them" • systems archetypes • causal loop diagrams • systems archetype exercises
• distribute learning journals	
What is Learning? • exercise in personal learning • overview of five learning disciplines • problem solving vs. problem articulation	**Management Flight Simulator Session**
Mental Models • how we perceive reality • as barrier to team learning • writing a left hand column case exercise • ladder of inference • balancing inquiry and advocacy	• overview of MicroWorld for product development • how to use computer interface (simulator controls) • strategy sheets • simulation runs • debriefing
Practice versus Performance Environments	**Learning Lab Debriefing**
	• discussion groups and reporting out, or • group dialogue

Practice fields are meant to take people away from everyday performance pressures and allow them to develop some new attitudes and approaches in a simulated environment. Just as a "flight simulator" training device prepares airline pilots for emergencies and pressures that would be overwhelming in real life (unless they could first have some training for them), a practice field helps people learn to cope with emergencies and management pressures before they occur.

LAUNCH MANAGER: In his speeches, Peter Senge asks: "How do great teams become great teams?" Well, they practice. Orchestras practice; baseball teams practice. Great teams tend to practice. But we don't have that capability in the business organization. So how do we become great teams? Well, we just kind of luck into it.

We wondered: "Is there a possibility for us to create an environment where we can create that kind of practice?" The way to do it is to start with learning labs: small groups in which we can begin to transform the way people think, behave and communicate in teams, and then create models that they can use to practice the behavior in reality.

Can managers incorporate some of these strategies into current meetings? And practice in that way? Or must it be done through formal learning labs?

[The Program Manager] did not directly participate in the learning labs. We were afraid his presence would inhibit the free flow of information and discussion in the group. Whereas apparently I was in a position where I would not have that effect. We were going to test this by bringing [the Program Manager] into a learning lab, but we didn't have the opportunity.

Nonetheless, [the Program Manager's] involvement was critical. He would always show up on the Thursday evening dinner. And we would have a guest speaker come in, generally from inside AutoCo: the Program Manager's boss, the segment director, or an operations person who has been a champion of this approach.

The participation of AutoCo management (from outside Epsilon) as guest speakers was repeatedly mentioned by participants as one of the most important things they remembered about the sessions.

◆ CHOOSING LEARNING LAB PARTICIPANTS

Originally, the learning lab designers (the Launch Manager, the Program Manager, and the Lead MIT Researcher) hoped to include everyone on the Epsilon team in the learning labs. Later, they realized that a critical mass of practitioners could influence the whole team, without having to put the whole team through the labs.

Participants in the labs were selected, rather than invited to volunteer. This contradicts one of the generally accepted tenets of learning organization work: That learners learn only what learners want to learn," and that forcing people into learning experiences would only backfire and produce resentment. Yet it seemed to produce little resentment here.

LAUNCH MANAGER: We had four Learning Labs for about 100 people in total. The first was in the Fall of 1992. We picked an interior team and an electrical team, deliberately choosing younger engineers whom we thought would be "early adopters": more open and receptive to new ideas. We conducted a two-day session. It had taken the Core Team eight months to learn to "stop being bosses": to begin trusting and communicating with each other. Now, how could we accomplish that with a group of 20 people in two days?

Well, to my surprise, the Learning Lab went extremely well. I was elated at how quickly they grasped the learning tools and began to use them—first, right in the Learning Lab, and then elsewhere on the team.

We went on to another learning lab with some very tough people: engineers who had been here many years, whom we didn't think would ever open their minds up to new learning. These were crusty people, who were sitting there wondering what the matter was with us.

We discovered that in only two days these engineers were very quick to adopt these new tools. One of my roughest and meanest team leaders had been there 35 years; we had to practically drag him into the learning lab by force. Afterwards, he walked up to me and volunteered, "Gee, [the Launch Manager]. If I knew how good this was, I would have brought everybody whoworks for me."

◆ THE SYSTEMS ARCHETYPES AND "SYSTEMS THINKING" SKILLS

At first glance, work on systems thinking is akin to "process mapping" and other quality movement methods. Participants uncover the hidden interrelationships that govern their own work. However, the mapping techniques are based on system dynamics theory, incorporating an understanding of the "feedback processes" that govern the growth and stability of systems over time. Thus, for example, systems thinking shows how a "fix" may unexpectedly backfire when it triggers an unanticipated "vicious cycle" or how unseen (but predictable) pressures may limit the growth potential of a desirable innovation. As one internal consultant put it: "The systems thinking work shows how you can't just throw people and money at problems."

The tragedy of the power supply

One of the first understandings to emerge from the Epsilon systems work was the "tragedy of the power supply," a case in which several functional groups on the Epsilon Team found themselves cast in opposition to each other:

LAUNCH MANAGER: The [overall Epsilon] team spent five months trying to resolve an electrical issue which they couldn't resolve at their own levels. Each engineer had a component they wanted to maximize. Each engineer's organization said to them, "Don't give in." So whenever they came to meetings, they argued the same issues: "No, I can't give up the air conditioning unit design. We need it to be the best in the world." Or, "I'm not going to change the headlight designs because they have to be the best in the world."

But we had a battery system which couldn't accommodate all these best-in-the-world components. Usage was 12 amps above capacity. If we had identified this earlier, we might have been able to put in a second battery, or a higher-capacity battery. But by then, the area available in the car couldn't be made any bigger. So they were trapped; they had to start compromising. And they couldn't resolve the disagreement, despite all their intentions.

CONTENT LEADER: Embroiled in these arguments at a Battery Charging Team meeting, I suddenly thought back to the systems work from the first Learning Lab. "Do you think

The multiple teams who were involved became caught up in advocating the importance of their own components, and thus could not reach an agreement that accommodated everyone.

An engineer who can't resolve a problem is considered to have "failed." Here, the engineers were in a double bind; the harder they struggled against their "failure," the worse the failure became.

BOX 4-3

MAPPING THE TRAGEDY OF THE POWER SUPPLY

In the two reinforcing processes (shown as loops with 'R" in the center) at left, each components group pursues actions which are individually beneficial—building their own electrical components with high functionality, and thus with high electrical requirements. In combination with the other components, this raises the total electrical load requirement to a point where the battery power available per component approaches (and threatens to overtake) the limit of total battery capacity. Facing these limits from an individual-component mindset, each design team adds even more functionality. This, they hope, will help justify allotting them as much battery power as possible from the common pool. The result is individual gain, but collective pain.

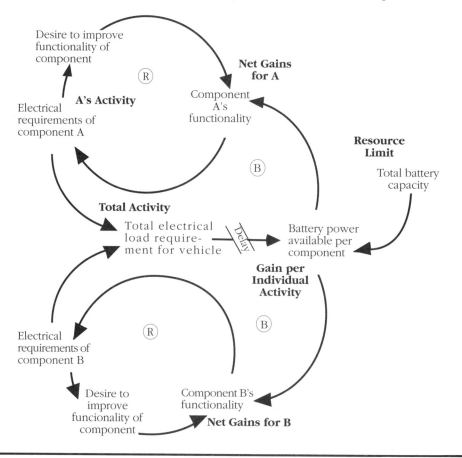

this sounds like a tragedy of the commons?" I asked. I talked about the Tragedy of the Commons systems archetype: The more a common resource is depleted, the more individual actors fight for a bigger share.

One of the process consultants, who knew the work, reminded us that it's very difficult to resolve a tragedy of the commons issue at the individual level. "How would you feel," he asked, "if we went to the Program Manager and the Launch Manager with this?"

"I'd feel really bad," I said. "I'd feel like I failed." But we realized how the system had created a "no-win" situation, and there was no shame in going to the Launch Manager and the Program Manager with this systems issue.

An insight into the structure of the problem helped distinguish among 1) authority imposed on participants; 2) mediation sought by participants; 3) the imperatives of the larger system, as seen and understood by participants.

PROGRAM MANAGER: Finally, they mapped the story for themselves. They laid out all their individual problems and their incentives: their organization's goals, how the results would be measured, and what the effects of a solution would be on that chimney and its performance measures. It was clear that they would all be individually right, but the car would fail. No one wanted to be criticized by his management for doing something foolish with his component to make somebody else successful. But they could all accept what they would have to do to make the car work—if the Program Manager told them to do it. They accepted my orders, even though the orders went against their chimney's objective, because they knew that's what it would take to solve the tragedy of the commons.

It might be useful to identify similar situations in other organizations and teams and to look at other ways that groups have handled this type of dilemma.

What difference does it make to have universal awareness of the system? What approaches offer more leverage?

Participants agreed that the value of this systems story, and others that surfaced in the learning labs, comes from the way they exemplified common real world dilemmas. There were many "tragedies of the power supply" at Epsilon. This just happened to be the first that came to light in such a dramatic way and was worked out in such a coherent form.

Once they were worked out, there was a tendency to package the systems stories for wider distribution. Unfortunately, this gave the impression that the stories had primary value as prepackaged lessons, rather than as learning experiences.

"I'm still hearing the same stories about 'the tragedy of the power supply,'" said an internal consultant. 'It's almost become a joke with some of those folks: 'Why don't you whip out the old 'tragedy' chart?' So now, people tend to think that everything is a 'tragedy of the commons,' when they should be investigating their own situations." A new technique can also get overused, limit insight, and undermine learning.

Did people use systems maps as a way to present problems to the Program Manager because they thought he would be better able to hear them?

What is the role of the manager in fostering better understanding of systems?

PROGRAM MANAGER: I had heard of a few examples of system mapping. About most of them I said to myself, "That's rubbish. They would have come to that conclusion any way." But in this case, if they hadn't mapped the problem, they would have fooled around for another couple of months, and it would have been too late. At the time of the EP prototype we would have discovered that the batteries went dead, and we would have had to do something drastic.

Another case was the battle between the chassis team and a development team that was struggling with noise, vibration, and harshness. Each side had a problem, and every time one side fixed it, it made the other side's problem worse. Both sides knew that if they had talked to each other earlier, they could have come up with a collaborative solution. But they hadn't. So both sides attributed motives to each other: "These guys are not willing to communicate. They don't care about us or our problems. So screw them." They stopped talking to each other.

Then we decided to map the problem together. It changed the way the two groups did business with each other. In fact, the chassis guys became very active with the development guys in design up front, instead of waiting back home for a transmittal from the development guys telling them what they had to do to fix the car.

There was nothing novel in the system diagram. Any of them could have thought of it by himself. But because they did it together, and because they could draw something they all could see, they changed the way they worked together.

◆ THE LADDER OF INFERENCE AND "MENTAL MODELS" SKILLS

The most effective aspects of the learning lab were the simple work on "reflection and inquiry" skills. In these exercises, participants "slowed down" their conversation and made a concerted effort to explicitly talk about the generally unspoken tacit attitudes and assumptions that drove many decisions. The discipline of "working with mental models" often has a large immediate impact with business people because it offers a tangible, accessible way out of the counterproductive defensiveness of many business conversations. Using conversational tools such as the "ladder of inference" and "left-hand column" (see page 24), people develop the ability to ask more effective questions and advocate their own positions with more openness and success.

TEAM LEADER: When you have the time to practice the "mental models" skills, they're not needed. But when you get into a crisis mode, everybody starts scrambling and worrying about their own thing; the communications fall off. You're facing off against body engineers not wanting to make a change, or another division, and people don't want to work together. That's where if you can retain a little bit of the skills, it helps you through a little bit.

   One tool from MIT that I think has helped quite a bit is the phrase: "Let me repeat what I think I hear you saying. Is that right?" We use that in meetings, and it helps in communication quite a bit.

It seemed to be a consistent issue throughout Epsilon (and AutoCo): behavior and thinking during high-stress times were very different than ordinary behavior and thinking, and it required a different approach to get things done in moments of high stress.

Might some people unconsciously engineer high-stress situations because if gave them power over others during those times?

TEAM LEADER: For an engineer, the material was very hard to grasp; it was so intangible. But the presence of MIT, as a respected university, gave it a little bit more credibility. The learning lab project wasn't just [the Program Manager] and [the Launch Manager]; it wasn't just an internal, whimsical, fly-by-night plan.

Few universities, in an engineering culture, would be as respected as MIT. Yet the learning lab was not built on mainstream MIT ideas. What kind of imprimatur is needed to give new ideas legitimacy?

CONTENT LEADER: The ladder of inference was worth its weight in gold for me. If you wanted to make sure that the other person wasn't just saying a conjecture or

Many people commented on the usefulness of the ladder of inference. Epsilon team members used this conceptual device to create different possibilities in their own minds for communicating more effectively with suppliers and other engineering teams. See page 24 for a description of the ladder of inference.

The ladder of inference concept created a possibility in the minds of engineers that the ways they "saw" things might be different than how others saw them. This led them to inquire before they jumped into action.

The example illustrates how a hierarchical culture and the attitude that "other people are idiots" seem to reinforce each other.

assumption, you could ask him to go down the ladder so the conversation got back "down" [to data]. All of a sudden, things would clear up.

ENGINEER: One of my suppliers—an excellent supplier, by the way—mentioned under his breath at the end of a meeting that a part would be two weeks late. He didn't want anyone but me to hear him. I gathered my wits for a minute, because it was really a shock. We hadn't had any problems with that part. I asked why it would be late, and he said, "I'm not sure." I could see everyone's eyes in the meeting hitting the roof. They were saying to themselves: "God, [Supplier] is an idiot. What's wrong with him? We thought he was a good guy."

At that point I could see we needed to bring things down on the ladder. [Supplier] was not going to tell us any more. Why would he? He had already risked enough, and made himself look foolish. So I consciously brought things down to observable data.

"Look, [Supplier]," I said, "If you don't tell us where the problem is, we'll never get to the root of this issue." After a lot of prodding and pleading, it came out that he thought it was a problem with paperwork that we [at AutoCo] had lost, and he didn't want to be the one to tell us.

So I went back and checked. AutoCo's system had misplaced not only his paperwork, but a lot of paperwork. It was causing parts to come in a little later than anticipated, just enough to mess up the build. [Supplier]'s honesty allowed us to make sure everything coordinated on time.

Traditionally I would have thought, "I don't want to hear about [Supplier]'s problems. He is an idiot." I wouldn't have checked the reasoning which led me to that assumption. I would have said to him, "Just make sure the part's on time." There would be nothing he could do about it.

It's very difficult to use the new approach when you're the only person in the room who knows what it is.

For instance, someone will make a statement like, "Oh, [Supplier]'s seat belt's going to be late." Everyone in the meeting says, "[Supplier]'s an idiot." You've jumped right up those rungs. No one even says, "Why are we saying this?" When I'm by myself, I'm more hesitant to step out of my comfort zone and ask that question in the group.

But if you have at least one other person who has been through the learning lab, you can bounce comments off each other without people in the meeting knowing what you're doing. It builds and builds and you see it taking effect. I'll be in a meeting with "X" [an engineer I work closely with], and he'll call someone else a moron. I might say, "X, you're at the top of your ladder." No one else knows what that means. But he'll think about it and say, "You know, you're right." Then we discuss why the "morons" might have done what they did, before we carelessly jump all over them.

Moving conversations among groups of people from beliefs and assumptions to "observable data" was particularly helpful in an engineering world where people design and produce tangible, technical automobile parts that need to work together.

CONTENT LEADER: When the learning lab ended, I said, "Well, that was neat. Let's get back to work." Very little of it seemed to stick with me.

But after a couple of days, I started thinking about it. We gave it a try in our meetings. "Come on guys," I would say. "Let's start talking about observable data here instead of our opinions or our belief systems." Because you don't make any progress at all by shoving your opinion at the other guy. By now, we recognize right away now when that's happening. We used to sit in meetings for hours, and everyone walked out pissed off.

Terms like "jumping up the rungs" or "where are you on the ladder?" were used to ask people to tell one another about the data they had to support their assertions.

◆ THE "MANAGEMENT FLIGHT SIMULATORS"

Some of the work of the learning lab centered around "simulation" exercises programmed onto computers by a core team of Epsilon and MIT people, in which different strategies and approaches could be tested. Research conducted on these computer simulations at MIT has shown that there are innate difficulties in converting a computer-based "management

BOX 4-4

WHAT IS A "MANAGEMENT FLIGHT SIMULATOR"?

A management flight simulator is an interactive computer simulation of business situations, used to provide managers the opportunity to "test" a variety of decisions and develop greater insight about the range of possible outcomes and the sources of possible leverage. The Epsilon learning labs used a management flight simulator based on the product development process in the automobile industry.

Menu Bar: Click and hold mouse button on the menu choice and drag the mouse to the desired command. Start a new game by selecting the restart option under the explore menu

The "Cockpit"

Decision Area: Select the decision you want to change and enter the new value.

Click on the step button to advance the

Reports show the current project status. Click on the desired report.

Graphs show history of the project. Click on desired graph.

Use up and down arrows to scroll through choices.

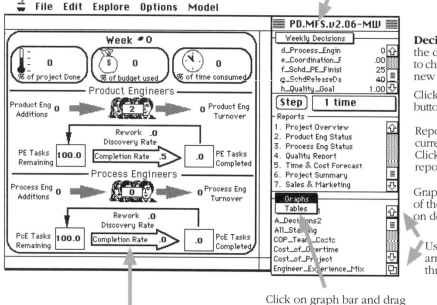

Click on graph bar and drag to desired viewing option

Main Viewing Area: Any graph or report selected in the "cockpit" will appear here. To close a graph or report, click anywhere in the view, then click in the box that appears in the left corner of the gray bar at the top of the viewing

Underlying the computerized "cockpit" (the simulator controls) is a system dynamics model of interrelationships among critical forces in the system. Mathematical formulas represent the links between different variables in the system. These interactions have been tested and calibrated through extensive field work in a variety of organizations. Nonetheless, like those of anymodel, they represent a simplification of the reality that the model is intended to describe, and part of the model-building process involves continual refinement of the model to make it match more closely the interplay of causal relationships in a real-world system.

A crucial feature of the management flight simulator is the design of the session (in this case, the learning lab) in which people work with it. Instead of simply "testing new strategies," as if they were playing a computer game, participants should be asked to articulate their strategies ahead of time, and the reasons why they have chosen their course. Managers are not calling upon the model to give them a "correct" answer, but to helpthem see their own tacit, deeply held theories about their business environment and organization, theories which guide many of their decisions in real life. For example, the simulation revealed that, under pressure, many managers slipped the schedule because overspending cost targets was so strongly punished. Yet, in the overall life cycle of a vehicle, a delay in getting a car to market was costly in terms of lost revenue that could never be recouped. Discussions with other team members help everyone see how those tacit theories affect the entire operation.

The illustration opposite shows the "cockpit" (the on-screen command center) of the Product Development management flight simulator. The left-hand part of the screen shows indicators of activity in the project (for example, the percentage done). The right-hand part allows the participant to enter decisions (for example, about the number of process engineers to hire) and select reports or graphs for viewing. These reports and graphs show, in detail, current status and historical data.

flight simulator" from one business environment (such as the insurance business) to another (such as the automobile business).[2]

For that reason, the Epsilon leaders and the MIT consultants designed and programmed their own computer-based "management flight simulator" just for product launches. In general, the computer models weren't considered as crucial as the systems and mental model conversations. At first, this surprised the designers of the learning labs. Later, in retrospective interviews, it was almost taken for granted by all participants: The computer models did not yield nearly as much insight as simpler exercises, like the Ladder of Inference.

CONTENT LEADER: I thought one beneficial thing was the computer game we played at the end, where we could see the consequences of our decisions.

Many people said to me that they think that the thing that changed their outlook on things the most was the computer game. They had thought they had all the answers, but they plugged them into the computer and all of a sudden the red flag came up. We didn't do as well as we thought we would.

This is one of the few remarks singling out the computer models as a valuable factor. Perhaps different learning styles need to be taken into account in laboratory designs. Some people may remember information presented in this manner more easily.

It was comparable to the "beer game" that MIT uses in its courses.[3] I had a fellow in powertrain sitting three chairs away from me in the "beer game." He was absolutely unmanageable, positive he was doing every‑ thing right. He made decisions and, in the end, he messed up pretty bad. And after that he was a totally different per‑ son. He wasn't so adamant about things.

◆ REINFORCEMENT: A LEARNING ROOM

To provide opportunities to continue and support the learning process, AutoCo program managers created a "learning room" where they held weekly breakfast meetings. This "learning room" was a conference room without a table, with flip charts from learning labs on the walls, and chairs set in a circle to create and encourage an atmosphere of peer-to-peer con‑ versations. For the breakfast meetings senior managers on the team brought doughnuts and invited engineers to "drop in" to ask questions and to take part in more free-ranging, unstructured conversations.

How can reinforcement be designed into a manufacturing environment, so people have a chance to practice learning skills as part of everyday work?

RESEARCHER [in mid-1994]: We're trying to put support mechanisms in place: conversations to continue and rein‑ force the understandings which people gained in the original labs.

LAUNCH MANAGER: Once a week, Wednesday morning, we asked members of the team to come to the learning room.

There they could discuss anything they wanted, but they had to leave the baggage of the conventional way of operating behind. "Bring your problems and use the tools. Practice them."

◆ LEARNING LABS: HOW DID THEY CONTRIBUTE TO THE CHANGE PROCESS?

General reactions to the learning labs were mixed. Some people we interviewed weren't even sure whether they had been to one. Most remember being skeptical, yet being impressed that the boss was in front of the room talking about mistakes and learning from them. In the end, were they influential? The quotes suggest they were, but in a subtle, often overlooked way.

Some of the learning lab participants commented that the changes they saw in management (particularly the Program Manager, the Launch Manager, and the Chief Engineering Manager) were much more significant than their own changes from the learning labs. Other participants talked at length about changes in themselves: an increase in openness, less tendency to blame others (or themselves), a better understanding of their own biases and mental blinders.

ASSEMBLY LAUNCH LEADER: When I learned about these "dog and pony shows," I thought, "Oh, they're flag waving." I laughed at it. "My God, what a waste of time and money."

But I saw it work. The labs got people talking to each other early on, picking each others' brains. They found out what things had gone right and wrong from prior launches, what we could do to make things better, and what pitfalls to watch out for. We had not only the engineering fraternity but the people from Assembly and all divisions trying to talk to each other and air their dirty laundry up front. That built the team.

Later on, other groups, like the truck people, used to needle us: "You guys having another cake and party? Another offsite boondoggle?" But even though you didn't have to believe in it, it did work and it's showing here. Would I do it again? No. I plan on retiring. But I'd advise

Even when people found they learned in the learning labs, it was seen with great skepticism by their peers in other groups. AutoCo people did not want to talk openly about "learning" amidst their prevailing corporate culture, with its strong emphasis on technological "answers."

Some managers and engineers at AutoCo (and at its suppliers) recognized Epsilon's unusually capable performance and attributed it to a variety of factors. The "MIT method," as mentioned here, was one factor, but they also had their success attributed simply to "making an effort" (as here), to having more innate capability ("Epsilon had some good people"), and to stronger willpower (as in the next comment).

another manager to go for it because it's proven out on the Epsilon.

EPSILON PRODUCT MANAGER AT A KEY SUPPLIER: Companies like AutoCo are so authoritarian in their nature, that anything you could do to blast them off of authoritarianism and start to move them towards participation and teamwork is a good thing. I don't know about the MIT method, but I see it as having created a kind of level of credibility for teamwork, for the team effort. They might have done that using other methods, too, but the main point for me is that AutoCo is making the effort.

If people do not apply the techniques covered in the learning lab, is that cause for concern? Or not? If it is cause for concern, does it suggest that changes should be made in a) the design of the AutoCo learning effort and learning labs? b) the MIT implementation of these tools? c) the learning approach in general?

INTERNAL CONSULTANT: I talked to a couple of folks who were not part of the learning labs. They might have gone to an offsite or two. They said, "We don't do much of the MIT stuff, except when [the Launch Manager]'s in the room. [The Launch Manager] will say, "Where are you on the ladder?" And people start talking about that for a while. It's not that they don't think about it; it's just that they're focused on their day-to-day jobs.

A couple of the hard-core engineers say things like, "I don't know why you credit this MIT stuff. This is a successful program because we set dates and held them." That's the engineering mindset.

CONTENT LEADER: When people go to learning labs, there's no light bulb that goes off: "Aha!" The change stems from the subtleties that go along with it. People go back to work thinking about trying to be more open, more honest. Maybe they're just more open to the possibility. They see themselves interacting differently with each other. They don't say, "And now I'm going to use the ladder of inference," but the tools creep up in the backs of our minds.

In the face of these considerations, how might one assess the effect of the learning labs?

MIT RESEARCHER: This is the tough part of measuring learning. If you learn something that sort of changes the way you see the world, it may look like nothing has really happened. Yet everything has changed. Paradoxically, the bigger the change is, the less visible it may be. The change may take place in so many subtle ways, so diffusely, that you can't see it until, over time, you gradually see a bigger picture. It's much less visible than a problem solving effort, where you can show visible progress on how you solved that sucker.

LAUNCH MANAGER: You remember how in the Wizard of Oz film, the scarecrow got a diploma to legitimize his learning? Maybe we did something similar here. Maybe, by bringing in MIT, we legitimized our focus on process improvement much more than we could have done on an ad hoc basis. Without MIT, I would not know how to use these powerful tools. I could have read about them in a book, but without somebody showing me how we practice them over time, we would not have realized the tremendous power that is in those artifacts.

PROCESS LEADER: What does it mean to be a learning organization? I think we fall short on several dimensions.

When you hear folks describe the left-hand column, for instance, it's not even close to a textbook descrip-tion. They say things like, "If they can expose their emotional stuff, we can get to the real truth." As opposed to how I would describe the left-hand column: the things that people haven't said because the environment is not emotionally or politically safe.

If we don't understand what a tool really is, how can we use it very effectively? I may make too big a deal of the textbook, but I think that we need to do a better job of helping people learn what the tools are really about. MIT and AutoCo are learning this together; and the difficulty is that there's not a lot of patience around here for struggle. That's not just true of AutoCo; it's an organizational reality. MIT needs to understand that organizations like AutoCo will fault MIT for not providing enough support or for not teaching us well enough.

I rarely use any of the tools in a meeting. I wish I could. I think about them. If I tried to use them in a meet-

There was value expressed by participants in the experiential component of the learning process. Although managers and engineers often ask for materials to read and don't take time to attend workshops, having the learning labs partially facilitated by managers and focused on current work issues made it feasible for people to find the time to participate.

Several articles lionized AutoCo, and Epsilon in particular, as a good example of a "learning organization."

Were the modifications people made to the textbook definitions helpful in adapting the learning materials for the AutoCo culture?

How might those changes have influenced the effectiveness of the tools?

This comment was typical. People appreciated the learning tools, but given the short exposure they had, they struggled when they tried to use them back in the work setting.

Attitude, as well as aptitude, influenced the effective use of learning tools.

ing, I'd go home with my head in my hand because I'm not good enough. I'm not facile enough with archetypes.

The tools you'll see used most are the communication tools: the ladder of inference and the left-hand column. The ladder of inference is helpful, but unfortunately, we generally use it during our spare time.

If we're in a meeting and things don't go well, we don't use the tool then. We walk away from the meeting and on the drive back to the office together in the car, I might say: "Well, wait a minute. You know, we're way up here on assumptions. Let's come back down to behaviors and try to understand why so-and-so did that."

Or people may use the tools sarcastically: "Well, let's get into our left-hand column and see if that helps, heh, heh, heh." And then they obviously don't.

In other words, the tools are very powerful, but until we can use them accurately and on the spot, we haven't gotten there. We're still on the learning curve.

I think the results are better. I hear both sides. Some folks from the pilot plant, who built the EPs, say this is the best product they've had come down the line. It looks better than an EP ever has before. Other people say, "You guys are flat on your ass. There's holes where they don't belong [in the auto body] and so on." In terms of hard measures, the one you can look at is the percentage of parts that were ready the day we were supposed to start building. I've heard numbers that say we're at 80 percent. Typical is more like 40 percent. If that's accurate, then we are much better.

Now, is that a result of what we've done at MIT? It beats me.

Again, this comment is typical of how people made linkages between learning tools and business results. The learning tools helped, but were diffuse and subtle. No one, other then the program managers, attributed the Epsilon program's achievements to the learning tools. Yet, people often talked independently about the efficacy of the learning tools for product development management issues and achieving metrics which were significantly better than many other vehicle programs.

How could the connection between learning and results be examined in this type of setting?

CHAPTER 5

COMBINING ENGINEERING INNOVATION WITH HUMAN RELATIONS: THE HARMONY BUCK

An innovation developed by the Epsilon team, the harmony buck, has become standard practice at AutoCo. Harmony bucks are a part of most new interior programs at AutoCo, beginning in 1998 and beyond.

The team's interviews suggest that large-scale technical innovations like this one are possible because of two factors: a willingness to break established methods and the opportunity to collaborate across functional lines.

The harmony buck story begins with the program managers' efforts at the beginning of the program to set common goals and objectives and to establish something intangible—a vision of what it would be like when they accomplished their program goals.

PROGRAM MANAGER: In the early stages of the launch, we asked people at every level of the team for their image of an ideal launch. What would make this launch successful, in their minds? Ultimately, the team settled on the image of a Maytag repairman, from the well-known Maytag commercials. When the car moved into the assembly plant, everything should be so well established that there wouldn't be anything left to do.

Then we asked ourselves, "Ignoring the fact that we don't think it would be possible, and ignoring the problems we anticipate—how would we make this "Maytag repairman" future come to pass? We said we would have

How do such visioning processes affect team innovation?

This simple image (the Maytag repairman) was used repeatedly during the Epsilon launch to describe their desired level of simplicity and reliability.

to redefine the schedule. Engineering changes should stop at the point when prototypes are in progress. During the period of building prototypes, the suppliers should be learning how to make the parts. Then during the stages of pilot production, the assembly people should learn how to assemble the car.

By the time we got to the launch date, we hoped, all that would be left would be training the assembly people to produce the car faster. Everything depended on setting things up so the engineers wouldn't make changes after the prototype phase. But how could we accomplish that?

◆ GETTING APPROVAL: BUILDING CONFIDENCE TO MAKE A CASE FOR TAKING A RISK

Making the case to upper management for additional investment is not always easily done.

Top management approved the request for a concrete technical innovation, like the harmony buck, more easily than they approved a more abstract and general request for support of learning process initiatives.

This comment about the Program Manager's predecessor illustrates the importance of individual personalities and management styles. The systematic nature of the learning

ENGINEER: The harmony buck story started back in June 1989, at the very beginning of the Epsilon project. The question came through our department: What would it take for us to meet and exceed the standards for components of the past? This was the most complex car that we had ever done. It was pushing the edge of so many different component technologies that the electrical community was very nervous about it up front. We recommended a full harmony buck from engine to rear; the idea went up to the program manager at the time, [the Program Manager's] predecessor. He was not very interested, but some of the other team leaders were. They realized the impact the harmony buck would have on the quality numbers. Different engineers from different parts of the car began to push for this thing.

Later, after [the Program Manager] was there, there was a meeting of supervisors, managers, and executives at world headquarters. The senior managers asked again: How would we raise or exceed past standards? Once again, the harmony buck answer came out.

RESEARCHER: One of the engineers who initiated the harmony buck told me that he would never have had the audacity to propose it, except for the encouragement he had received during the previous months at Epsilon. [The Program Manager] had been saying: "Look we're not going to beat up on you. We really want to know what you are thinking."

CHIEF ENGINEERING MANAGER: We presented the idea in a meeting with our Vice President. We said, "We think we can save money downstream by finding the problems earlier. But we can't tell you exactly how much it is going to save. You are going to have to trust us on that, and put up about one million dollars up front."

He turned to the controller and said, "I think I am projecting to underrun my budget by about $2 million, so let's go do this."

VICE PRESIDENT: I am pleased that I approved it. The idea was to make sure that parts fit well before they ever showed up in a prototype, or later in Assembly operations. If you had a problem you could go back and, with a master grid, finesse your design until it fit. The buck was over budget but the team found a way to offset it. And it was a good idea. It was probably one of the very positive things the team came up with. They committed to downstream savings in change count and PCR provisions which they wouldn't need. The first time through would be more expensive, but we thought it was right for quality and I think the cars turned out very well.

ASSEMBLY LAUNCH LEADER: The harmony buck let the engineer fit a wood mock-up or whatever of his part onto that buck before we ever had a physical unit going down the line. The engineer could try it out and see: Would it really work? How would it package with other components? We proved out so many parts on the harmony buck

efforts with MIT were only possible, like the harmony buck, because of the Program Manager's willingness to support innovations. The importance of this is not to be missed —it appears that the success of organizational learning depends on the predisposition and temperament of the few key senior leaders, as much as on any other factor.

If there had not been a cushion, would the harmony buck have been approved? Should it have been approved if there were no cushion?

To obtain approval, the Program Manaager had to make a personal commitment to "take $4 million out of the provision for changes." This meant, in effect, offering a guarantee that the harmony buck would be effective.

Box 5-1

WHAT IS A HARMONY BUCK PROCESS?

The harmony buck Process (HBP) is an engineering tool to assist in design efforts. It is a "full body" design aid encompassing the entire car, on which engineers and designers can test part prototypes and diagnose engineering issues that were generated after the first set of prototype parts have been delivered.

In the past there might have been many individual "bucks," representing different sub-assemblies of the car. Having a single "harmony buck" vehicle, accessible to all team members, provides a central focal point for improved coordination among engineers.

With this early non-driveable "vehicle," an assessment of each component and system can be made much earlier. Issues such as: basic design concept inadequacies ("My part doesn't actually work the way I assumed it would on paper. . ."), design incompatibilities ("My part clashes with another part . . ."), and system interactions ("When I get these parts all together, it just doesn't look right or function right . . ."), can be evaluated and corrective actions taken early. In addition, the experience assembling and maintaining the harmony buck is invaluable at the build site.

On Epsilon, the HBP identified almost 300 issues, including about 30 "no-builds" —all corrected before the actual builds. At the end of the program, more than half of the $90 million provision for changes at launch time was returned—unused. The HBP deserves a portion of the credit for this accomplishment.

The harmony buck is not just a technological process. It gives engineers the ability to raise cross-functional problems and think through mutual solutions. This required budgeting time for engineers to "hang around" the prototype, letting solutions to problems emerge. The harmony buck process encouraged relaxed, comprehensive thinking.

---

before we ever built our first unit. Usually, by the time you get to 1PP the engineers are still going back and changing the entire part again. But the parts that were in our car in early 1993 were pretty much the same as in the package now [in September 1994]. Certainly, a lot of changes happened. Some of them you would see, some of them you would not. But the basic vehicle layout, including the wiring, did not change a whole lot.

◆ IMPLEMENTATION REVEALS RESISTANCE WITHIN THE TEAM

Approval by top management did not mean that the innovation was supported by everyone involved.

ENGINEER: At first, there was an internal struggle. The current buck program was a current Epsilon body with a new front end and front underbody. We were looking to expand that to a full new body and new interior. The people responsible for the front end resisted, I think, because we took the buck away from them for a month and rebuilt it from scratch. "Don't interfere with my job," they said. "I don't see any benefit in doing this anyway. I don't want to have anything to do with it." Every day somebody would tell us, "This is just not worth the money. I don't know how you're going to do it."

But those of us who had a clear vision of what it would do kept pushing until we got it through. We had to keep telling ourselves that it would work. We knew it would pay off in the end. We got into a few meetings about the buck. At one meeting, [the Chief Engineering Manager] said, "No, go ahead. Go on with your program. You'll get your body back soon enough and it won't lose you that much time." I think that was a big turning point.

CONTENT LEADER: If something hasn't been done before, we tend to be negative about a new idea. I heard some people say, "Why do we need another prototype? We already have enough prototypes." Well, we haven't implemented a bad idea on the Epsilon program yet.

ENGINEER: The harmony buck was a great tool. It was AutoCo's first harmony buck. It allowed a total car to be reviewed up front before we built the cars. Previously, the company had used partial bucks. By having a full car package buck, all the engineers could understand the interactions between their part and the surrounding parts. That allowed us to build VPs on the assembly line—which

The idea of yet another prototype was interpreted by some people as meaning more work, taking more time, and costing more money. It meant changing the way things were done, and there was resistance.

Over time people found that the harmony buck helped, and they were more overtly supportive of the effort.

Does this comment suggest that corporate people need to push themselves beyond the comfort zone—beyond the measures that they think may be realistic?

If so, what management systems and corporate cultures reinforce people for this? Could reward systems create incentives that lead to new behaviors?

The harmony buck was linked by many with achieving better results on subsequent prototype builds.

had never been done before. Typically all the VPs are built off line because the parts are not ready enough to go into a car and maintain line speed.

◆ THE HARMONY BUCK AS A COMMUNICATION TOOL

Having a single, physical prototype provided a place for people to meet, talk, and test out the compatibility of their parts and sub-assemblies. This created opportunities for communication and collective problem solving.

It was an advantage to hire someone from outside the team for this critical position, involving not just his own experimentation, but fostering experimentation among others.

How can companies cultivate and reward these in-house "pollinators" of ideas?

CONTENT LEADER: We hired a manager from outside the team to take charge of the harmony buck. He developed a lot of processes that we had never used before [involving computers and checking points]. He got a lot of cooperation from just about every group in the company, but it was largely a one-man effort. I hate to say this, but I don't think that we could have found anybody on the inside who would have been willing to take as many chances with as many new ideas and processes. He really showed us a lot of stuff.

ENGINEER: We hired outside prototype shops, instead of the suppliers, to make many of the prototype components for the harmony buck, because they could do it more quickly. When we started getting those prototype parts in, it was a big turning point. You could see the interest ramp up. We had to fight to schedule time for people to get in there to see their parts.

Coordination became a critical factor in making the buck successful.

Once we started the buck build, people were in and out of that room frequently. It was a good place to resolve a lot of problems because again, we made it accessible. [One content leader] stressed that to us: "Let the people get at it. If they want to call you up and come on down, don't resist." You could go down there anytime in the day and there'd be from 10 to 15 people around this thing, all doing something different. We made sure we set up a process where someone could easily change a part. "Just let us know about it," we said.

PROGRAM MANAGER: When we started the harmony buck process, we added a whiteboard to the buck room. Whenever someone found a problem on the harmony buck, it was written on that board. And the rule was that you couldn't ever erase something from the board unless you had placed a concern number behind it. Once you make it a concern, everyone can think about it: "Now, how might that affect me?" Everybody can work on it together.

Did the white board in the harmony buck room help people in voicing their concerns formally as well? The record number of change requests (see page 99) may have been exacerbated by this device.

CONTENT LEADER: After the harmony buck was set up, the engineers loved it. They were swarming over it. We found all kinds of problems, way in advance of even the first mechanical or evaluation prototypes. We paid that $2 million back in a week or two, finding concerns early enough that we avoided major expenses in retooling. This was probably one of the big reasons we have underrun our investment target.

While a diffuse and subtle learning effort might not be linked to business results, a single innovation like a harmony buck, can be directly associated with financial results. Is the benefit from a harmony buck plausible only in an environment created to be conducive to learning?

◆ EXPANDING THE COLLABORATORS

As the first harmony buck evolved into a more complete (Evaluation Prototype) build, the coordinators deliberately set up the car's process to involve all of the constituents, including the Plant A assembly people and suppliers, in the design of the car from the beginning. Suppliers could see problems before they reached assembly. Suppliers met with assembly people at the buck, and depended less on telephone calls to one another.

ASSEMBLY LAUNCH LEADER: In the past, assembly was the neck at the end of the funnel. Whatever transpired early on in design and engineering eventually gets into the assembly plant and we have to assemble all these dreams. And they don't always fit. With the harmony buck, we moved the neck of the funnel up into the prototype stage.

When we found problems, we called in the suppliers and told them where their mistakes were and what we required so that we could assemble the thing. We did this up front; we didn't wait six months to find these problems. To me, that was one of the biggest keys.

Are people more effectively involved if there is an upfront communication and planning process?

ENGINEER, CAR PROGRAMS MANAGEMENT: Two guys who worked with us actually worked for the supplier that did the sheet metal body. They just stayed on site for a year, which is very uncommon, and they got very familiar with the car.

When we reached the EP phase, we wanted to develop the build sequence basically as if we were running it down the line. Those of us who were managing the harmony buck insisted that the engineers and suppliers come to Plant B and install their parts. We told them: "Come and do your own part. Try everything out yourself."

So we scheduled times. We started with the wiring guys—engineers and suppliers. We had planned a half day for them, but they begged and pleaded for us to give them more time, because they started to find things that wouldn't have permitted us to build the car.

For example, a harness of 120 wires hanging out the door. There was no way to loop it around and attach it; we had to rework all the parts. If we hadn't noticed it on the harmony buck, it would have meant boxing up all the parts for the EP build, stopping the build, and shipping the parts back to the supplier.

How much time would that have taken? How much money would we have lost? I don't know how to quantify it, but we found quite a few of these problems. We put together a list of the significant stoppages that we averted because of this program. We tried to quantify this list as well, but we could not come up with a dollar value.

PROGRAM MANAGER'S BOSS: The whole process was built around having the individual engineer who was responsible for a component or a system go in and actually participate in assembling that component. It gave the engineers a lot more familiarization than they would have had otherwise with how their parts fit within the vehicle.

VICE PRESIDENT: It allowed the engineer to check the finish, or the robustness, of the fastener. Could he jerk it? Would it rattle? It allowed them to look at wiring to determine routing robustness. It wasn't a prototype that was here for three days and then off on another test; it was there all the time. If you had a problem, you could go make another part, and put it back on again.

CHIEF ENGINEERING MANAGER: It was at either the EP or the VP harmony buck that the President came out to review the status of the program. I remember that he talked with us while sitting in the back of the harmony buck. He thought it was great to see this level of parts that you could look at for fit and finish issues, and to get the hard stuff out of the way before you cut production tools.

CONTENT LEADER: We used it as our golden car. We kept it up to date. We put all the VP components on the EP and proved those out ahead of time. This ensured much more up front quality of the electrical system and we're continuing to use the VP car right now [September 1994].

ENGINEER IN PROGRAM MANAGEMENT: It was a phenomenal success. That was evident in just the amount of attention it got from other programs. People from the other vehicle programs, and one of the truck programs—everyone was dying to get in to see this thing. It was like a miracle we'd pulled off. And it really wasn't that hard to do. It was just common sense when you really think about it.

Significantly, these senior AutoCo executives, external to Epsilon, were highly aware of the harmony buck's significance in retrospect.

Other comments suggested that the Epsilon harmony buck did not always attract interest from other program managers. Some had to be told by the Vice President to go to take a look at what Epsilon was doing.

What factors might make it easy or difficult to replicate the harmony buck's success?

The harmony buck was integrated with other practices that opened technical communication with outsiders. Before each of the three builds the team held a big suppliers' meeting to coordinate information, with the buck as a central (but not exclusive) coordination point. They also implemented a process called "Must-See-Before": engineers had to visit the suppliers' plants and see the parts in production before the build. Several engineers suggested these processes made an enormous difference.

◆ THE SECOND HARMONY BUCK: APPROVAL AND DECLINE

A subsequent harmony buck, used in the transition from design to the assembly plant, was not as widely successful in terms of producing new insights as the first buck had been. The second buck was less of a "big deal"—it was a way of "doing business" for the team, rather than an innovation. Did the first buck raise expectations so high that no subsequent process could meet them, or was the social innovation of meeting and talking—and problem solving—around the first buck less developed in the second buck?

Can the success of the harmony buck be attributed to the team's learning efforts? The quotes thus far show that the link is subtle: At every stage, the buck was successful to the extent that people felt free to raise questions with each other, suppliers, and assembly people.

Some argued that the concept of a buck was more appropriate and innovative for engineering design than for coordinating assembly and production.

ENGINEER: We had to have a second meeting with Vice President to ask for additional money to continue the program. We found we couldn't quantify exactly how much money the buck had saved us in time, labor, changing tools, getting parts, etc.

So instead, we walked [the Vice President] through the program. We got stories from every engineer: "Here's what we started with. Here's how we built the car." And we had a board full of photos to show the process: "Here's the engineer putting his own part on the car three months ahead of schedule." The engineer wouldn't be standing back, watching an hourly guy hammering the part on the car because it didn't work; the engineer would be putting the part on the car.

"The benefit is just phenomenal," we said. "We know the EP came off so smoothly in large part because of this. We'd like to continue it through to the launch. Doesn't it make sense?" They couldn't argue with it. He agreed, and they gave us funding to let us keep going.

ENGINEER, CAR PROGRAMS MANAGEMENT: I don't think they
were able to generate the same amount of information in
the second phase of the harmony buck. They were not
able to generate the same interest and involvement that
we had gotten before.

When communication broke down, the advantages from the harmony
buck also seemed to diminish. According to some interviews, that communication breakdown happened in this final stage. There was less
emphasis after the VP build on drawing engineers in to test their components on the buck and making them feel as if it were "their buck."

In the end, the harmony buck process was one of the most generally
agreed-upon positive noticeable results from this program (as listed on
page 9).

CHAPTER 6

PARTNERSHIPS

Several Epsilon efforts could be seen as attempts to develop infrastructure to support communication and partnership between functions. Two efforts stood out in participants' minds:

- The market research clinic expanded the team's opportunities to learn from customers and dealers and to pursue cross-functional conversations.

- The collocation effort showed how physically changing the infrastructure is not sufficient in itself. It's also necessary to develop new habits and attitudes to help people get the most value from collocation.

◆ THE MARKET RESEARCH CLINIC

The engineers designing the Epsilon were exposed to customers early in the development process. The impact of this effort was reflected in the interviews:

BODY ENGINEERING MANAGER: Most of the engineers are young and have no plan to ever drive a [luxury vehicle like the] Epsilon. It's not their type of car. Their mindset is oriented to [lower cost passenger cars]. How can you feel a certain allegiance to making this the best car in the world if it's just another car to you?

Yet, none of the people designing the cars ever drive any of those cars. Only the senior management types drive them. I don't know if it went anywhere, but [the

Epsilon leaders obtained eight of the most competitive cars to the new Epsilon so that team members could drive them overnight and on weekends. The cars were continually in use for the next two years.

Program Manager] was going to get a fleet of luxury cars for people on the team to experience to get a sense of what this car was all about.

LAUNCH MANAGER: After we go through a number of ideation sketches and start honing in on some favorite themes, we usually go out and do some market research. We invite people to sit behind a mock-up of the interior and the trunk. Ordinarily at AutoCo, we would have had a market research expert create a qualitative report. The bosses would have read it and told the engineers what to change.

Instead, we had our background in vision work. We had asked ourselves: "What do we want this car to be and how do we want to engineer it?" The best way to learn, in that context, is to take our 40 engineering team leaders and have them spend a week talking to the customers. "Why do you drive what you drive? What would you like from your next luxury car? What do you think about the price? What do you think we should do?" The specific answers were important, but less important than making our engineers feel connected to the customer. So when they're engineering those cars, they remember John, Bill, Mary, or whomever they talked to. They have a face in their minds, not just an engineering drawing.

MARKET RESEARCH LIAISON: They took the Epsilon to a market research meeting way earlier than I would have done. At the time, I fought them on this event. I wanted valid research and I knew the engineers weren't trained to do that. But in retrospect, it was brilliant. The engineers couldn't have gotten any of the feeling they got by looking at a video or reading a book. I thought that was extremely valuable. That was the first time I had seen that done.

They also wanted us to have dealers and media present at the research sessions and that worried me a lot. It's really a risk because the dealers are very influential. Had they disliked the car, it would have really hurt our launch. Had the media disliked it, that would have hurt us too.

It turned out that the dealers and media made suggestions. I found out at the launch meeting yesterday that the team had responded to each one of the suggestions. When we bring the car close to market at the end of this year, I can go back to the dealers and say: "When you told us this, this is how we responded." Suddenly the dealers and key members of the media are a part of the team.

ENGINEER: I went on the market research clinic in April 1992. I thought it was great that they let engineers [attend], because we got a chance to talk to the customers. People were complaining about sluggish performance in the way the vehicle felt. From the powertrain area we already knew that it might be substandard, and we had proposed fixes and they were gonna cost X amount of dollars. It was hard to sell that point to the program people, but after the second clinic I think the point came across. We weren't just talking out of our hats; this was real. When a customer agrees it's a lot easier to say, "Hey, maybe he's right."

MARKET RESEARCH LIAISON: The Epsilon team members always attend research, whether it's theirs or ours. You expect them to attend their research, but they attend our research. They want to be involved in the launch. They want to be involved in the delivery. They want to have their people learn for the next program.

Once the engineers had met and worked with marketing people, they maintained the contact and interest well into program development activities.

◆ COLLOCATION: OPENING A NEW REALM OF ISSUES

Collocation—the assignment of engineers from a variety of functional areas to workspace near each other—is not as simple as merely putting everyone under one roof. Because of the timing of its start-up and launch dates, Epsilon had not been designated to be collocated; this was still a relatively new practice at AutoCo. Thus, collocation came late to the Epsilon project. It might not have been introduced, people agreed, if the learning organization ideas had not reinforced the need people felt for intensive collaboration across functional lines.

Epsilon approached collocation a little differently than other teams. Instead of being seen as a cross-functional team because members were collocated, collocation was seen (from inside the team) as a first step.

Once collocation began, people were responsible for coordinating old loyalties, and protecting new ones, in unprecedented ways.

In retrospect, many people on the Epsilon team expressed a wish that the collocation process had taken place earlier and had included representatives from more functional areas.

Epsilon was one of the first teams to be collocated. AutoCo has learned from these earlier experiences that collocation is effective and full collocation is valuable.

CONTENT LEADER: Some of the value of collocation is [intangible]. But there is a real advantage to being in the same room with other people. If you need to ask someone a question and you have to call and they're not there, and they call and you're not there, that can go on for days.

ENGINEER: The politics disappear. You don't have to go through another layer of management to resolve an issue. You just walk over and have a one-on-one discussion. It also helped to have the major suppliers on site during launch: Prince, the body shop people, Motorola, etc.

Collocation provided an opportunity for improving how people worked together. However, as this quote illustrates, other factors were needed for people to benefit from their proximity with one another.

TEAM LEADER: When you see somebody every day, just by human nature, you build a bond because you're in each other's offices all the time. "Let's grab a coffee," you can say. There's an undertone because you're physically located. Sometimes you find yourself actually not talking about the car, but about the ballgame last night. You just become friends. Trust-building is really encouraged by this collocation.

CONTENT LEADER: However, a lot of our problem is not related to proximity; it's the chimneys. We started buying doughnuts and coffee on Wednesday morning and having the team leaders hang around for people to bring problems to. That was not really working. People came in for doughnuts and coffee, but they still didn't say what was on their mind.

CHIEF PROGRAM ENGINEER: When someone is afraid to tell you that he's got a problem, it doesn't matter if he's sitting in the next cubbyhole or sitting on the other side of town, he's not going to tell you. If he is willing to tell you, there's an advantage to being together because a lot of time is spent in the halls talking together, instead of formal meetings. There's a great power in collocation, but collocation doesn't fix the lack of openness and honesty.

CHIEF ENGINEERING MANAGER: It was a late collocation. There were a lot of people resisting it. The program is already off and running, they said. We can't collocate every team. Maybe this is one we don't collocate.

In fact, we never really did assemble a fully collocated team. Our team was halfway in between. Those who felt strongly that it would be beneficial moved in. Those who didn't want to move resisted. But I noticed that those members who were collocated got things done faster and smoother.

CONTENT LEADER: Collocation hasn't helped in any substantial way. When [the Program Manager] was trying to pull all this collocation together, we resisted until we were basically kicked out of our building. We came over here because we had no other place to sit.

The reason I resisted was this: 90 percent of my parts in body structures are made by Metal Stamping Operations. Those suppliers were right in our old building and sat next to my engineers. They were the tooling experts. When somebody asks us for a change, we have to ask an expert: "Is this feasible? Can you make it?" Now,

People talked in the interviews about the effect of collocation in much the same way that they talked about the benefits of the learning labs. Could collocation have been effective without the work on "trust" and "openness?" Could trust and openness have been developed without the reinforcement from collocation?

To what extent were team members affected by the ability and influence of the team managers to get top management to support their request for collocation, despite the fact that it wasn't planned or budgeted?

Collocation pulls some people together and still leaves some people out. Does the benefit from collocation depend upon the interdependence of the work of the people that are being put together?

If people didn't see feel compelled to move toward greater interdependence with other Epsilon sub-teams (as in this quote) it was easy to miss the value that collocation provided.

As with the other innovations in this program, there was initial resistance by both those whose approval was needed (top management) and by those who were affected (engineers).

And, as in the other cases, people only recognize benefits afterwards.

What enables program managers to continue despite the resistance they encounter at various levels?

after collocation, that tooling expert is a 15-minute drive away.

TEAM LEADER: I was in the experimental vehicle garage when the team collocated. It was interesting because most of the vehicle development people did not want to collocate. They were set in their ways; they had the EV garage and all their creature comforts. Who wanted to go to another building? From my perspective I saw a lot of resentment. This was not going to work.

But over the last couple of years I've seen a lot of positive changes. My manager asked vehicle development [in summer 1994] how many people, if they had to do it over again, would prefer to have stayed in the garage. I think about two-thirds of the people wanted to be here. That proved that in the end, the team cooperation that you get when you're all under one roof, along with the dedicated facilities that we had, really worked out well.

CHAPTER 7

PROCESS INNOVATION IN THE CONTEXT OF A LARGE ORGANIZATION

In creating a new approach to managing the Epsilon team, one deliberately different from traditional AutoCo management culture, the leaders came to feel isolated from the senior levels of the AutoCo system. This left the Epsilon program manager, in particular, feeling isolated. The launch manager, while he received many inquiries from others as to what Epsilon was doing, felt the inquiries were superficial because most people appeared to be waiting to see how things would turn out.

The Epsilon team leaders felt that senior managers sometimes applauded them, sometimes supported them, sometimes ignored them, and sometimes invalidated their efforts. The team leaders tried to explain their approach, but they did not gain sustained interest or attention from senior managers. The Epsilon team coped with their position as innovators by assuming that their excellent results would make them popular, influential, and acceptable, legitimizing their alternative methods. Unintentionally, this became a strategy of isolation: it meant holding back from engaging anyone in AutoCo until they could point to unequivocally outstanding results. However, even the best results in the auto industry might not have made enough of a difference; Epsilon could not be isolated too much from the larger AutoCo system.

This section of the learning history shows how an innovative team like Epsilon needs an advocacy from above that fulfills the spirit, not just the letter, of mentoring. Since their work, by definition, challenges the established rules of the game, the team needs help anticipating potential frustrations and roadblocks, in time to find strategies for managing them well. They need safe, open communication channels for raising difficult questions—and committed advisors who can help stop them from going off into organizational dead ends. In the end, the tension raised by an effective change effort represents opportunities, for improvement within the team and in the larger system. It is a challenging task to take advantage of these opportunities, but we hope future teams can build effectively upon Epsilon's experiences.

There is a temptation to view this story as a "David vs. Goliath" narrative—"the innovative team versus the rest of the organization." However, that is just one perspective on a fairly complex and multi-faceted story. In reality, nearly every participant felt that Epsilon accomplished a great deal but could have achieved much more.

The Epsilon team leaders explicitly hoped that they might recreate their positive team experiences and results in other AutoCo settings and were disappointed not to be given that opportunity. Others in the company felt that the difficulties perceived by Epsilon team leaders were just that—perceived difficulties. They felt that Epsilon was appropriately supported and nurtured, like all AutoCo teams.

◆ POSITIONING THE PURPOSE OF THE TEAM

Before his assignment as the Epsilon program manager, the Program Manager held leadership positions with other vehicle programs. He had been the Planning Manager for one of the most popular AutoCo cars—a car whose market success was generally attributed as having "saved the company." These experiences strongly influenced his goals for the Epsilon team.

The priority of these goals were consistent with the objectives set by top management at AutoCo.

The Program Manager's goals did not explicitly include impacting the larger organization—but is it not inevitable that anyone who succeeds at process innovation will want to see that success replicated on a larger scale?

PROGRAM MANAGER: I wanted to accomplish three items on this launch.

The first was to make the car as good as I could get it, given the total program constraints.

The second was to run an orderly, "no-surprises" program.

The third was to take a better approach in managing people in the product development process.

What I really wanted to accomplish was to build a team like [the Theta car manager] built on the Theta in

1984. I was on that team. He didn't know any of the tools or theories that we used on Epsilon, but he loved us. That was important! He created an atmosphere such that no matter how he yelled at you and what he did, it didn't matter because he loved you. And I thought if I could ever build a team like that, that would be the crowning touch of my career. But I wanted to create that spirit through a reproducible process: one that we could spread to other teams without relying on personalities.

Those main topics are exactly what I described to the team at our very first meeting. I never changed those goals.

The management style of another process innovator influenced the Program Manager

People often talk about what it's like to be on a "great" team; it seems to be a basic human experience which people then often seek to replicate.

◆ ENGAGING SENIOR MANAGEMENT

In retrospect, some critics of the Epsilon project have suggested that senior management should have been more involved from the beginning. There should have been more attempts to help senior managers understand the theory, tools, and process associated with the five disciplines of a learning organization (see Senge, *The Fifth Discipline*, 1990).[1]

As early as the Project Engagement Clinic,[2] in September of 1991, when the Epsilon learning effort began, this problem was discussed. Chris Argyris, Professor at the Harvard Business School and an advisor with the MIT group, cautioned that the strategy of excluding senior management from direct involvement might not be effective in the long run. The Program Manager and the Launch Manager were aware of this problem. They said that AutoCo culture generally valued results over theory. They felt they could not effectively include senior managers in their effort, or even talk much about the MIT "learning" theory, until they had some tangible results to demonstrate. If they tried, they would be viewed as "a holy crusade" and as not paying attention to what senior management held as paramount in developing a vehicle—the financial and technical details. This put an extra burden on the team, because if results failed to measure up, it would call their judgment in working with MIT into question. In effect, the leaders of the project were betting their careers not just on the success of the launch, but on the ability to product results through the learning initiative methods.

That early decision, which drew a "curtain of silence" around the Epsilon team, may have been more damaging in the end than team members expected. Of course, it will never be known what would have happened if the team had opted for a more visible approach. Suppose they had not moved forward until senior executives understood and accepted the new way of working. They might never have been allowed to attempt the necessary amount of innovation. In the end, the Program Manager and Launch Manager felt that they had no effective way to involve senior AutoCo executives and no alternative but to proceed without their full involvement.

Throughout the next two years, they continually but quietly tried to raise the value of learning at senior levels of AutoCo, with varying degrees of success and interest.

The strategy that was broadly advocated at AutoCo was to take the risk by trying a new approach, and to justify it retrospectively with the results it produced.

PROGRAM MANAGER (at project definition clinic): There have been lots of studies in the company in the past that have highlighted the fact that there's a lot of fear in the organization. Nothing changes [people's minds] unless you have data ["noticeable results"].

LEAD MIT RESEARCHER: But this is not a problem of data. You will never be able to present hard evidence of a causal link [between your innovations and the positive results]. It's epistemologically impossible.

When is the most appropriate time to engage senior management?

LAUNCH MANAGER (later): We were asked: "How much success can you have without involving senior management?" We admitted we didn't know. We were asked whether we would be prepared to involve them at some point in time. I think our answer was that when we thought we were ready we would be prepared.

The tension between "hard" and "soft" results leads directly to this dilemma: the need to justify investment of time and money in new approaches before the results can be quantified in conventional "hard" measures.

PROGRAM MANAGER'S BOSS: I think one of the reasons that we didn't spend more time trying to get management support is because this process was "soft." As I look at this project and other similar projects within the Company, the people involved are clearly very, very large supporters of the process. Our approach was to let the results speak for themselves basically and not go out and try to preach the process because it could be viewed as soft.

PROGRAM MANAGER: I tried to be the buffer for the team. I said, "Wait until the results come in. When they see the results, they're going to start asking "How did you do that?" Then they'll be ready to listen."

Since all proof is ambiguous, both the Program Manager and the Program Manager's boss found themselves cast in the role of buffers. Note the way this role gravitates from person to person throughout this chapter.

But when results began to show up—as new records of achievement for the program—it was still difficult to talk about them as substantiation for the value of the learning effort. Achievements were not acknowledged in the way tha Epsilon team leaders had hoped for. And the link between process work and engineering results seemed to go unrecognized.

PROGRAM MANAGER: I brought the team leaders in [for a one-hour presentation to a group of senior managers, including Vice President, on the value of the learning effort]. We told them all the things we had accomplished, what we had done to accomplish them, and how much poorer we believed our results would be if we hadn't tried to do it a new way.

Two things seemed to make an impact on [the Vice President]. One of our engineers' stories dealt with immense reductions in development time because of what she had used from the learning lab.

Secondly, my perception was that he never got the chance to hear firsthand stories like this. They were always filtered through so many levels of management that this was a rare occasion to hear directly from the people who did something. I think that had an impact in itself. And we got him to agree to money for more training.

Nonetheless, at the end of that meeting he told us we could keep working on this stuff. But we shouldn't let it get in the way of our real jobs. After that comment, I didn't think I had a prayer of convincing [the Vice President] other than with hard data and results.

The Vice President's response was not seen by the Program Manager as an endorsement, but rather as a missed opportunity to see or accept the linkage between the learning approach and product development accomplishments.

Experience from a variety of companies suggests that executives who can educate themselves in the rationale behind an innovative pilot project tend to become more effective champions—not just through their support, but through their advice and judgment.

But how can senior executives justify the time that merits such close involvement? And how can they draw the distinction between close involvement and micromanagement?

◆ EVALUATING EPSILON: MISCOMMUNICATIONS AND
MISUNDERSTANDINGS

By the second year, the Epsilon team had fallen into a pattern of relative
detachment from the larger system. Now there were recurring misunderstandings. In some cases, Epsilon team leaders thought the larger system
was micromanaging them from above (as AutoCo routinely did with other
car programs). From the perspective of the launch, it seemed as if AutoCo
were: dictating requirements that didn't really apply to Epsilon, such as
conventional quality and production metrics, because the new management practices made those requirements obsolete. Other car programs
also thought the requirements were obsolete. But for lack of better measures, Epsilon and others continued to comply with conventional reporting requirements.

At the same time, some of the senior leaders perceived the Epsilon
team as withdrawing into its own "true believer" perspective—as if
Epsilon leaders felt that they had some special insight that the rest of the
AutoCo organization did not or were falling prey to "group think." They
seemed to speak a special, elite language about "ladders of inference" and
"systems archetypes." Their unconventionality was particularly worrisome
to senior leaders because they felt the jury was still out on Epsilon's
"unique successes." They did not know whether it would do better than
other, more conventional teams.

These misunderstandings and doubts seemed at first unrelated to each
other, but over time they built upon each other. Epsilon leaders began to
feel that the system would not let them communicate their ideas up the
hierarchy. Their attempts to tell top managers did not meet with the
enthusiastic reception they had hoped for. Instead, they were told not to
let these efforts "get in the way" of their real jobs of producing a car. The
more they persisted, the more difficult the Epsilon leaders found it to get
time on executives' calendars to make their case. Some within product
development worried that the Epsilson team might be falling prey to
"group think."

> INTERNAL CONSULTANT: I got the impression that [the Program
> Manager] and [the Launch Manager] were saying to them-
> selves, "We did everything right. Everybody at AutoCo
> should be pleased. When they see the results, they'll

knock the doors down trying to learn how to do what we did." I'm sure I shared in some of that attitude myself.

But in retrospect, that was a naive approach. If we expected results and teamwork, in themselves, to communicate our message to the rest of the company then we were setting ourselves up for disappointment. And we have to be careful not to blame everyone else for not recognizing us the way we hoped they would.

Change, by its nature, is painful. It means going against the flow from beginning to end. And results are always more ambiguous than we'd like. Perhaps we should have prepared for the ambivalence that outsiders would feel and adopted less of a missionary attitude about what we were doing. On the other hand, if we hadn't taken that attitude, we might never have begun the learning effort.

PROGRAM MANAGER (in an interview in mid-1993): I have taken to discussing problems openly with my boss and the Vice Presidents. In one meeting, I told an Executive Vice President that there weren't enough resources on this program from body engineering. I showed him how that might jeopardize the program, how we were trying to recover, and what the risks were.

As the Epsilon managers and engineers learned to be more open and direct among themselves about the problems they faced, they began to practice some of that same behavior with their bosses and others outside that team . . . with varying degrees of receptivity.

I felt the VP wanted to hear, instead, how we would make it with the head count we had. A year or two before, I would have told him what I thought was politically wise to tell him. This time, I was telling him what to realistically expect up front.

He seemed to think I was being uncooperative. But other people in the room—the Vice Presidents from chimneys I had to work with—responded more positively. Later, when I called them and said, "Hey, I need a hand," they helped in a way that they've never helped before. I think it's because they remembered me as having talked to them candidly.

Changing in a larger organizational system seems to require both an awareness that individuals are part of a system and that changes need to occur at individual and organizational levels.

As it happens, we did make up the problems with the existing head count—because of process things we did that had nothing to do with what the rest of the com-

What conditions are required for individuals to sustain new behaviors?

Why is it a risk to be open in a large firm like AutoCo? What are the implications for improvement if being open is risky and only a few people take those risks?

pany was doing. In essence, we did what that Executive Vice President wanted us to do in a way he didn't expect.

If I were 35 years old and worried about getting promoted, I couldn't have taken those risks. I guess I'm old enough and I've been around long enough, and some of the things I was doing with MIT were changing my mindset. The change wasn't with them. The change came from within me.

Can people find a way to talk about individual change without seeming like "cult" followers?

VICE PRESIDENT: I felt a bit like "the outsider." It became almost cult-like to me. People would sit in meetings, look each other in the eye, and talk about the "ladder of inference." Meanwhile, I was trying to run the business. I had a lot of tough decisions, and I was very tight on my time.

Does the language that was used to describe the tools for learning become a barrier for others when it isn't understood?

It almost seemed that the tool became more important than the end result. The team became so process-driven, so mechanistic, so much like disciples of Peter Senge, that I think it got in the way of what they were trying to do. I know the team would disagree, but that was the view from the outside. There was critical time spent away from work in some cases.

Learning approaches are based on developing a level of skill in conversation and inquiry. What happens when people in other parts of the organization, those who are relied on for support and approval of resources, have not had an opportunity to learn those new skills (and may not be interested)?

When I was there as a senior person I got the impression that they were letting the process overwhelm the solution of their problems: "Make sure we follow this process, so we're aware of what we're doing." I think that's dangerous when that happens. That is my only personal experience with the whole thing. To an outside observer, if you weren't part of it, and if you didn't buy into all this, you were wrong and they were right.

The learning approach was based on a philosophy of openness and acceptance of differences.

I think that's where training can go bad. If you're going to expect performance changes or behavioral changes from the people you interface with, then you better make sure those people go through the interface, the process with you, at least so you understand it. Had I known it was going to be as broad and deeply spiritual as it seemed to turn out to be, then I should have been a part of it. We shouldn't have done it unless we all agreed to go through it together.

Did I ever call [the Program Manager] on this? I don't recall any specific discussion.

◆ IMPLEMENTING THE NEW "CHANGE REQUEST" POLICY

Traditionally, AutoCo programs tend to be judged by the numbers. Ultimately, the final measure of success is in the marketplace, but prior to launch, product development progress is closely monitored. Metrics are the major form of communications between program teams and senior management and are the primary way for senior managers to see if a program is meeting objectives and "under control."

When a team innovates to improve the process, it changes the rules, as Epsilon did. This stymies the rest of the organization's ability to measure the team's progress. If the rules are truly changed, then traditional measurements no longer represent the team's progress and can no longer be effective predictors of the quality, efficiency, and cost-effectiveness of the final product. The Program Manager and the Launch Manager assumed that if they got the people process right, some intermediate metrics would be spectacular, while other metrics would become less relevant. In the end, they expected to produce a great car, whatever the intermediate measurements predicted. Unfortunately, these attitudes about metrics were never explicitly talked about.

PROGRAM MANAGER: We brought the Vice President in early in the program. In our very first meeting with him, we downplayed all the normal predictor charts. We talked for two hours about all the processes that we were putting in. We told them that we were meeting all our indicators, and everything else was on time and under control.

But when we left the meeting he reportedly said to [the program manager's boss' predecessor] that he was worried about us. We were doing all this soft stuff and we were going to lose control of the hardware. We were not going to deliver the hardware.

At AutoCo, company-wide metrics are used to ensure that all the programs develop a disciplined level of quality performance and predictability. These statistics are gathered and compared across programs at corporate headquarters. But these metrics may not apply as well to program's like Epsilon's. If process innovations involve behavioral changes, how would a system of quantitative

When I heard about that from [the program manager's boss' predecessor], I didn't feel threatened by it. I was disappointed. Isn't it unfortunate, I thought, that he can't understand what all this means? But we would show them; we wouldn't lose track of anything.

This problem came to a head around "change requests" or "concerns." (At AutoCo the two terms are synonymous.) These "change requests" are the notes entered into the computer system, documenting issues, problems, and impending changes on auto components. They include lists of associated parts that might be affected by changes in the original part.

Back in 1992, the core team had determined through systems analysis (see page 21) that engineers were slow in reporting concerns because of the unwritten expectation that they should resolve concerns shortly after they were logged. The Epsilon Program Managers decided that it was better to have engineers report concerns as soon as they knew there was a change in a part. This meant going against a long-standing, unwritten practice at AutoCo. Conventionally, engineers who reported concerns without closing them out quickly were punished. That was like reporting a problem without supplying the solution—something that, in AutoCo's culture, should only be done for grave, unresolvable situations.

Epsilon's leaders were determined to encourage engineers to report change requests early and to wait for the best solutions. They felt that this would allow better coordination among changes in parts and lower overall costs because fewer of the very expensive, late tooling changes would be required.

This account of how change requests were traditionally used and perceived by engineers and managers, and then the change in the ways in which the Epsilon team used the change requests and associated reporting system, illustrates the influence of reward systems on behaviors.

ENGINEER: The change request (CR) account reached 500 because we were all encouraged to bring our issues out and to stop keeping them on the hidden log that every engineer has. In the past, engineers would keep a hidden log of their problems until they knew the answer. Then they'd put them on the CR with an answer at the same time. To say we were not rewarded for revealing CRs would be an understatement. Typically more than one person would be trying to solve the same problem. And a lot of people would do a lot of different things, not knowing what each other was doing, because there was no common document out in the system that tracked the problem.

I might be working to solve something and it might involve sheet metal. The sheet metal people wouldn't know because I didn't have it on a CR out to the world. I might not even have known it effected sheet metal. When I wrote the CR, they might say: "Wait a minute. We can't do this. It effects us." If I had known that a month ago it would have changed my solution.

Thus, with this process we were encouraged to get CRs out in the open sooner. This meant everyone else understood that you knew what your problem was and what you and other people were doing to follow it.

Other programs may require every CR to go through the Program Manager. [The Program Manager] empowered us to handle our own problems; if we couldn't handle them, we brought them to him. But he didn't need to see them all.

Not only were [the Program Manager] and [the Launch Manager] strong proponents of getting the problems out there on "pink" [the color of the change request form], but they went to bat for us. My organization, body engineering, is very meticulous about tracking CRs and how long they've been on pink. We have daily meetings on this. It can become very punitive when you have a problem out there for a long time.

[The Program Manager] and [the Launch Manager] went to my organization and said, "Look, we're telling our group to get the problems out there right away. That means they're probably gonna be on pink a little longer." That circumvented a lot of problems.

When one group (like Epsilon) changes the way it manages a metric (like change requests), they automatically affect the other groups that use the metric.

What does a shared perception of what a metric means require of groups who seek to innovate processes?

◆ EPSILON IS "OUT OF CONTROL!"

At Epsilon, the dilemma about how to use intermediate metrics escalated. This gradually led to a judgment, by people outside the team, that the program was "out of control." This was one of several circumstances in which Epsilon managers and senior managers elsewhere in the corporation held different interpretations of events.

ASSEMBLY LAUNCH MANAGER, interviewed July 1993: In vehicle operations we have a metric that starts with green and goes to yellow and goes to red. Well, I called [a top manager] the other day and said the Epsilon program was "purple." "That's the other side of red [worse]. The other side of red! You can make all the processes you want, but there's zero substitute for experience!"

The Epsilon isn't ready. I've had a unique ability for the last 10 or 15 years to say what's ready and what isn't ready and be right 95 percent of the time. The patient is terminal. My recommendation is to move the launch date back six months. If that's not an option, then move the launch date back six months after you crash.

CONTENT LEADER: Initially, I felt really good about our CR count. We were using the Engineering Release computer system, which made it much easier to write a change request.

Since these were pre-release CRs, management wasn't following them. There was no threat to engineers. It was fantastic to find out about all these things and have them documented, and then have them sent over to car management people and designers. We knew that they were being worked on, and we could manage them daily right there in the Engineering Release system.

This comment comes from an interview conducted at the same time that the "out of control" perception was brewing, by a manager outside the Epsilon team.

The launch date was not moved back six months. The car eventually came out on time, and without the "heroic effort" that is typically required at the end.

Why did the AutoCo bosses continue to be troubled by the large number of CRs, even after the managers' explanations? What sort of executive agreement or "buy-in" is appropriate for unproven experiments like this?

If managers from other functions argue convincingly that a program is in trouble, what is the next best step?

Through his approach to change control, the Program Manager let engineers make their own decisions about what changes should go into the system. He trusted them to put in only the problem reports that were important, and he interpreted the quantity of change requests as an accurate reading of the state of the vehicle's progress.

It was difficult for the Program Manager to communicate the significance of the way that Epsilon used the CR system. At a program review meeting in March 1994, the Program Manager described his approach.

PROGRAM MANAGER: In the normal course of events there are anywhere from 50 to 150 concerns in the system during a program. We went into that meeting saying, "We have 500 concerns, and that's good. We've encouraged engineers to tell us when they have a problem, as soon as they have a problem. Based on the measurements we were using, we've had the best quality evaluation prototype that we've ever had in our history, so we were able to do concerns that involved fit and finish earlier than in the past. We're closing concerns early enough so that they're still in design without affecting hard tools. They're costing thousands of dollars to close instead of millions."

I went through our accomplishments at the meeting. We had an exceptional MP [mechanical prototype build] and EP [evaluation prototype build]. We met our quality goals, and we had the highest number to date for MRD [delivery at Material Requirement Date]. "By encouraging engineers to write concerns," I said, "We're actually getting work done earlier and we'll have a better quality product. This is a change in our system and we want to keep it that way. We want it to be not punitive for an engineer to write a concern early."

[The Vice President] nodded and listened. But after the meeting he still said the program was out of control.

VICE PRESIDENT: I wouldn't have found the change request situation to be that unusual. It wasn't too different from Kappa [another program]. The Epsilon program was not out of control in my view. Nor did I find the experience of working them back down to near zero again any different from what the Kappa team wanted to do.

The ethic that everybody was trying to follow was: There is a right time for change and there is a wrong time. You ought to be following a curve where changes get less numerous as you get closer to Job One. Before every milestone, such as a prototype build, you're bound to have many changes where people rush to get things in to make a prototype date. One of the biggest problems that

The way the Epsilon team used the change request metric was the opposite of the way it had been used by others. The more change requests on the system, the earlier they were logged, the better.

The results from early prototype builds, and logic behind the way they were using change requests, seemed to indicate that the innovation was sound and successful in achieving results.

The Vice President's perspective on the same incident is at right. To him, the Epsilon project was not "out of control": it was simply going through the normal expansion and retraction of changes.

This description of how the change request system was used illustrates the expected behavior of program managers—to perform managerial tasks so that the change request system follows a predictable pattern.

any Program Manager has is to get hidden changes and problems out of engineers' desks onto the top of the table, so you can get them resolved and closed. That pushes the number up.

Then you just have to hammer them back down again. This would have been eight months before Job One. At that time, from a manufacturing standpoint, the engineer's job is done. Now let us do our job in manufacturing, and you keep the product stable—which means no changes. Let us optimize the product and process so we have a quality launch. That's the way it's supposed to work. It never does work that way. The engineers keep changing things, most of the time for good and relevant reasons. Manufacturing drives some changes. And so you have this constant battle of late failures, problems, fits, and finishes. There is huge pressure from Assembly to drive the change count down.

◆ FREEZING AND REDUCING THE CHANGE REQUESTS

In March 1994, under increasing pressure from AutoCo corporate management over the high number of change requests, the Program Manager and the Launch Manager instituted a change in procedures. Engineers were told to stop everything else and resolve changes.

During an intensive weekend, the engineers reduced the number of open CRs from 350 to 50. At the time, this enhanced the program's reputation. For example, at least one senior Assembly manager gave the team a lot of kudos for driving the changes down to a lower level. In his eyes, a program that had been a disaster now inspired confidence—the metrics were what they were expected to be and the Program Manager had demonstrated that he was in firm control.

Ironically, however, the appearance of solving problems early may have contributed to an outbreak of late-breaking problems when changes that had been "pushed underground" resurfaced later in the game.

CONTENT LEADER: But when management takes that approach you drive your engineers underground. Nobody will write a CR that they don't have a solution for if they know that their supervisor has been told to come to them three times a week to ask them about their open CRs. The engineer won't tell me about it. Thus, after we got through the VP build it reverted back to the old "hidden" system.

PROGRAM MANAGER: Instead of calling them concerns from then on, we called them investigation issues or some other name so we could identify what the concerns were. That's better than nothing. But that's not what you really want.

What you really want is for everyone to know that there was an issue. Once the whole company system knows a concern exists and it's a problem, they can all think about, "Now, how might that affect me?" Everybody can work on it together.

I even went back to [the Vice President] and said, "The magic of this system is we capture everything, I mean everybody knows about it from the day we capture it." He thought that sounded terrific, but he still didn't like open concerns!

In physics there is a law which specifies that any action is met by an equal and opposite reaction. Does this law from the physical sciences also apply to the behavioral arena of managerial action? What is the reaction to pressures to reduce CRs?

◆ THE EARLY RETIREMENTS

AutoCo announced major organizational structure changes in early 1994. These changes were part of efforts to become better at managing in a global marketplace. One effect of these changes, as they began to be implemented in the summer of 1994, was that approximately one-third of the middle managers would no longer have positions. The criteria for program managers was a strong background, and proven track record, in technical contributions. In August, the Program Manager was informed he would not be promoted, and he was given an option of taking another assignment with less responsibility, but at the same pay, or early retirement. He chose to take retirement. The Launch Manager faced a similar situation and chose the same option several months later.

When executives were asked, they said that these events had nothing to do with reactions to Epsilon's achievements, and nothing to do with the perceived effectiveness (or ineffectiveness) of the MIT learning efforts.

However, the early retirement options occurred around the same time that the Epsilon project was garnering notice in the press. The Program Manager and the Launch Manager had begun to give speeches about the process, both inside AutoCo (as part of the activities promoting the car to dealers) and outside AutoCo (often at MIT-sponsored events).

The early retirement was taken by many on the team as a signal, albeit unintentional, that the Epsilon effort, and its process innovations, had not been valued as much as team members hoped. Epsilon team members struggled to understand what it would mean to their future. Other people in AutoCo began to wonder if the Epsilon team performance had been as high as the hype suggested. And there was general confusion about how much AutoCo could learn from the Epsilon experience. In hindsight, the timing of the reorganization sent signals which senior managers wish had been interpreted differently.

Is it possible to go through a significant change effort, in which you come to believe you are special because of your experiences and your achievements, and still keep the perspective of the traditional organization? In this case, does success simply mean, "You've done your job?"

PROGRAM MANAGER: I never expected to be offered early retirement. I still expected that, after seeing the hardware results we got, they'd see that we did something special. When [Vice President] called me over for a one-on-one meeting, I thought I was going to get promoted. Instead, he gave me a brief presentation, told me I would be demoted [sic], and handed me a retirement package for consideration.

I honestly don't think there were any ulterior motives. They simply didn't regard what we did as so special. They had to reduce the total number of people at my level. They wanted engineers in the program manager roles. I'm not an engineer. I don't think they thought about it as a terrible thing, or even as hurting my ego. They created a formula and then carried it out. They just didn't think we did anything much different from what any other team does.

Once given the opportunity to speak and act freely, will people be frustrated if they feel they cannot maintain that same level of openness in their next assignments at AutoCo?

CONTENT LEADER (interviewed September 1994): I'm not sure that we are coping with it very well. There are a lot of morale problems right now. We were so proud of what we had been able to accomplish, and then to get slapped in the face like this. It was like every one of us got fired. We feel unappreciated and totally demoralized. Yeah, we were extremely successful. We made a lot of break-throughs. We had tremendous success in just about every measurable you want to throw up. Then to be told that "You really didn't do anything special at all. Oh, and incidentally, we're getting rid of your Program Manager," was a terrible experience.

VICE PRESIDENT: I think the team spirit witnessed itself in a negative fashion once it was clear that [the Program Manager] was going to retire. The team reacted not as individuals, but as a unified group. Individuals were not incensed; the whole team was very upset.

A lot of people associate some of the disadvantages that the people on the Epsilon team went through with the MIT organizational learning experience. That is absolutely wrong. The perception is not correct, and we ought to correct it.

PROGRAM MANAGERS' BOSS: But we haven't done anything to correct it. All we did was take the top guy and hammer him. That's what people see, and they believe what they want to believe.

I think we have taken a major step backwards from showing the people out there that we support improving our processes. They are all scared to death. When the reorganization started I argued that we ought to take some overt action to support organizational learning. Because we have a lot of people who are unsure whether they ought to be involved in any of this kind of stuff.

Senior executives confirmed, in interviews, that they supported the "learning organization" efforts. Why, then, did their actions present another picture to Epsilon team members? One hypothesis suggests that the lack of time spent by top managers and Epsilon Program Managers in trying to understand each other was a factor. To AutoCo, Epsilon was one of many projects, and hardly the highest-priority project. To Epsilon, AutoCo was an organization badly in need of ideas like theirs. These perceptions led each side to exhibit the type of behavior that reinforced the other side's most negative attributions, thereby producing an escalating ciurcuit of misunderstanding and mistrust. However, some argue that there is no plausible way that Epsilon could have influenced AutoCo. As one low-priority project among many, it was preordained to be ignored.

◆ IN THE END: ASSESSING THE INFLUENCE OF INNOVATION

VICE PRESIDENT: If the MIT course is something that everyone should be following, then I think not only I, but each of the vehicle center people, ought to go through it. And we at [the top management staff level] ought to adopt it as the process that we want to follow for human interaction and team building.

With all the different consultants and approaches used in an organization, how do top managers most effectively learn to evaluate them?

But if it's equivalent to other approaches, and there are 40 different ways to achieve the same results, then it's not so important that we choose that specific course. I don't know which is the right one. That's the confusion factor.

Does the anecdotal data from the Epsilon team mean that organizational learning will be effective in other circumstances?

PROGRAM MANAGER (interviewed October 1993): We'd like to get the kinds of things we're learning to spread in the company. We're showing some of the new Program Managers what we've done and the results that come from it. We're saying, "I know this works. It has worked for us. It has changed our teams. I have lots of hard data and war stories from different people." I don't know really what to do to spread this any further, but I know if I could it would be an extremely valuable tool for the AutoCo.

Others on the team weren't convinced that the "learning organization" approach made a critical difference. It was experimental, not that clearly explained, and there were concerns that it could be reproduced in other teams.

LAUNCH MANAGER (interviewed in April 1993): Maybe if the Epsilon were successful, there would be more open minds about the approach. But my great fear is: Others may not have the patience, inclinations, and discipline to go through what we did. They'll expect a two-day learning lab to produce a miracle. They'll see no miracles, so they'll say, "That stuff doesn't work," and go back to the old ways.

PROCESS LEADER: We haven't made a strong enough case of the benefits to cause anybody to say, "Let's do this on every team." Worse still, they don't understand that "doing this" means developing your own systemic understanding, commitment, and in-depth reflection. They see "doing this" as: "Okay, you guys have tested it. Now we can go train everybody." So, we have not done a credible job of presenting the learning process.

PROGRAM MANAGER'S BOSS: I spent quite a bit of time with the Epsilon program team. I was able to watch their progress versus the progress of the other programs for which I was responsible. I saw a measurable difference in the way the Epsilon team went about their business, and the way they reached closure on issues. The interaction of all the cross-functional participants on the team was much more supportive, much less confrontational, and much more focused than it was on the other programs.

I guess I didn't see the same kind of chemistry relationship on [other successful programs such as the Kappa. Kappa had excitement and cohesiveness because everyone rallied around the product, and it is a great product. It was more difficult for [Program Manager] to rally people around their product. Yet I didn't see the same type of positive relationships within the Kappa team. As far as I'm concerned, it is important for us to have those kinds of relationships on every launch team.

VICE PRESIDENT: If you look back at the history of the team, they went through some periods where they went over cost. As a team they pulled it back to objective and in the end they've even beaten their objectives. [The Program Manager] went through some very positive sessions with suppliers to make sure that each supplier knew what he had to do, specifically when he had to deliver it, and at

As they reflected on the program, corporate executives recognized the conditions that Epsilon was saddled with at the beginning. In the complex business of developing vehicles, it is difficult to separate the impact of initial conditions from the impact of an innovative process.

It is difficult for top managers to compare qualitative results from one program to another. They see the overt behaviors of the team. But the way that Program Managers are asked to report their progress and results makes it difficult to assess if an innovative process had any impact.

what quality level. He literally took 500 people in massive meetings and made sure each and every person understood it. That represents involvement of the people you depend most on.

Whether all this is Senge, or whether it sprang from the MIT experience, I don't know. But I think you could only do that if you operate as a very strong team.

The final situation of the Epsilon vehicle development effort and associated learning program leaves open many questions. Can a company, through a learning process, ask people to change their attitudes? What does real collective learning require? If it involves personal and internal changes, what is the role of a company and the work environment in promoting these changes? Can they be legislated? How are conditions created where people can examine their attitudes and make choices for themselves and others about their attitudes? Beyond the realm of individual change, what must an organization provide its innovative teams to allow them to sustain their innovation? What kinds of challenges does an innovative team present for an organization? If teams proceed, led by innovative managers, without establishing an organizational context for their efforts, what consequences might be anticipated?

One of the organizational consequences for the Epsilon team was that their accomplishments were not recognized by AutoCo in the way they had anticipated. This had a direct effect on the work lives of (by some estimates) more than a hundred individuals who had been part of the Epsilon team, had engaged in a learning process there, had undergone some personal or behavioral changes—and then found themselves, as the project ended moved into new teams, and back in the more traditional environment.

As the vehicle went on to manufacturing, it experienced several problems reconciling design versus manufacturing concerns. These issues, although described at first by some long-standing AutoCo observers as taking place in an atmosphere of crisis and heroics, were ultimately seen as much less traumatic and less costly than those of most other programs. The initial response from manufacturing was explained by design engineers as the typical "posturing by Assembly." In the end, the plant manager commented that Epsilon was "the smoothest launch he had ever seen." He said this shortly before he ended a 25-year career in Assembly and he, too, left AutoCo to retire.

The tangible evidence for a sound design and development process came when the production began one week earlier than planned. The factory had all the parts at hand, they were of the expected quality standard, and fit and finish concerns had all been addressed. The quality, from the syndicated independent research on competitive new vehicle quality, showed a 30 percent improvement in quality, a 9 percent improvement in satisfaction and a 50 percent improvement in surprise and delight features. The warranty data was not as compelling; the 1994 Epsilon had worse warranty repair statistics than the previous Epsilon model. Subsequent Epsilons, however, which represented minor variations on the major redesign undertaken in the1994 model, have had unprecedentedly good warranty metrics.

Also significant, perhaps, is the fact that organizational learning continues to be discussed in depth at AutoCo. This report, in fact, was commissioned as an effort to capture the Epsilon experience—so that the triumphs, along with the questions and difficulties, would not be lost.

◆ APPENDIX: SOME INITIAL QUESTIONS FOR GROUP DISCUSSIONS PRIOR TO MOVING FORWARD WITH LEARNING INITIATIVES

This learning history presents a story of what happened in the Epsilon Program. It also provides a context for considering important issues which surface as business organizations undertake explicit learning efforts. Provided below are four questions applicable to what happened with Epsilon, which can also be taken as a starting point for management team conversation in considering their own role in either leading or supporting process innovation efforts:

- How have the approaches taken by the Epsilon team added value to the traditional product development process? Can whatever value-added there was be recognized and accounted for by existing vehicle program metrics?

- Which methods and techniques used by this team can be transferred and used by other program teams? How do these tools get used to provide early improvement results ("quick hits")?

- Which methods and techniques require longer term investments to produce improved results? How does the value-added of "quick hits" compare with those produced by longer term investments?

- What action steps and resource commitments are necessary to achieve visible improvement results on both a quick and a long-term basis in other parts of large organization.

COMMENTARIES

CHAPTER 8

PRACTICE WITHOUT PREACHING

An organizational learning perspective on the AutoCo Epsilon Program

Peter Senge

Peter Senge's commentary reflects an in-depth knowledge of the theories, methods, and tools which were used by the AutoCo Epsilon team. Indeed, he was, at the time of this story, the director of the MIT Center for Organizational Learning and was closely associated with the "Lead MIT Researcher" who plays a prominent role in the story. Without Peter Senge's book The Fifth Discipline *(1990, New York: Doubleday), and his elucidation of the "five learning disciplines for organizations" and their relationship to practice fields and learning laboratories—and without his encouragement of people at AutoCo and MIT alike—the story told in this learning history might never have taken place.*

We asked Peter to offer a wider view of the implications of the Epsilon story in terms of organizational learning. As he notes in this essay, it represents one of the first cases where a full-fledged organizational learning process can be seen in action, and where its impact can be evaluated.

Peter is now the director of the Society for Organizational Learning (SoL), an international consortium of academic researchers, consultants, and organizational practitioners aimed at fostering the development of learning organization theory and practice. Based in Cambridge, Massachusetts, SoL evolved, in part, from the MIT Center for Organizational Learning. For more information about SoL, see the website http://www.sol-ne.org.

Peter is the coauthor (with Art Kleiner, Charlotte Roberts, Rick Ross, and Bryan Smith) of The Fifth Discipline Fieldbook *(1994, New York: Doubleday), and also coauthor (with the Fieldbook authors and George Roth) of* The Dance of Change *(1999, New York: Doubleday), a fieldbook of theories, strategies and tools for sustaining the momentum of learning organizations (see http://www.fieldbook.com).*

People always ask, "What do you mean by a "learning organization' approach?" I believe that reading this learning history provides one of the best ways to answer this question. There are many important insights here, and I believe no other description captures as well the reality and the complexity of implementing a "learning approach" in a working team.

The case of the Epsilon automobile launch highlights critical issues about organizational learning work. If I were asked by AutoCo managers, for example, to suggest the document's critical lessons for them, I would highlight the following four points:

- The tools and methods used in this project were quite effective in enabling a genuine "learning process" with the team. By that I mean that the tools enhanced both the team members' capabilities and their effectiveness. Thus, the Epsilon case shows how the combined impact of the learning tools and committed managers willing to genuinely learn and grow can lead to significant enhancements in local business results.

- New types of interrelationships, attitudes, and thinking can't just be decreed. They must be allowed to grow. There is no substitute for individual responsibility in learning. Senior managers can help most by giving people room to experiment within the constraints necessary to deliver the program and by striving to serve as examples for the behavior they're trying to produce.

- With a modicum of specific attention to "building better conversations," a flood of innovation poured forth. Managing the "softest" aspect of the team—the ways people thought and communicated together—gave the highest leverage for improving "hard" results.

- Having a great team is not enough, even when that team has as many as a thousand people. The relationship between the team and the larger organization is crucial. Diffusing learning requires extraordinary efforts on the part of team leaders to help executives understand new workplace innovations. It requires extra attention (for example, the willingness to talk through potential misunderstandings or to make themselves available "beyond the call of duty") because innovations can easily be misunderstood. Executives have managerial accountability for the team's business performance—performance that they fear might be compromised when they don't understand the new practices.

But the implications—for managers at all companies, and for researchers into organizational learning—go beyond these four lessons. Although it is not made explicit in this document, the Epsilon learning effort was actually a pilot project. Those of us who served as advisors to the project at the MIT Center for Organizational Learning (now the Society for Organizational Learning) didn't know before how it would operate in reality. Nor did the project's organizers. In some ways, the Epsilon team became more effective than anyone anticipated. Consequently, we also had little understanding of the consequences of such "success."

The learning history provides a wonderfully rich illustration of the tremendous complexity and difficulty of implementing and assessing this kind of work. Assessment of organizational learning and change initiatives will be a major area of research in the coming years. I expect this learning history to become a landmark document as this research develops.

◆   CRITICAL CASE INSIGHTS: DILEMMAS AND CHALLENGES

At the very beginning, on page 13, an AutoCo manager recalls telling Russ Ackoff that he still can't digest Ackoff's message. "You'll never get it," Ackoff replies. He goes on to say that the manager's children and grandchildren, less influenced by the prevailing mindset, would have a much easier time. This quote gives an immediate feeling of how challenging it is to develop a systems perspective, given our life-long conditioning as reductionists. Since our organizations have grown up around the skills of reductionistic managers, you can reasonably infer that organizations are biased by a reductionist tendency as well. It is enormously challenging, both personally and organizationally, to sustain a learning process aimed at reversing these life-long habits.

It is significant that the leaders of the Epsilon Program worked to change their own management style first. Only after they did that did they encourage other people to change their styles. Everybody preaches the need for non-authoritarian participative management approaches. But the Epsilon experience was quite distinctive. The approach produced a more non-authoritarian, participative management style as a by-product of people working effectively together in new ways. No one had to preach to the Program Manager that he needed to change. He changed because, once you really get engaged in this kind of learning process, you start to understand the interdependencies among things, which starts to produce a natural change in people's behavior. The tools and methods used at Epsilon, applied in the context of a "learning laboratory" or practice field, seem to have helped many people put a different philosophy into action.

The opportunity to create this kind of learning laboratory in a business setting is very rare. The scarcity of similar examples can't be overemphasized. To my knowledge, very few university business research projects have accomplished anything similar—especially with the scale of business impact seen here.

It is also rare for researchers to have an opportunity to work for three years in a real work setting. Although it's not mentioned in the document, the longstanding researchers' presence meant that the managers within AutoCo who worked on the Epsilon project gained sufficient experience to be able to take on the process of organizational learning themselves. Many of the learning labs were led by internal people, which contributed significantly to the results achieved.

Nonetheless, one overall goal of the project—the implementation of an ongoing learning laboratory—was only partially achieved. The lab, in fact, was a by-product of the work with new conversational tools, as this quote from an Epsilon leader shows:

The tools are very powerful, but until we can use them accurately and on the spot, we haven't gotten there. We're still on the learning curve. (p. 72).

This quote demonstrates why practice matters. But only a few members of the entire team (which I heard grew to about a thousand engineers) had the opportunity to practice in a regular, structured way. The top team created a "practice field" by extending their monthly staff meetings. Most of the other groups that were formally exposed to the "learning organization" tools and methods participated in an "Introductory Learning Lab"—a two-day workshop. The team did eventually establish a "learning room" where people could hold meetings and practice with the tools. But this came late in the project and benefited only a few.

In the learning history, there are mixed reviews of the specific conversational tools, expressed in varied positive and negative comments. In context, this makes a lot of sense; some people only used the tools for two days. Tools and methods do not produce change in themselves; it's the skills and capabilities that people develop from using the tools and methods that are important, and this takes time and regular practice.

◆ THE CHALLENGE OF FINDING TIME

One of the most important contributions of this learning history is the way it reveals many of the core dilemmas that confront people attempting to undertake this type of deep change work in organizations. For example, regular practice requires time. Many of the difficulties in implementation of an organizational learning approach have to do with people's ability to organize and control their time. This is a key issue because many people, even those in senior management positions, don't feel that they have control of their time.

Some argue that the issue of having enough time is a matter of support from top management. I'm less convinced. Even when given more visible symbolic support from the top, and even when they recognize that learning takes time, many people still find it difficult to take that time away from more urgent work. People have had a time clock mentality drilled into them for years: "If I'm not working, or if I take time off, I'm not doing my job." This is an inescapable core dilemma.

The Epsilon Team resolved the time issue in a way that forced them to cope with another dilemma: free choice versus full involvement. When the project management extended their monthly team meetings from a half day to a whole day, so that they could spend the time they needed to learn, people complied with the change, rather than acting in commitment to it.

In a situation like this, there is an implicit ideal at work: Real learning needs to be voluntary. If people are forced to do something they often will resist and find subtle ways to undermine it. Thus, the leaders would ideally talk to everybody individually and make sure people are on board before organizing the meetings for learning.

On the other hand, as the team leaders understood, having a regular opportunity for practice was important for the team. Since many people are unlikely to take the time away from urgent tasks, there may need to be some kind of mandated initial exposure. As they wrestle with this dilemma, line managers like the Program Manager at Epsilon often feel conflicted.

In this case, the manager mandated the longer staff meeting. He felt that his direct reports needed to move together in this work. But he also framed it as an experiment. He openly acknowledged that he wasn't sure it would continue. He encouraged people to express their qualms.

In the long run, it would be interesting to see whether people who were required to go to these meetings eventually developed real enthusiasm and commitment. This might be measured by the extent to which they initiated similar efforts on their own later in their careers.

◆ THE DILEMMA OF THE "BETTER MOUSETRAP"

Another core dilemma illustrated in the learning history involves the diffusion of insights from highly innovative projects. This could be called "the failure of the better mousetrap theory." It was framed well by a comment made by an internal consultant, on page 96:

> I got the impression that [the team leaders] were saying to themselves, 'We did everything right. Everybody at AutoCo should be pleased. When they see the results, they'll knock the doors down trying to learn how to do what we did.' . . . In retrospect, that was a naive approach to the world.

A moment later, he continues:

> Perhaps we should have prepared for the ambivalence outsiders would feel and adopted less of a missionary attitude about what we were doing. On the other hand, if we hadn't taken that attitude, we might never have begun the learning effort.

The enthusiasm that drives the innovation is precisely the same enthusiasm that becomes problematic. To those outside the effort, it can be interpreted as blindness or as being caught in a kind of a messianic zeal. "You've lost track of your real job," outsiders say. But without that zeal, people would never undertake daring experiments.

This dilemma is important for all of us involved in management innovation to understand. It relates directly to several endemic ambiguities around the role of senior management. At the end of the document, for example, there's a quote from the Program Manager's boss (page 107):

> I think we have taken a major step backwards from showing the people out there that we support improving our processes. They're all scared to death. When the reorganization started I argued that we ought to take some overt action to support organizational learning. Because we have a lot of people who are unsure whether they ought to be involved in any of this kind of stuff.

It would be interesting to know, what would have happened if the boss had really advocated more organizational learning. Would it have been ignored, as are many "good ideas" from senior management? Would it have turned people off because of the cynicism that has developed from one new change program after another "rolled out" from on high?

Alternatively, what could the Program Manager's boss have done differently? You might think that someone like him would be the perfect person to coach the Program Manager, to push him to communicate, and to give him feedback at doing a better job of spreading understanding of what he and his team had done. Relative to this sort of innovative effort, the boss might define his own role as helping the Program Manager manage upwards. In his position he would hear a great deal; he would know what was going on above the Program Manager and (for example) what concerns and perceptions the Program Manager would need to address.

On the other hand, to play such a role might also put the Program Manager's boss at political risk within the organization. The Program Manager has already put himself at risk. Those allied with him, especially those with management accountability for the innovative team's results, run a similar risk. It is easy for those immediately above innovators to be predisposed to a conservative stance regarding their innovations.

In some sense there needs to be an intermediary to the larger system. The local line leaders who are instigating, initiating, sustaining, carrying the flag for significant innovations need a coach. The coach could be very close to the team, but should not be part of the innovation itself. He or she should be senior and secure enough to remain free from high risk and capable of seeing how the team is perceived by the larger system. He or she could help the local managers deal with the negative perceptions held by people around them, perceptions which are often founded on incomplete views of the team.

It's hard to conceive of an example where effective senior management champions of this sort wouldn't be important. Yet, I think they are often missing in cases like the Epsilon story. Unfortunately, such senior coaches are often hard to find, even when the local innovators are looking for them. Moreover, because they are not deeply involved in the innovation process, they may have only superficial understanding of what the innovators are doing. At the same time, the innovators tend to be drawn not to senior coaches, but to other innovators—who, like themselves, are deeply immersed and from whom they can learn more about each others' innovations.

◆ EXECUTIVE LEADERS AND THE "KISS OF DEATH"

This lack of senior coaches suggests that there is much to learn about the effective role of senior management in the innovation process. There's a great quote from the Vice President, on page 108, that may hold some clue to the thorny dilemmas around senior management:

> If the MIT course is something that everyone should be following, then I think not only I, but each of the vehicle center people, ought to go through it. And we [at the top management staff level] ought to adopt it as the process that we want to follow for human interaction and team building. But if it's equivalent to other approaches, and there are 40 different ways to achieve the same results, then it's not so important that we choose that specific course. I don't know which is the right one.

When I first read the phrase, "We at the top ought to adopt it as the process that we want to follow," I wrote "the kiss of death" next to it on the document. In my experience, that sort of top management support is a surefire way to kill a real innovation.

The executive lays out two options: Either the Epsilon innovation is one of a lot of approaches that he doesn't have enough time for, or it's the answer to all of AutoCo's problems and should be rolled out through the organization. But none of us who were involved in developing Epsilon's innovations would advocate rolling them out through the whole company. There is still too much to learn. When you roll out a process like this, you standardize to the extreme. That doesn't allow people to go through the organic process of testing the new approach, improving it, and becoming committed to it. The new approach has to develop in a symbiotic way between different local line settings, their particular needs, and their different types of leaders. One person wants to emphasize the "management flight simulators"; somebody else wants to emphasize the ladder of inference. That's very appropriate.

In short, I think we see a huge failing in executive leadership here. It starts with a way of thinking that frames two options: Either standardize a new approach and make everybody follow it, or ignore it. Why would executives tend to think this way, especially if there are compelling arguments that standardization of learning can be problematic? One possible answer is the assumption: "the only way you get things done is through standardization."

I do not think there is anything wrong with standardization, but you have to

1. first have enough data and experience to know what and why you are standardizing, and

2. be able to distinguish certain highly replicable processes which are suitable for standardization and other processes which cannot be standardized.

You can standardize around the conventions for writing music, but you cannot standardize the process for writing music. Appropriate standards enable the creative process. Inappropriate standards impede it.

Another reason why executives often think you must either standardize or ignore innovations involves time frame. It might take 10 years to test a new set of ideas systematically, and allow them to diffuse organically. This means that it's not going to happen on any individual executive's watch. The executive thinks, "I've got big problems, and this can't possibly achieve the scale of impact that I need to achieve in the next two years—so forget it."

I believe that, in corporations today, there is a fundamental lack of stewardship for innovations that require a long time frame to have broad impact. Executives have difficulty supporting management innovations that might take 10 or 20 years to come to fruition. Conversely, it's easy to become addicted to "quick-fix" strategies. This is one of the major reasons for so much money spent on management consulting.

The issue of time frame is a bit more complex, however, when we consider the difference between investing in physical capital and in human capital. Investment decisions—like a major capital expansion in China—are often made with the knowledge that the benefits cannot be reaped for 10 or 20 years. If I'm an executive, and that kind of investment happens on my watch, I'll be remembered as the person who started it. With those kinds of big capital or technology investment decisions, executives can strike a balance between the long-term payoff and the short-term personal gratification of a legacy or reputation. It's much more difficult to acquire that gratification with the "softer investments," such as the innovations of the Epsilon Program. These are more diffuse, harder to measure. And there is not so much one momentous decision as a whole series of little steps that head in a coherent direction. Perhaps the real problem with learning is that no one or two "great leaders" can get credit for it. This tends to go against our "hero leader" mindset.

As long as these ways of thinking characterize the executive mindset, it will be difficult to galvanize serious interest in innovations like Epsilon's. Innovators will be "pulling teeth" to get people to invest any real time to understand a change effort that may take 10 or 20 years to have an impact throughout a large organization. If, at the same time, executives require proof of results and replicability to decide that this is the right thing to do, then the innovators are caught in a dilemma. You can't talk to executives about something new until you've had results, but you can't do something because you haven't had results yet. No wonder innovative line managers adopt the attitude, "It's better to get forgiveness than permission." Meanwhile, the executives are adrift: They're paralyzed as long as they keep this way of thinking.

These difficulties are quite typical of many significant innovations. They indicate a flaw in the management system, not a flaw in individual managers' attitudes. There is no clear accountability for "management research." One way out of this paralysis is to see the role of executives shift. Their jobs could, in part, have to do with the serious assessment of potentially significant new innovations like those of the Epsilon program. This would not be an easy shift to make in a world where executives are under the gun for short-term profits. But if knowledge-based management really has a future, one key will be clearer managerial accountability for serious study of significant innovations that hold promise for improving knowledge generation and diffusion.

◆ THE DIFFICULTIES IN ASSESSMENT

One reason I think this would help is that there are also significant dilemmas around assessment itself, many of which are also illustrated in the learning history. These dilemmas tend to interact adversely with the dilemmas around executive decision making, as it functions today. If there were clearer executive accountability for helping the organization learn from its own innovations, people would wrestle with the assessment dilemmas more seriously.

The difficulties in assessment have to do with one of the cornerstone principles of systems thinking. In situations with "dynamic complexity" (where cause and effect are not closely related in time and space), it is difficult to see causal relationships. For example, the first problem with assessment arises from time delays. A significant management innovation takes a long time before there are demonstrable results. It takes time to understand what a tool can accomplish and how to use it effectively, and only then can it be evaluated. MIT and AutoCo are learning this fact of life together. But it is difficult to see how long it can take, and there is not a lot of patience for the struggle—either at AutoCo or MIT. So we end up assessing very partial progress because it takes time and patience to achieve significant progress. If there's not enough patience and commitment to stay with the learning process, then the assessments themselves may be incomplete and misleading. As retired CEO Bill O'Brien puts it, "Managers are always pulling up the radishes to see how they're growing."

Second, it may be hard to distinguish causality because so many other things have happened during those years. The pressure to find clear causality makes it difficult to assess any significant innovation. Not only are there time delays. These experiments occur in a complex system where there are many things going on, interacting with one another and with the internal dynamics of the organizational system. Why, under such circumstances, do we expect to be able to say: "This is what is causing the consequences we observe?" Yet, the underlying epistemology evoked by people in the organization is this: "If it works, we'll understand how it works, so that we can make it work the same way everywhere."

This is illustrated in many quotes in the learning history. When people make comments like, "Well, I don't think the Learning Lab did this" or "I don't think the tools did this," they are invoking a particular causal frame. To say that "the real fundamental thing that made a difference in this case was the changes in the behavior of the senior management" is hard to argue with. Yet it totally misses the point that the senior management core team went through a particular learning process involving more than nine months of intensive work.

Moreover, self-assessment is innately tricky when you're dealing with changes in mental models. In many cases, when people go through slow gradual evolution in their mental models, we've seen that it's extremely difficult for them to look back and remember that they didn't always think the way they now think.

Then there's the problem in quantifying results. There are some quantifiable results, but most of the really important results are difficult or impossible to quantify. A related problem concerns the difference between obvious innovations and more subtle innovations. The harmony buck is an example of obvious innovation. Many people talk about it as being extremely successful. But more subtle innovations might have been essential for making the harmony buck effective. Why did the team take the risk and invest a million dollars in the harmony buck in the first place? It wasn't a new idea, yet no one else had done it before them. They stuck their necks out because they had made some headway in their working methods and believed this would help further. Moreover, the communication skills, openness, and trust they were starting to develop may have been vital in making the harmony buck work. The obvious technological innovation was indeed important, but so were the subtle changes, which may cause and enable the obvious innovation.

This distinction becomes especially important as people make informal assessments. What do observers at AutoCo say when they see the harmony buck? Somebody could come along and say, "We should standardize this idea." But, in fact, the key factors that allow the harmony buck to work occur at a more subtle level. You can't standardize communication skills, openness, and trust; you can only standardize the formal innovation. By doing so, and stopping there, you end up propagating something that will probably have minimal impact.

I think this happens all the time around significant innovations. That, in fact, is why tools like learning histories are so important. They can begin to address some of these core dilemmas around assessing innovations, by providing a richer, more realistic documentation of the multidimensional nature of significant management innovations.

Lastly, there is the difficulty of assessing innovations that might, by some traditional measures, make things worse. When a team innovates to improve a process it changes the rules. This stymies the rest of the organization's ability to measure the team's progress.

In Epsilon, this was especially evident in the increase in change requests. The team felt that this was a direct result of increased trust and meeting deadlines in prototype builds: People saw that they needed to make changes earlier in the process than otherwise would have occurred. But this same data was interpreted, by many outside the team, as the team "being out of control." If this type of misinterpretation through conventional measures is joined with the desire to find what works, standardize it, and roll it out, then the organization is held in the grip of a deadly duality that could destroy opportunities for really significant innovation

◆ THE PROJECT GOALS AND STRATEGY

Of course, all of these dilemmas and challenges must be viewed in the context which characterized Epsilon. We saw it as a very early pilot. We were seeking a basic "proof of concept." Remember, one reason we started projects like Epsilon was because we wanted to see if we could generate some basic evidence for our basic notion that the tools, methods, and practice field approach, taken together, could produce some significant enhancement in a real organization settings. Those of us involved believed that these weren't just a bunch of good ideas that make nifty three-day workshops. We believed they were well enough developed after 15 years to begin making a difference with real people doing real work. But, we were also "prototyping." When you are prototyping any new innovation, you cannot expect to get everything right the first time out. We mainly wanted to see if it "could fly"—not necessarily to prove that it would fly perfectly.

Also, it's important to keep in mind the essence of a learning orientation toward fundamental change. To pursue a true learning approach, we simply must give up the goal of "finding the right answer" or "the right approach." The overarching goal is to continually enable people to shape their future—not to find all the right answers.

Our first goal, in developing the Epsilon project was to test a particular concept for creating learning infrastructure. We wanted to establish a long-term project in which we could develop a learning process in collaboration with a group of people within a company, implement it, and observe and study the results. In particular, we wanted to test the concept of a learning laboratory—the sort described in Chapter 4—in conjunction with several specific tools and methods: system archetypes, some basic inquiry and advocacy techniques, and the "microworld" computer simulation. We wanted to study how effective this design would be.

Secondly, we had some questions, which are perhaps easier to articulate in hindsight. What happens in a real organization—with a real set of cultural dynamics, inertia, views, biases, and traditions—when a particular set of people go through a process like this? As they integrate a learning environment, like a learning laboratory, into their work setting, what happens to them personally? What happens to them organizationally? How does it shift their relationship with their local organization—their team—and their larger organization? This second set of questions grew in importance as the project unfolded.

These questions were informed by an overall theory about how to enhance organization-wide learning. This theory was originally articulated in *The Fifth Discipline Fieldbook*, in the lead essay. According to this theory, the essence of the work on learning organizations involves deep changes in how people think and interact, a so-called "deep learning cycle" which involves developing new skills and capabilities, new ways of seeing the world, and eventually new underlying assumptions and beliefs. Put differently, all deep organizational change involves deep changes in the ways that people think and interact.

Why would a learning orientation or a learning approach matter to corporations? Because creating a deep learning cycle is literally what it means to be alive. As noted above, we are very skillful reductionists. We see a world of things, of isolated phenomena, and we have the attendant beliefs and assumptions: "I can fix this over here, and by golly it will stay fixed." We acquire these attitudes and beliefs through a profound learning process that continues through our lifetime. We learn to be reductionists, to break problems apart and analyze the parts, and we become quite successful at it. Most of our environments, in turn, are continually supportive and conducive to that learning process.

The essence of a strategy for transforming organizations, according to this theory, is to move people toward more systemic ways of thinking and seeing. This can't be done by fiat or by command. It requires creating new workplace environments which will support and sustain different types of learning processes, as shown in Figure 8-1.

Figure 8-1
Strategy for transforming organizaitons

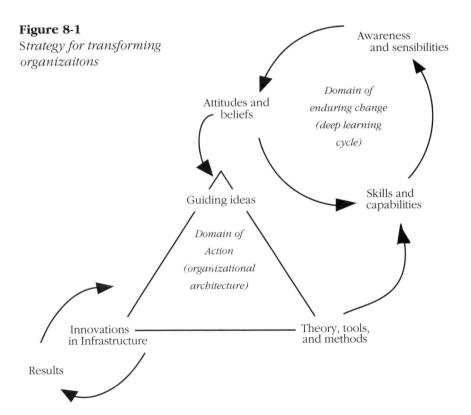

Appropriate tools and methods based on suitable underlying theories constitute one element of such an environment. Much of our learning occurs through the tools we use, as they shape the ways in which we deal with practical problems. Hammers, saws, and screwdrivers are basic tools of carpentry, but they are also primary ways of developing carpenters. They force their users not just to build a house, but to think and operate and interact in new ways—that, in the end, add up to learning carpentry.

A second element of this environment is the infrastructure through which you can organize the resources—time, energy, and focus—so that people actually have the support they need to use the tools and methods. In the Epsilon story, the first innovation in infrastructure was the monthly core team meeting. This meeting, originally held for a half day, was extended to a full day. This meant that the core team members had time at regular intervals to begin practicing tools like the ladder of inference, left-hand column cases, and system archetypes. This experience wasn't like a training program, because the practice occurred within the work team and at the regular work setting. They had their regular staff meeting, then reflected on the meeting and the issues it raised using these tools.

Later on, the team developed other infrastructural innovations, like the Learning Room. Learning infrastructures may be physical like this but they don't have to be. The simplest way to answer "what is infrastructure?" is to ask how time and other are resources made available. If people have no time to reflect, to sit down and ask each other, in effect, "Why the heck did that happen?," then they have no infrastructure for learning and they are not going to learn.

A third element of the environment consists of the guiding ideas that help people make sense of "why we're doing this." Guiding ideas have always been a core function of leadership: articulating a story that says, "Here's why we want to do something differently," and "Here's what we're hoping to accomplish." In any setting where people are seeking change, success depends on the ability of leaders to construct a sensible story, to explain why resources must be organized in a somewhat different way. The Program Manager had to do that right at the outset of the Epsilon project, just to give some credibility to the decision to extend the monthly staff meeting.

Tools like those used in the Epsilon meetings can be very effective, but they're limited without a particular set of appropriate guiding ideas. The traditional guiding ideas of running an organization— which do not usually include openness, making reasoning well known, and working as peers to learn together—these tools actually have a potential to feel more manipulative. "Tell me your reasoning," can be a very intimidating mandate from a control-oriented manager.

Of the three elements of the triangle, guiding ideas are the toughest to pin down because they evolve over time. There is a good reason for this. As you develop and start to sustain the deep learning cycle, people's understanding of their progress will steadily deepen. Hence their guiding ideas will steadily change. Initially, the Program Manager might have just said, "We're going to meet for longer than usual because there are new ways we need to learn to work better together." As time goes on, the story shows how different guiding ideas were needed: around openness, the need for trust to functioning as a team, reporting of lateness, and so on. But few of those guiding ideas were present at the outset.

One last point which is not evident from the learning history bears noting. I was never present on site with the Epsilon team, except for an introductory one-day session about six months before the project started. The main MIT researcher on this project was a graduate student in the midst of completing his Ph.D. He was very talented and skillful with the basic theories and tools. He had written quite extensively about systems thinking. But he was a far cry from an experienced consultant with 20 years of experience at a major consulting firm.

To have somebody with only a few years of consulting experience accomplish this intervention with the Epsilon team was very significant because our goal was to test an approach. Often, experienced consultants can help groups to change, but you never know the extent to which the effect came from the approach used or the consultant's savvy and experience. Often, I feel it is the later. Here, the results were more demonstrably replicable.

Moreover, as the process unfolded, many of the introductory learning lab sessions in the firm were led by internal people. This showed that internal capacity was developing. In other words, the "deep learning cycle" was working. In fact, today, there are quite a few very skillful internal facilitators and consultants within AutoCo who can trace some of their experience back to the Epsilon learning labs and similar sessions elsewhere.

Lastly, we've done our best to try to make the process of the Epsilon intervention transparent. It is impossible to document in detail of every meeting, every learning lab, and every change that went on with every individual and team. But the tools and approaches have all been explained here and elsewhere, and the learning history provides a rich documentation of some of the key dimensions of the process as it unfolded over time. This sort of evidence is rare, especially for field projects that involve significant personal, interpersonal, and business change over many years. I think we have all learned a lot how to do this better in the future, but I also think this learning history is a significant first step.

Developing a team learning process is the most significant contribution that the Epsilon project has made. In their action, the team demonstrated what a learning approach is; in their results, they showed what it can accomplish. They did it themselves. The tools, methods, and processes which they used are clearly documented. There is every reason, on principle, that this success could be replicated. It would not be trivial to replicate, or automatic that it would be replicated, but other teams could pick up nearly everything that the Epsilon team did and apply it to their own learning approach.

◆ THE CHARACTERISTICS OF A LEARNING APPROACH

LEARNING AROUND BUSINESS ISSUES

A learning organization orientation is focused on key business issues. The need to change and improve the team's ability to realize business goals drives the whole process. For example, the learning exchanges that stood out here involved either key business issues (like getting parts on time) or key interpersonal problems that were limiting business results. The priority is always the practical results the "learners" are striving to achieve.

SURFACING RATHER THAN SOLVING PROBLEMS

In a learning approach, people focus on assumptions and assessments, not just on solving their problems. This delicate balance is explained very effectively and then illustrated in the quotes in Chapter 2. The leaders and consultants resolved to place their attention on the differences among the assumptions and assessments they were making, rather than trying to solve the problems in the same old ways they'd been trying to solve problems for years. Only then is there a hope of reaching deeper insights and more enduring "solutions."

LEARNING THROUGH DISCOVERY

In a learning orientation, learning is driven by self-discovery, rather than teaching. Over and over, this case shows people discovering for themselves the ramifications of the assumptions and assessments they had been making individually and collectively, rather than having someone else tell them. People must discover for themselves how their assumptions and habitual actions contribute directly to some of their most pressing business problems—as occurred with the "tragedy of the power supply" or the way low trust was undermining the goal of getting parts on time. Although the practice of learning through discovery defines a learning approach, it's relatively rare in practice.

FIGURING OUT "HOW TO DO IT"

Fourth, focus on "how to do it," not just what should be done. So much has been written telling people what they ought to do to be effective, and so little that gives examples of how people actually go about changing their behavior. This represents a fundamental difference between learning and proselytizing. Anybody can preach "we should be trusting."

The learning history illustrates again and again the tools and process- es that were used that caused people to reflect, and made it possible over time for them to be more open and trusting. This is actual knowledge, not conceptual knowledge.

This does not imply that there are "three simple steps" to build trust. Every situation is unique and the solutions will also be unique. But there are guiding principles and practical approaches which people who are committed can apply—guided by a common body of underlying theory, such as the feedback theory of complex human systems, and the theory of how mental models shape perceptions and action.

DISCOVERING AND SEEING INTERRELATEDNESS

Next, focus on the interrelatedness of problem symptoms, rather than just trying to solve isolated problems. One of the toughest learning challenges is overcoming the fact that people think in a fragmented way: "I'll do my piece, and that piece is somebody else's problem." When you realize that the way you do your piece creates somebody else's problem, you're start- ing to see interrelatedness.

DRAWING ANSWERS FORTH FROM THE COLLECTIVE

A sixth point comes out very clearly in the learning history: no key person has all the answers. There's a great quote on page 37: "The boss was learning with us. He didn't have the answers. We were going to do this together." That also defines a learning approach. Nobody's got it all figured out. We're all ignorant at some level. We may understand pieces, but nobody, including the boss, understands everything.

HAVING CONCERN FOR THE WHOLE

In organizations, openness based on trust and genuine desire to cooperate is another element of a learning approach. What is the purpose in learning? If it is solely for self gain, the health and effectiveness of the whole system cannot improve. To cooperate requires trust, and trust comes from openness.

Openness is often advocated. But there are two types of openness and, over time, they go together. It is important that people be able to express their views without fear of reprisal. But it is equally important that they be able to inquire into their views, that they be able to move beyond the "normal state of affairs" where they believe their views are right and work to get others to adopt them. The foundation for real openness is reflectiveness and humility, two features in short supply in most management situations. Without these, people may simply argue for their own points of view in a more "open" way a hollow victory. Again, these are not conditions which can be legislated; they evolve from a consistent leadership which acts with integrity for the organization as a whole.

CREATING AND GIVING FEEDBACK

This means having a community of people who develop individual and collective skills, and hold each other accountable for those learning behaviors. The members can articulate what they are trying to do and why; their colleagues can respond with candor and awareness. This concept involves the "community nature of the self," a fundamental systemic notion about which Fred Kofman and I have written. Teams like Epsilon, over time, develop a community of people who support one another in the learning process. Giving feedback, and holding yourself and others accountable, is one part of that support. Continually seeing what others have accomplished and understanding what problems they are wrestling with is another.

SEEING FAILURE AS OPPORTUNITY

Another defining aspect is a shift in attitude toward failure. As one team member put it, "If you know you're not going to be punished, you'll try harder." Fear is a powerful element of most work settings. And fear cramps imagination. Reducing fear of failure is vital to innovation and learning.

But reducing fear of failure also involves a more subtle shift around the available time for learning. As the learning history shows, in an engineering culture where "you don't say you have a problem until you have a solution," just getting people to talk about problems openly is a big step. But, the real gain comes from the learning opportunities inherent in seeing unsolved problems and acknowledging mistakes. It takes trust, a genuine desire for mutual support, and a good deal of reflective time to convert those mistakes into significant innovations.

The first step is for people to be able to sit with, acknowledge, and tell the truth: to acknowledge themselves and to be able to talk about things that aren't going well, or about which they are perplexed.

CONNECTING PERSONAL DECISIONS TO SYSTEMIC RESULTS

Using simulations to encourage people to connect their personal decisions to systemic results is another characteristic of a learning approach. Actually, it is a specific example of a more general principle, the role of "practice fields" where people can learn through doing. The section on the role of simulation in the document was very short, but it was indicative of results that we have seen in many other settings. People may think they have all the answers, but then they try their strategies out in the computer and they don't do as well as they thought they would. If this leads them to then discover shortcomings in their own understanding of the larger system, this can lead to real learning.

BUILDING RELATIONSHIPS AND FOSTERING PARTNERSHIP

The importance of building relationships and fostering partnership is highlighted in many sections of the learning history. There is a simple assumption that lies a bit below the surface here: that the quality of decision making depends on the quality of thinking and that the quality of thinking depends on the quality of relationships. In other words, real trust and mutuality are not just nice qualities that we would prefer in any work setting. They have a first order impact on the results people are able to produce.

DEVELOPING GENUINE INTEREST IN EACH OTHER'S REASONING

Lastly, there is the need to gradually develop genuine interest in one another's reasoning. A simple example of this in the learning history occurs in a learning lab, described on page 64: "One of my suppliers . . . mentioned . . . that a part would be two weeks late." Rather than dumping on him, or telling him to shut up and perform, the Epsilon engineers eventually got him to explain why he was going to be late. It turned out that AutoCo was making a great many mistakes in the paperwork. Rather than blaming the supplier, they could learn how to fix a problem that affected lots of people.

CHAPTER 9

WHY THE BATTLE WAS WON, BUT THE WAR WAS LOST

An organizational change perspective on the AutoCo Epsilon Program

Rosabeth Moss Kanter

From her earliest organizational studies of communes to her groundbreaking 1977 book Men and Women of the Corporation *(New York: Basic Books) to her strategic guides to becoming a "Change Master" and helping corporate giants "Learn to Dance," Harvard Business School Professor Rosabeth Moss Kanter has been one of the premier strategists in organizational innovation and change. She was one of the first to show how a place could be made for the entrepreneurial spirit to thrive in industrial-era corporations—a perspective which led, indirectly if not directly, to the climate which allowed Epsilon to thrive at AutoCo.*

Here, she offers a strategist's perspective on the opportunities and pitfalls that faced the Epsilon team, and the ways in which they met their fate. This commentary is particularly valuable for leaders of teams which, like Epsilon, seek to create change not from the top of an organization, but from within the ranks of middle-management, enmeshed in a middle-level project. Sustained change is feasible from that position, says Dr. Kanter—but only if a sharp strategic eye is cast upwards in the hierarchy.

Dr. Kanter is the author of Rosabeth Moss Kanter On the Frontiers of Management *(1997, Boston: Harvard Business School Press);* World Class: Thriving Locally in the Global Economy *(1995, New York: Simon & Schuster);* When Giants Learn to Dance *(1989, New York: Simon & Schuster);* The Change Masters *(1983, New York: Simon & Schuster); and other significant books on corporate dynamics and change.*

Many dimensions of the AutoCo project were very successful, which represents an impressive accomplishment. But there were major difficulties in translating a successful project into organizational change. The battle was won, but perhaps the war was lost.

There are three main issues to consider from what happened at AutoCo.

First, how much did the particular learning tools and approaches used in the project contribute to its successes? The tools employed were very useful, and on the face of it are valuable as a way to help people stretch their thinking and understand the underlying dynamics of situations. An important question to ask is, "Could the tools have contributed more?" How could the system dynamics perspective extend learning beyond individuals and the Epsilon team to the AutoCo organization?

Secondly, what can the team's changes and success be attributed to? It is implied that the success of the team was based on the tools which people learned. This explanation is limited, particularly given that there was little evidence that system tools were used in diagnosing and changing the larger AutoCo environment. And how much of the project success was due to new elements in the organizational environment for teams at Epsilon, rather than the learning tools themselves?

Thirdly, there are two sides to learning and change—being learners and teachers as well as change targets and change agents. Participants in organizational learning and change will inevitably find themselves in all these roles. How does what they are taught, and the skills they learn and practice, help them to be effective as teachers and change agents helping others to learn—and not just as users of new tools themselves? How can "change agent skills" be added to learning labs to help people become even more effective at getting results and producing long-term organizational capabilities?

Each of these issues are considered in more detail in this chapter.

◆ EXTENDING A SYSTEMS PERSPECTIVE TO THE PRACTICE OF FACILITATING LEARNING IN ORGANIZATIONS

The AutoCo Epsilon Learning History is a valuable account of a good systematic way of teaching people to stretch their thinking, take more responsibility, and see system forces and root causes instead of engaging in quick fixes. AutoCo and other companies are already starting to work in team-based, cross-functional ways where traditional rules are suspended, which contributes to helping them achieve a faster product development process and a higher-quality product. As an organizational change paradigm, however, the learning approach as described here appears limited. Very little is changing about the AutoCo organization as a whole. People are taught a way of thinking, and there's nothing in the case about the practice intervening in a single system dynamic.

The Epsilon Project itself might be considered an example of the Quick Fix systems archetype. The "command and control" leadership style was resolved in some ways by a learning lab, but it really did not address the issue of participative style. It provided a quick fix. The people who went to learning labs felt a temporary sense of satisfaction as they learned and understood something. But things could get worse because people could be lulled into a sense of "We have the answer, we have the tool." Things could also get worse because the people being educated develop their own language and behaviors, and can become a cult-like group within the larger organization.

In some ways it is ironic that given the MIT Center of Organizational Learning's, now the Society for Organizational Learning, understanding of systems dynamics, many of the tools in this case are not addressing organizational learning or organizational change. The tools and the project are aimed at individual learning and individual change, with a hope that people will carry that learning back into a team, behave differently in a team, and that team will then somehow magically figure out how to change an organization.

The Society for Organizational Learning should add "organization" to the learning, and think about organization change, and how one goes about it. Until that happens, in part, the practice is not compatible with the theory. The practice is not addressing any underlying system dynamic. The diagnosis work that people do in the learning labs is still only having an impact at level of individual awareness. There was a supportive new social organizational context surrounding the Epsilon Project. It was more team-based and cross-functional, but many other companies have also discovered this to speed up product development. Clearly these tools can support that process, but there is still a gap.

A locally supportive environment made Epsilon work, but the lack of a wider supportive organizational context also killed it. That larger organizational context seems to be the missing piece and the place to focus. That context can mean addressing political, governance, policy, structure, and even supporting systems. Do people need a different communication media? Do they need to use information channels differently? Sometimes the opportunities for consultants to have an impact are limited because of what a client will allow you to do. If the client gets excited about teaching individuals to change their thinking, then it's hard to say, "Well yes, but as part of that we also must create new vehicles in the organization." It's hard, but it's not impossible, and it is an important how to in creating learning organizations.

◆ TOOLS AND SOCIAL CONTEXT CREATE LEARNING ENVIRONMENTS

A second how to is how to sort out the intrinsic value of the tools. They are good tools. The mental model tools, from the ladder of inference to the systems archetypes, help people understand what's really going on and open up communication. They are very powerful and insightful. The tools grab people. But what makes an organization work is that people use common tools.

One of the great values of total quality was simply that it gave people a common vocabulary. They had shared meaning and ways of going about approaching and solving problems. That combination by itself had a positive impact on outcomes, regardless of the tools themselves. When tools are shared, people can communicate in code, immediately depersonalizing tense situations by their common understanding. As they develop a way to solve problems together, they immediately solve problems faster.

It is hard to determine or separate the value of a particular discipline or tool from the value of simply having shared meaning. Creating shared meaning around tools is one of the kinds of impact the Society for

Organizational Learning is having on individual learning. Yet the approach doesn't help assess whether it's these tools, or the use of the tools in a supportive context, that speed up the development process. There were a set of bosses suspending rules, and places where people could gather to communicate without hierarchical barriers. These practices leap out as critical just by themselves and may conceivably be more important than specific tools.

One trap a project like this can fall into is to be identified with only one concrete manifestation of a tool. The MIT team was brought in to do learning labs. The learning labs were concrete and tangible. Every manager understands that training programs are deliverables. The bosses in that division could say, "That's what we're doing." But people not only said the learning labs weren't the most important thing, they often said, "I wasn't even sure I was that comfortable" or " I can't remember. Did I go to that?"

Other possible explanations exist for the success of the team. Perhaps the most important element of the learning project was to contribute to the creation of an environment in which managers behaved differently. Maybe one should be honest about that and say, "What we provide is an environment which allows managers to behave differently. The learning labs provide the occasions for people to share common perspectives and build common vocabularies. One of the most important things about change is creating environments that support people using what they already know. It is less significant that people were taught anything differently."

The dilemma, of course, is that explanation doesn't distinguish the Society for Organizational Learning from anyone else using new tools to do team building. Research groups and consulting groups want to be known for their particular approach to the world and to sell their particular tools. There is a great temptation to say, "We provide learning labs and learning tools because they make us distinctive. This approach has a Peter Senge or a George Roth theory stamp on it." Instead, the Center for Organizational Learning ought to offer a way to organize people so they can take advantage of whatever tools they already have. The learning task is creating the supportive environment in which you can use whatever it is you're learning, not a particular set of tools which people are taught.

◆ LEADERS AND FOLLOWERS: PREPARING PEOPLE AS CHANGE AGENTS

Change in organizations has many dimensions. One question to consider is how participants are prepared to be teachers, not just learners, and system change agents, not just change targets. This issue concerns what's taught in the learning labs. There is a considerable gap between the system archetypes, which promote a style of thinking and can be used as a macro diagnostic tool, and techniques like the left-hand column case, which is a more micro diagnostic tool, and relates to interactive communication. To what extent are participants taught to be agents of change, to understand how to apply what they do, to work with other people, to understand the frustrations, to see why other people are going to resist, and to learn to be ambassadors? These skills give participants the capabilities to practically apply their knowledge behaviorally. In the Epsilon example participants are not explicitly taught these skills, and there is nothing that fills the gap between macro change and micro behavior.

Not having those intermediate skills might lead to people being excited about new tools which make their team work well, but rather than being ambassadors of what they have learned, they become converted cultists. They promote ideas like "The rest of the organization really stinks," or "I have changed so significantly that you really need to look at this." The implications of these messages are that you need to change. Pilot team members are seen as zealots, and their own thinking and questions are no longer aligned with the greater concerns like, "How do organizations really change? How do you do projects?" "Why do people resist change?" "How do you help them overcome it?"

For example, asking these questions would go along with the kind of thinking that says, "We can't just conduct learning labs. We must also sell senior management, so we need an advisory council. Senior management isn't going to come to learning labs, but in that advisory council we'll let them know what's going on. We'll get their objections. We'll tell them what the people in the learning labs are saying, and what the policy implications might be. Maybe they will want to change a practice or a policy to support what's coming out of these learning labs."

Arming participants to be better organizational change agents, rather than people who are converted or educated, is a very important piece of what is needed to actually build a learning organization. The change agent skills relate to flexibility in when and how new tools are used, emphasizing the depth and breadth of the skills people learn. They also help establish mechanisms within the organization for feedback and assessment of the effort.

◆ DANGER IN RIGID APPLICATION OF TOOLS

A common trap in the replication or application of a change effort is to say, "Let's just implement the conclusion." This approach overlooks the importance of the lessons the original participants learned, and the significant challenges they faced in reaching their conclusions. What is important is the process people went through, and their involvement in shaping the outcomes. Learning along the way is a part of what makes the conclusions acceptable to participants. If a "solution" becomes too rigid or is imposed, it doesn't have the same impact.

Many companies bring in people to teach strategic thinking who use some very good, state-of-the-art group dynamics and other kinds of tools. But often these tools are applied so rigidly that they immediately start creating organizational "haves" and "have nots." It becomes a great cult of those who "got it," which makes it very difficult for anyone to be skeptical in the programs themselves. Programs like these aren't teaching underlying principles, they are just teaching another form of rigid conformity in the service of liberation.

At one point, we were working with a company in a regulated industry, where one of these rigid programs was in progress. Our project was one of the counters to that dynamic. We were saying, "There are many ways to get things done." In that particular case, the work force became so distressed by this other project that members complained to regulators. The company was eventually taken to court, and the whole change effort was brought to a halt. That outcome illustrates one of the dangers of not addressing the organizational context. That result gives all change efforts bad name.

◆ BUILDING LONG-TERM CAPABILITY THROUGH BREADTH AND DEPTH

In order to be lasting and effective, change efforts have to be effective both on their own terms and in building the longer term capabilities of the organization. Clearly the Epsilon project was a great success on its own terms, but how it contributed to long-term capabilities is questionable. In fact, the learning project appeared to have some immediate negative consequences. One issue concerns not waiting for the rest of the organization to see the value of a pilot project. If you think of the project, learning labs, and the tools as organizational interventions, you can begin diffusing what is effective without training every part of the organization in-depth. Other projects could be put in motion by communicating and using only a small portion of what helps people and teams be more effective in learning.

A challenge in change efforts is to have simultaneous breadth and depth. Both are required at the same time—show what it is you're doing and do it fully, and at the same time communicate something to everybody in the organization. Communicating to others helps them feel included and gives them the ability to act on new ideas. That communication creates organizational momentum.

A temptation which counters communicating simple messages is thinking you have such a great theory and model that you do not want to dilute it by saying, "We can give you the five-minute version." But if you don't let lots of people have at least the five-minute version as a way to take a tiny baby step, it creates an incredible gap between the fully educated, fully developed perfect people and those who have nothing until two years from now when it's their time to find out the learning.

That gap is going to create the maximum tension between the people in any project in which the rules are suspended, and the rest of the organization. People in the rest of the organization may hate the project not just because its participants act like cult members, but because they may be having more fun than everybody else. They're creating something new, they have fewer rules, they're getting these terrific fun workshops, they've got real live dialogue rooms, and their managers are different. That can create resentment on the part of the "have nots." And one of the ways people may deal with that resentment is by discrediting the whole process—"they're just a bunch of out-of-control hippies," or "They're just lucky that they got those results."

◆ SETTING UP MECHANISMS FOR ASSESSMENT THAT ENGAGE THE LARGER SYSTEM

Another piece of the system context surrounding the project is selling senior management. It's important to get them involved, to create vehicles for them to play a constructive guiding role, and then to create ways to make policy changes based on what's coming out of the discussions in the learning labs. When you try to set this up in the beginning, senior management may say, "No, this takes up too much time, we're doing all the rest of it, we just want the training." So then you say, "Well, how can we connect with the rest of what you're doing?" And this comes back to how to number three, about making participants in the learning labs change agents themselves. If you've got a portion of the time spent in helping them be change agents, you'll soon find out what's really going on, and surface a lot of suggestions. You might be able to organize or mobilize the participants in the learning laboratories and beyond to do some of that work.

It would be important to set up mechanisms so that the learning lab is a systems diagnostic event for the whole organization. There need to be some agreed-upon measures in advance. How do we know that things are going to be different? And since some results are going to take two or three years to get, what are the interim signs that tell you that something you're tracking is going well or not?

Although it's difficult to get much time from senior management, you can get a lot of other people's time. It has to be built in to, and set up early on in, a project. A senior management council, composed of people who are committed to meeting every two or three months, should be the board of directors. Then task forces can be set up surrounding it. The task forces could be middle managers, including some skeptics and critics, who will also help define the measures and the communication vehicles. There are probably a lot of people with insights into what doesn't work in AutoCo who would flock to be on the measures task force. What they know has implications for these larger policies, but right now there is no mechanism for those insights to be communicated.

Once you have the measures, you can take five minutes of senior management's time, and bring in some pretty hard-nosed information.

Thus, for instance, at the end of the first year you would hold the learning organization conference trade fair and include everybody in the organization. You get senior management support by making them look really important, and giving them a role to play. They're going to convene and kick off this event that shows off what Epsilon's got so far, asks people for feedback on what Epsilon can do to improve, and showcases other group's initiatives—so there isn't a sense that this is a closed system. You could videotape the whole event, and send the tapes out.

You need different measures because this is a different process. But you need to do it in a form that's very familiar to people. These are the kinds of vehicles and mechanisms that build your communication channels, your support base to influence the system.

◆ SUMMARY

What bridges the gap between individual learning and organizational learning? AutoCo demonstrates two things: 1) the tools and the right context can produce very powerful results, and 2) without attention to these other organizational variables and context projects like this may not build long-range capabilities, and in fact may lead to negative outcomes that can discourage people from using the tools further. In this case, although the tools were phenomenal, it was the tools, plus the commonality, plus the "learn together," plus the social context that made up the total picture.

The Society for Organizational Learning doesn't want to be the Society for Individual Learning Inside Organizations. Presumably, readers of this learning history want to learn to actually build learning organizations and arm people to be better organizational change agents rather than converted cultists. This would be the next leap forward.

It is significant that Society for Organizational Learning and AutoCo are attempting to learn from the Epsilon experience together in order to improve upon the practice. Mental models are often rigid set frameworks, and breaking out of those set frameworks and thinking and working across boundaries is what it really means to be world class—a cosmopolitan thinker and a cosmopolitan leader able to see and influence the broader organizational system.

◆ FURTHER READING

R.M. Kanter, *The Change Masters*, 1983: New York: Simon & Schuster, especially Chapters 3, 8, 9, 10.

R.M. Kanter, *Rosabeth Moss Kanter on the Frontiers of Management*, 1997: Boston: HBS Press.

R.M. Kanter, *World Class: Thriving Locally in the Global Economy*, 1995, New York: Simon & Schuster, especially Chapters 2, 3, 11.

R.M. Kanter, B.A. Stein, and T.D. Jick (Editors), *The Challenge of Organizational Change*, 1992, New York: Free Press, especially Chapters 10 and 14.

R.M. Kanter, *Men and Women of the Corporation*, 1997, 1993, New York: Basic Books.

R.M. Kanter, *When Giants Learn to Dance*, 1989, New York: Simon & Schuster.

CHAPTER 10

CHALLENGING THE CATCH-22 INSIDE OURSELVES

An action science perspective on the AutoCo Epsilon Program

George Roth

Underlying the design of the learning laboratories at AutoCo Epsilon were well-established on principles and practices of "action science"—a 30-year-old set of theories about the relationship between attitudes, beliefs, talk, action, and the innate "theories of the world" which people hold within themselves. Chief among the developers of action science is Chris Argyris, coauthor (with Donald Schön) of Organizational Learning: A Theory of Action Perspective, *(1978, Reading: MA: Addison-Wesley) and (with Robert Putnam and Diana McLain Smith) of* Action Science *(1985, San Francisco: Jossey-Bass). Chris was also an advisor to the AutoCo Epsilon project who, significantly, dropped out of his advisor role when the team opted not to challenge the assumptions of AutoCo's senior management right at the beginning.*

We asked Chris for an explanation of the reasons behind his demurral and for an "action science" perspective on the Epsilon Program in general. He agreed that such a perspective would be valuable but suggested he would not be the best person to write it. George Roth, one of the coauthors of this learning history, had been Research Director at the MIT Sloan School's Center for Organizational Learning during the course of the Epsilon story. Trained in both process consultation and action science at MIT's Sloan School, George had followed the Epsilon story, from the beginning, from the action science perspective. This commentary combines the researchers' close understanding of the issues with the core action science inquiry: Where are the limits placed on innovation by management defensiveness? And how can that defensiveness be broached?

George is currently the Executive Director of the Ford/MIT Collaboration, an innovative $20M, five-year partnership between Ford Motor Company and the Massachusetts Institute of Technology focusing on research in the environment and the impact of information technology and globalization of the workforce on engineering work and education. The project involves linking Ford and MIT together through research teams in creating new knowledge that will, in part, serve as part of a catalyst for change in both institutions. He conducts research and teaches at the MIT Sloan School and University of New Hampshire in Durham.

From the moment they began, the project leaders of the Epsilon car launch were caught in an impossible situation—a storyline out of Joseph Heller's novel *Catch-22*. Heller's protagonist Yossarian pretended to be crazy to be discharged; but no one who wanted to get out of the war could possibly be considered crazy, and therefore his requests were ignored. The Epsilon leaders put on a front of being "normal" managers in order to influence the company—but no one who wanted to change the rules they changed could possibly be considered "normal," and, therefore, they too ended up ignored. Or so they felt. The challenges they faced, like the challenges faced by many leaders within corporations today, have less to do with the results they created than with the perpetual dilemma of demonstrating the value of their methods, no matter what the results might "prove."

"Don't try to change the boss's minds," many well-intentioned managers decide, "until you can back up your argument with results." This approach appears to be an ultimately sensible strategy—why would corporate executives change "the rules" without solid evidence that the rules weren't effective? And, indeed, the Epsilon leaders followed this course. Unable to see any other way to communicate, Epsilon managers sought to eventually convince senior managers they were "right." As their own narrative suggests, they didn't feel they had much choice. Opportunities for engaging senior management were limited, even about practical "hard" technical matters—let alone the critical need to think about the nature and value of an effective learning approach to launching a car. The bounded nature of the relationship between the two management levels made it easier for researchers and Epsilon managers to avoid saying anything meaningful about their increasing difficulties until they had evidence which would allow a more traditional—and, seemingly acceptable—form of engagement. When they had their evidence it was too late—or, at least, when it emerged, senior management didn't recognize it as compelling evidence for accepting their approach, and even less so for changing the nature of product management at AutoCo.

Epsilon's experience shows not just the pitfalls of taking on fundamental change, but the pitfalls of playing halfway—of being willing and able to challenge deeply held beliefs, but not being willing or able to effectively engage senior management in that challenge. The approach used by the managers was based on an espoused belief about the way their organization worked: That the route to success depended upon setting out to win every argument, being rational, not expressing negative feelings to higher-up leaders, and making sure you achieved set goals. Some of these beliefs may, in fact, be accurate, but when the methods and aims included learning, the combination ended with a self-defeating outcome.

In the end, the senior managers branded the project leaders as "cult figures"—exactly the label that the Epsilon leaders were trying to avoid. When you look at the actual behavior of the Epsilon project leaders, they were the opposite of cult leaders within their own team: They managed to draw forth and encourage, for example, subordinates who questioned their own behavior. (See, for example, the "Modeling new behavior: I don't trust you" segment on page 48) Yet their approach to learning, the implicit beliefs they seemed to hold about learning, and their approach to working with senior management somehow undermined the very learning they fostered.

The catch-22, in short, is prevalent throughout organizations, not just in product management teams but in every type of team that tries to develop its own and the organization's capabilities as it accomplishes something significant. Indeed, there is a branch of management theory called action science which looks at this practice and focuses specifically around these seemingly impossible catch-22s. Action science suggests that organizational learning, even when well-supported and well-staffed, is impossible to sustain unless we learn to challenge the internal beliefs that guide our own actions around fostering and nurturing organizational change.[1]

◆ THE PRECEPTS OF ACTION SCIENCE

Action science research is a branch of social science research, focused on designing and executing actions whose consequences are systematically studied. An aim of action science's pioneers was to create better organizations and societies with "citizens" who were responsible for becoming inquiry-oriented as they participated in public experiments to improve the nature of society. Thus, action scientists have worked to create "communities of inquiry" where people better understand the principles and premises embodied in their attitudes that influence their actions.[2] Action science researchers have found that the conditions needed to promote learning and create new knowledge for improved action do not exist naturally in most organizations. Sustaining learning in organizations requires adopting a new set of values and using them consistently in guiding behavior and holding conversations which are open to inquiry about one's own and each other's assumptions.

What kinds of values are needed to govern these conversations? The precepts of action science[3] suggest (1) that people be able to test the explanations for each others' behaviors (empirically disconfirmable propositions), (2) that expected behaviors are capable of being produced in workplace settings (knowledge that humans can implement), and (3) that people chose to participate based on their own volition and desire to act consistently with their beliefs (alternatives selected in light of freely chosen values).

As researchers in organizational learning, Argyris and MIT professor Donald Schön[4] developed theoretical frameworks for meetings and encounters in which they posited that some types of interactions and conversation enable learning, and others limit learning. The difference between the two types of interactions depends upon the degree of consistency between what people actually do (informed by their deeply held "theories-in-use" about the world), and what people say they do (informed by a more superficially held set of theories called "espoused theory").

For example, in the AutoCo Learning History, the company had an espoused theory in which teamwork is valued. Teamwork was praised and endorsed by just about everyone interviewed, from senior managers to low-level engineers, usually on the grounds that, as one Vice President puts it (page 109), ". . . you could only [beat your objectives] if you operate as a very strong team."

But early in the document (page 33), we see an implication that two very different theories-in-use about teamwork are influential throughout AutoCo. One theory, held by many Epsilon team members, holds that teamwork is an anarchistic, candid, freeform process: "Everything that we know is thrown on the table. We thrash about, and issues sound a lot worse than they really are. This is our way of sharing what's going on."

Another theory, held by outsiders, is voiced by a project manager (in the following paragraph) who joins Epsilon as a newcomer: "You've got to be kidding me. If anybody had said anything remotely like that on [my previous program], he would've been killed. Programs would have to reach a level of disaster before people would ever talk candidly."

From this example a reader could infer an implicit belief found between the lines of this last remark—candid conversation is a sign of disaster, and true teamwork requires civility and mutual support, even at the expense of mutual understanding. Which theory-in-use is "correct"? That doesn't matter, as much as recognizing how the discrepancies between them shape behavior at AutoCo. As long as people talk about teamwork as beneficial and act as though it were an anarchic horror, their ability to learn, and long-term effectiveness, is limited.

So what could you do when you find yourself in the middle of such a set of theories-in-use? Action science proposes that there are two predominant ways that people in organizations might respond. Argyris and Schön call them "Model I" and "Model II" behavior, and each has its own theory about what people have in their mind that determines how they behave.

In Model I, for example, a senior manager tells people how they will conduct themselves as a team—in this case, by saying, "Here's how we conduct teams here." Yet despite the manager's "team" rhetoric he makes sure he is in control, and holds himself above reproach should the team experience problems. The unspoken assumptions and ideals that guide his behavior are based on Model I theories-in-use—that one view (the manager's view) is always right and other views are always wrong. The basic assumptions that underlie people's thinking (governing variables) and types of management behaviors that come from them (action strategies) are shown in Figure 10-1.

Model I, which has been studied by action science researchers in thousands of settings, explains the most typical way in which managers in organizations think and act. These Model I theories-in-use are the "nat-

Figure 10-1 *Theories of action for learning in organizations*[7]

Model I Theory-in-use		Model II Theory-in-use	
GOVERNING VARIABLES	ACTION STRATEGIES	GOVERNING VARIABLES	ACTION STRATEGIES
Define goals and try to achieve them	Design and manage the environment unilaterally	Valid information	Design situations where participants can be origins of and experience high personal causation
Maximize winning and minimize losing	Own and control the task	Free and informed choice	Task is jointly controlled
Minimize generating or expressing negative feelings	Unilaterally protect yourself	Internal commitment to the choice and constant monitering of the implementations	Protection of self is a joint enterprices and oriented towards growth
Be rational	Unilaterally protect others from being hurt		Bilateral protection of others

ural" or normal way people think and behave in organizations, an explanation why firms are generally unable to learn. When people operating with Model I theories-in-use deal with difficult or threatening problems, they not only create limiting conditions for solving those problems and becoming more effective over time, but also create conditions that keep them unaware of their own limitations and ineffectiveness.[5] People say one thing, act in another way, and are unaware of the gaps between their words and deeds.[6] Model I theory-in-use is a source of ineffective operations, the kind, in the automotive industry, where when the car goes to launch problems suddenly surface, AutoCo expends enormous efforts and funds, creating torment for all that toil in this chaos.

For people and organizations to sustain their ability to improve, they must learn how to learn together, and for effective learning to occur, real world behaviors must become consistent with Model II (see Figure 10-1). When individuals interact on that basis, they can create an organizational system which allows members to deal with difficult issues productively, thereby enhancing long-term effectiveness.[8] Model II involves raising theories-in-use to the surface at all the critical levels of organizational relationships—making the gaps between what is said and what is done a topic for conversation, dealing with difficult issues productively, and suspending the coerciveness inherent in people's positions. In this way, all views about the nature of (in the example) teamwork can come to the surface without fear of reprisal. The manager's desire for better team behavior would include him telling team members what he saw as problematic, how he experienced his role in the team, and creating settings that allow others to express their views and collectively develop and monitor new team behaviors.

In all of the studies that Argyris and Schön have conducted, one thing is clear: Good intentions are insufficient to bring about learning. Those intentions go against experience, are subverted by Model I, and lead to disillusionment. It is not, in their experience, until people in an organization learn to move to Model II values, strategies, and assumptions that typical defensive routines are disrupted and supplanted with productive learning patterns.[9]

Producing Model II behavior, however, is difficult precisely because people and organizations are socialized to operate according to Model I, even when Model II is espoused and some people act according to Model II theories-in-use. To shift behavior and to enhance validity and learning, action science researchers must help clients learn by producing actions consistent with Model II Theory-in-use.[10] Intervention is essential, by consultants, researchers, or skilled individuals, to help people in organizational systems consistently think and act according to Model II.[11]

The theories and techniques of action science research have a great deal to offer the "data" from an experience like AutoCo's Epsilon launch. The scholarly and theoretical literature is divided on organizational learning as an effective means to organizational change. Authors who are proponents of organizational learning often uncritically presume that capabilities can be appropriately taught to help those in organizations draw valid, useful inferences from their observation and experience, and then convert that to effective action. Those who are skeptics treat any challenges to teaching and learning needed skills as unalterable features of organizations. Clearly, a robust test of premises about organizational learning would involve making people in organizations aware of, and helping them learn how to overcome, the problems that have heretofore gone unnoticed and remained uncorrected.

In the course of their studies, Argyris and Schön[12] have identified three potential threats to an organizational learning effort, such as the effort at Epsilon. First is the communication difficulties associated with hierarchical and cross-divisional relationships, which makes it much more difficult (or impossible) for middle and top managers to produce coherent action. Second is the managers' own limited abilities to understand, comprehend, and produce organizational learning in business settings—not because of innate deficiencies as people, but because they lack opportunities to question and test their information, assumptions and interpretations together. Lacking the chance to consider alternatives, people often persisted on courses of action despite their uncertainty. Finally, organizational patterns of defensive behavior, or defensive routines,[13] effectively block most attempts to identify and correct the lack of awareness which leads to errors. Those errors go undetected, and thus remain impossible to correct.

As a formal "learning project," the Epsilon learning history gives us a unique opportunity to consider the extent to which these traditional challenges were met in an innovative setting.

◆ What guides does action science have for the Epsilon project?

The direction for the Epsilon learning project derived from Peter Senge's book *The Fifth Discipline*, and from research developed by associates at the MIT Center for Organizational Learning. Senge's learning approach is a synthesis of five different "disciplines" whose combined study and practice of which enhance overall effectiveness. The discipline combine elements of action science ideas (inquiry into "mental models") with creative processes, visioning, group dynamics and systems concepts. The synthesis of ideas proposed in *The Fifth Discipline* creates a different emphasis from that of pure action science, and does not explicitly seek to implement Model II values, strategies, and assumptions.[14] However, more careful examination of action science and Model II concepts can provide valuable insights on the AutoCo Epsilon learning initiative. My commentary focuses on four particularly significant and relevant aspects of the approach used and processes developed for instilling learning at Epsilon:

1. The initial establishment of the learning project by MIT researchers and Epsilon managers which took place in a project engagement clinic.

2. The development of the Epsilon program core team and its use of learning techniques as part of its management approach.

3. The diffusion of the learning (mainly through learning labs) from the core team to other engineering teams who were part of the Epsilon program.

4. Going beyond the teams that were directly part of the Epsilon program and communicating with others, particularly AutoCo senior management.

In a fifth and final section of this commentary I return to the precepts of action science to propose alternatives for initiating and diffusing learning practices within large organizations.

Initiating learning with engagement

The joint project between the MIT research group and the AutoCo Epsilon team began with a project engagement clinic (see page 15).[16] The purpose of this meeting was to assess a "readiness for learning" on the part of AutoCo and to explore possibilities for "business improvement and research results." The clinic provided an opportunity for researchers to meet and work with managers and engineers, which in turn led to the formation of the core team for the project— the top managers from all the different functional areas responsible for Epsilon.

The engagement clinic helped develop a relationship between managers and researchers partnering on the project. It also tested the ability of both parties, conceptually at the inception of the project, to hold business improvement and the development of theory as equal priorities. While managers felt primary responsibility for business improvement, and researchers for the development of theory, both agreed on the importance of supporting each other in working toward these goals. The assessment of readiness to support learning in the engagement clinic developed the relationship and conditions for experimentation in applying learning tools to business improvements. From an action science perspective, this initial agreement, which was partly explicit and partly tacit, itself paved the way for the team's ongoing success.

One subject of discussion in the clinic was the extent to which improvements from learning, and the development of theory about learning approaches in product development, would affect other vehicle development programs. Preliminary interviews had raised questions about whether the learning initiative should focus on a particular prototype build or the product development process in general. Ideally the learning project would provide both improvements for Epsilon and key insights for all vehicle development activities at AutoCo. Influencing a larger arena at AutoCo, however, required the support of overall vehicle program management. The executives who headed vehicle development operations were not all aware of the Epsilon team's learning initiative. Some of them accepted and supported the decision to work with MIT and test the learning approach—as long as the team met their technical and financial program objectives.

Even when it was not specifically required, the Epsilon managers felt they needed to have tangible and measurable improvements in their own program before asking for further involvement from their bosses. After all, as the learning history shows, tangible measurement of progress was critically important in both the MIT and the AutoCo cultures.

The question of involving bosses raises an important consideration for learning project activities in business organizations (see pages 87–89). The executives who oversee Epsilon are responsible for the quality, technical, and financial performance of multiple vehicle development programs. They judge the progress of individual programs based on their own experience in managing and controlling these performance statistics. This created a dilemma for Epsilon program managers. They wanted their team leaders and engineers to focus on technical details and to make decisions that were usually the purview of executives. They considered creating a learning environment where engineering teams were making these decisions as part of the learning approach they had committed to. Since this was different than the way programs were typically managed, the learning approach would have to operate "under a shield" until they could substantiate their countercultural approach by achieving demonstrably superior results.

A focus on results as a demonstration of the effectiveness of learning was discussed in the project engagement clinic, as well as in subsequent meetings. It says something about the effectiveness of "learning organization" work that the ability to demonstrate superior results did not seem to be doubted much. Instead, project leaders worried about their ability to communicate their success. They thought that the senior executives' acceptance represented an appropriate level of support, and they agreed that "results" should matter in business more than any other consideration. But they also felt that the support they were getting from executives was qualified, or even lukewarm. Comments about the need not to let the learning process "get in the way of our real jobs" (page 95) were interpreted as a demonstration of executives' lack of interest in learning processes, their continued emphasis on immediate business results, and their reluctant acceptance of the project as contingent upon those results. Epsilon managers "heard" that they could experiment and learn as long as they didn't make mistakes—executives didn't want to hear about their process; they wanted technical and financial achievements.

In short, while Epsilon managers could create learning conditions and practice new communication skills with their subordinates, they could not easily create those conditions with superiors. They acknowledged that their bosses' responses didn't rule out the possibility of candid conversation, but they held the perception that senior executives were not interested in a learning approach.

These interchanges about executives and program mangers, and the thinking behind them, are examples of Model I.[16] Each person unilaterally manages his own success criteria, seeks to control tasks, and to protect himself. The executives remain unyielding in their criteria for evaluating program managers, and despite executives' questionable support for their efforts, the program managers pursue their own desired course of action.

Epsilon program managers needed intricate conversational skills in order to talk with executives about their learning approach and its link to the technical and financial data used to evaluate their program's achievements. Unfortunately, while the learning lab and other conversational "tools" provided a practice field for better conversations within the team, there was never an equivalent practice field for conversations in the larger system of AutoCo. The new "learning organization" approaches were sufficient for changing behavior within the team, but were not strong enough to overcome defensive routines and other barriers that arose when Epsilon leaders approached their bosses and peers on other car projects.

Could another type of "learning lab" have made a difference, a learning lab in which Epsilon leaders learned to effectively confront the larger system? Action science suggests that it could have, but only if other factors were at work. Those factors include the participation of executives and the adoption of Model II theory-in-use. What is not clear is if the Epsilon leaders would have put aside time for such a learning lab, whether they would have been able to fully adopt a Model II theory-in-use, and whether they would be able to engage executives to join them as a group of mutual "learners." The complexity of this task, particularly given the enormous pressures in developing vehicles, makes it seem unlikely. What else could Epsilon leaders do, and what were the limits of their learning approach without executives' direct involvement?

Creating a learning agenda as part of a team's work

The research project initially focused on helping managers of the Epsilon program team work together. They were introduced to learning techniques and tools by the MIT researchers (see "Learning in the core team," "The systems map," "The transition to openness," and "Creating the atmosphere of trust and cooperation," pages 19–31. The members of the core team chose to expand their monthly meeting time, develop their own learning agenda and decide what the focus of their efforts would be.

Besides solving problems and making decisions about the Epsilon vehicle's development, the team considered ways to improve their process of working together. The use of the learning "tools"—systems archetypes (page 22), ladder of inference and left-hand columns (page 24), K.J. diagrams (page 26), approaches to problem solutions (page 30) and system diagrams (page 32)—gave them insights into how actions they took might relate to a larger organizational system. The eight months that the core team worked together were repeatedly described as significant (for example, see description of finance and program manager interactions, pages 23 and 28). As the core team managers worked together, the behaviors they learned and practiced with one another in their monthly meetings influenced their thinking and behavior in other settings. Sharing their insights and thinking about the overall program with engineers, for instance, extended elements of the learning environment beyond the core team.

Essentially, the core team members spent those months developing their ability to span cultural boundaries.[17] Although all the individuals on the core team shared a common AutoCo organizational culture, they also came from different organizational subcultures (e.g., finance, purchasing, marketing, manufacturing, engineering, general management). Subcultures create and maintain their own identity through the development of specific understandings. However, the understandings that allow a group to operate effectively within its membership may also limit its members' effectiveness in other settings. Members of the core team, for instance, used the same words, but often misunderstood one another at very basic levels (again, see description of finance and program manager interactions, pages 23 and 28).

Cultural boundaries are largely conceptual and thus "generally less visible and less easy to define" than physical boundaries.[18] The invisible nature of cultural boundaries makes it harder for "newcomers" or "foreigners" to realize when those boundaries have been violated, while natives of the culture will notice immediately. If misunderstandings do develop, they are often covered up and not discussed. When cultural boundaries are not addressed in teams, the shared understanding required for effective collective action takes longer to develop, or may never develop at all.

The learning process the core team undertook helped them articulate and deal with these differences. By understanding one another more accurately they could design more effective ways of working together. As Argyris and Schön[19] have noted, these types of open social conditions are necessary for the learning that allows organizations to improve over time. The conditions that developed within the core team—valid information, free choice, respect, and integrity—became part of what Epsilon managers sought to recreate to facilitate learning within various program engineering teams. Creating conditions for learning became part of the team's "learning agenda."

Engaging engineers and diffusing techniques through learning labs

A learning approach became an integral part of the way Epsilon core team members worked with their own teams and with engineering design teams and a part of the overall way in which the Epsilon program was managed. Their "learning approach" was guided by *The Fifth Discipline* concepts. This approach included articulating problem symptoms fully rather than simply solving them, discerning solutions by involving those people who would be affected rather than getting answers from outside experts, as well as integrating and synthesizing efforts by searching for interconnectedness and interrelatedness of issues, rather then decomposing issues into their elements and fragmenting efforts. Once they gained insights, rather than rolling out these answers and their new insights, they let the vehicle development timeline "pull" the diffusion and consideration of what they learned naturally.

The time that the half-dozen core team members spent together changed their behavior—which was noticed by many of the 300 others on the larger collocated Epsilon team. As other Epsilon engineers became interested in the concepts which had influenced managers' thinking, the core team prepared a two-day workshop in which they would teach engineering teams what they had learned. These sessions were based on the managerial practice field, or "learning lab," concept—providing a safe environment and dedicated time for teams to learn and practice new skills that applied to their real work settings. Core team managers, together with the MIT researchers, taught these learning labs. Taking a role in teaching gave managers an opportunity to talk about their own learning process. While engineers were asked to consider new behaviors for themselves, they also heard first-hand accounts of how managers' thinking had become more insightful and how it related to their new behaviors.

All of the new learning activities had a common thread—they were used by program managers to interact with engineers in a less hierarchical manner. The resulting "show and tell" approach supported the ability of engineering teams to raise issues which might be difficult to do in more traditional meeting sessions. Interactions between engineering teams and the program managers were opportunities for mangers to support openness, as well as to model it for others.

Coupled with other initiatives, Epsilon project managers began to create a climate conducive to learning and thinking more broadly. In effect, this new climate offered a new balance between two types of anxiety prevalent in organizational life. It promoted "survival anxiety"—the fear of not learning essential new skills and capabilities when change is required —and played down "learning anxiety"—the fear of incompetence which accompanies learning new skills.[20] Managers were more willing to try new approaches because they understood the need for doing so and they felt they had more freedom in which to innovate.

One significant innovation that emerged from this activity was the harmony buck (see page 76). The engineer who proposed the creation of this unusual prototype credited the learning environment created by program managers: "He would never have had the audacity to propose it, except for the encouragement he had received during the previous months at Epsilon. [The Program Manager] had been saying, 'Look we're not going to beat up on you. We really want to know what you are thinking.'" A supportive managerial atmosphere also helped the engineers gain approval to fund developing the idea, which was not part of the budget. The harmony buck also proved to be a social innovation. As engineering teams tested their subassemblies on the prototype, their communication and interaction with other teams increased. Many people commented that the communication techniques and skills taught in learning labs also helped engineers resolve other complex issues.

The creation of an environment conducive to learning extended beyond learning labs. The Epsilon program managers seemed to hold a kind of "gestalt" for new styles of work that, given their approach, would facilitate better learning and project results. The market research clinic and the collocation of engineering teams (see pages 85ff.) were also unusual innovations—for the Epsilon team in particular and for AutoCo as a whole. Other activities that helped create this overall "learning environment" included a three-day offsite for creating a shared vision of Epsilon; weekly Wednesday morning "doughnuts with the managers" drop-in sessions; interviews of engineers by managers to ask them for their ideas; including suppliers in prototype review meetings; and the furnishing of a conference room solely for "learning" activities (page 68).

These activities often required special efforts and approvals on the part of the management team. Individually, none of the new approaches were much different from what was going on elsewhere at AutoCo. Taken together, however, they represented a dramatic shift from "business as usual" on other programs.

Engaging others in AutoCo through learning

Epsilon program managers were pleased with the learning approach. Not only could they gain insights into themselves and the impact of their behaviors, but they could see the impact of the approach on others. They had created an environment on their teams which was leading to better results (as recorded by prototype milestone measures). They were working with and receiving the attention of a group of researchers from MIT, as well as from the consortium of large American corporations who sponsored the MIT Center. Their peers at AutoCo had heard about their results and wanted learn how to apply the ideas to their own programs. The efforts were intrinsically and extrinsically satisfying and producing better than expected results.

Why then did the Epsilon managers struggle in learning with their bosses? Five issues become apparent in looking at the Epsilon story through an action science lens.

STARTING THE LEARNING PROJECT WITHOUT BROAD PARTICIPATION

Involving senior management was particularly important, at least as an "espoused theory," to MIT researchers. They expressed the desire to diffuse the learning from Epsilon more widely in AutoCo. Epsilon provided a test site; the results of this test were expected to yield insights that would be helpful to learning approaches at corporations in general and the product development process at AutoCo in particular. In order for that to happen, researchers needed the support and involvement of those at AutoCo with the power to help make it happen.

The senior managers on the Epsilon project also espoused involving senior management from the beginning—and they asked for help in doing so. Yet when the subject of involving senior managers in the learning initiative was raised in the project engagement clinic (see page 15), program managers wanted to delay talking with them. Given generally fearful attitudes toward "bosses" in AutoCo, they felt that it would be difficult for engineers to be open about problems and issues around senior managers. They also believed that senior managers valued results, and were not very interested in theory. They assumed it would not be possible to engage them at the start, much as they wanted to do so.

A number of participants in the engagement clinic recognized that if senior management was not involved, the project could founder. A transcript of that session (not included in this document) shows Chris Argyris, for one, expressing the view that the project should not go forward unless senior management at AutoCo were more involved. But there was neither time, will, nor an agreed-upon method for engaging them. To be fair to the Epsilon leaders, most of the researchers were equally uncertain about how to engage the larger system. There was an atmosphere in the room that, somehow, people would know how to cross that bridge when they got there. Epsilon was the first project for the newly founded MIT Center for Organizational Learning, and researchers were anxious to get started. Their interest was a proof-of-concept for a largely theoretical set of propositions about learning in organizations. The Epsilon program team was in place, already behind in the schedule for producing the vehicle, and eager gain MIT's help. An agreement was thus voiced by MIT and Epsilon participants: Involving senior management was important, and it would occur as soon as there were results to show. "We'll be vindicated when they see our results" (a form of the ends justify the means) creates inherent inconsistencies for learning, inconsistencies in management behavior which are particularly difficult to criticize when the means are as benevolent as facilitating learning and the development of human capability.

CREATING A CULTURAL ISLAND

Instead of challenging their superiors, the Epsilon program managers created a "cultural island" in the midst of AutoCo's vehicle program operations. From the engineers' perspective, program managers had created a receptive climate and new norms that supported learning. This is apparent, in the document, from the ways that engineers, program managers, and senior management all described their differences from the other vehicle development teams surrounding them.

Engineers talked about the opportunities they were given as part of the project: the chance to make design and technical choices not usually within their control; learning techniques for communications, visioning, and learning; conceptualizing system properties of social and managerial systems; and working with one another in "practice field" settings. They found their ability to take more responsibility and work with more latitude both inspirational and highly satisfying.

The engineers' positive response reinforced program managers' supportive disposition for a learning approach. They could identify critical leverage points in their management policies and behaviors which helped them achieve, or exceed, their expected business results. That they were able to do so without the chaos, turmoil, and financial and personnel costs that generally accompanied a vehicle launch was highly significant. By paying attention to how they managed their people and what behaviors they exhibited (see Chapter 2) they achieved technical, financial and business results. Using the learning techniques, they gained insights into their own behaviors and the potential impacts of those behaviors on other individuals and the system around them.

Despite all their insights into the forces of the larger organization, the relationship between program and senior managers grew steadily more difficult. Epsilon managers could not set the conditions for engagement and discussion. The explicit and implicit rules in the AutoCo organization governed when and how program team and senior managers communicated and interacted. In general, program managers presented progress updates for their programs at scheduled meetings. When senior managers had questions, they called reviews. Otherwise, their interactions were informal, and generally infrequent.

Epsilon managers needed to find a way to break this pattern and create an opportunity to engage senior managers in their experiment, starting with thinking how an experiment to be more effective could be important to them. As it was, when the Epsilon passed through milestones, the program manager regularly sent senior management electronic mail messages with accomplishments. None of these messages, from the program manager's recollections, were ever responded to or acknowledged.

DISTINGUISHING BETWEEN LEARNING AND PERFORMING

The dilemma that emerged between Epsilon program managers and senior managers is a recurring problem with learning efforts in hierarchical organizations. A manager who tells his boss he wants to try a new approach, but isn't certain what the results will be, makes himself vulnerable. Conditioned to avoid that situation, many well-intentioned managers proceed with complex projects believing, or at least representing, that they possess the knowledge and ability to be successful.

This situation is related to what Chris Argyris describes as limiting learning and creating defensive routines in organizations—errors are "covered up on purpose as nonerrors . . . to prevent players from experiencing embarrassment or threat. To admit that there is a need to cover up embarrassment or threat is itself embarrassing or threatening."[21] These routines create self-sealing patterns which inhibit learning. When a learning initiative is undertaken, the same kinds of thinking and behavior can come into play, but they take place before any mistake has an opportunity to be made.

Telling a boss you don't know something as you embark on a new project is an indication that you may make a mistake or create an embarrassing situation. Under typical organizational conditions, this is potentially threatening for your boss. Not only is he associated with you, he is partly responsible for your results. Raising this issue with your boss puts him in a difficult situation. By supporting your efforts he is being overtly asked to take on part of the risk and responsibility for your success or failure. When that effort is an experimental approach with potential implications for others in the organization, he knows that everyone involved will be exposed to a high degree of public scrutiny.

Argyris[22] has identified three levels of thinking and action that limit learning in organizations. All three levels come into play in this situation. First, mistakes are covered up. Next, the act of covering up the mistakes is undiscussable. Finally, the undiscussability of covering up mistakes is itself undiscussable. Most senior managers don't need to be told about these three levels; they "sense" the looming difficulties, when asked to be supportive of a learning initiative. They are often unable to articulate this sense or their reasoning and are uncomfortable with substantive discussions around learning issues. They have a tacit knowledge of the norms and shared assumptions which govern behaviors. They know that the process of learning—making mistakes, initial incompetence, and possible embarrassment—is itself undiscussable in most organizations. And they generally don't have or can't take the time to learn the skills needed to safely address what they innately sense as "dangerous" situations.

Thus, the prudent action is to avoid any of this risk altogether. "I'm not going to talk much about learning," they might think. "I'll just quietly let them learn—as long as they don't get too threateningly visible." As a result, though the senior leaders may be conceptually supportive, they may also send mixed signals—espoused levels of commitment with behaviors that don't support what is said.

From observation and interviews, senior managers at AutoCo are both feared and revered. They are revered in that sense that only critical or urgent issues are deemed worthy or appropriate to bring to their attention. Opportunities to engage in more in-depth conversations are limited, and those opportunities and their conditions are controlled by senior managers. Subordinates feel limited in their ability to express disagreement or voice concerns and have witnessed the repercussions of senior manager's authority to make unilateral decisions. They fear creating negative impressions which may have lasting career implications.

Fear also has an affective impact. Epsilon project leaders could practice constructive dialogue, surface assumptions, and balance advocacy with inquiry except when talking to executives. Although role plays and coaching built their skills and confidence, these carefully practiced approaches gave way to conventional reactive and confrontational responses when the managers actually faced their bosses. Certainly, with neither the ability nor the authority to create learning conditions including executives, the prospects of Epsilon's managers influencing the greater AutoCo system was limited.

THE FALLACY OF "PROVING" INNOVATIVE EFFORTS WITH BUSINESS RESULTS
Producing good results, even spectacular results, is not enough to get people to change the rules by which they operate. Story after story of corporate success include "breaking the rules," the hero becoming an anti-hero, being banished, and only later recognized for his or her contribution.[23] Consider, for example, the not often told automotive industry story of the Ford Taurus and the team that developed it. Lew Veraldi, its program manager, led a team that produced what became the best selling car in America. The success of the Taurus is credited for having saved Ford in the late 1980s. Yet, within Ford, Team Taurus was not recognized for its achievements, but was instead admonished for failing to meet several cost targets. Many of the team members credited Veraldi, a leader with a willingness to challenge Ford's status-quo, for their accomplishments. Veraldi reached a pinnacle in his career, built a vehicle that was one of American industry's great success stories, but was subsequently demoted[24.] The team "bent" rules in product development to build the car, but, even with the car's success, the utility of those rules was never examined.

The decision to wait to involve senior managers until there were business results proved to be flawed. Epsilon managers were unprepared for senior management's growing concern regarding the program managers' focus. During the course of the development program, senior managers continued to rely on traditional data to inform them of Epsilon's progress. Epsilon managers were unable to engage senior management in productive discussions about the data, how it was perceived, or the decisions it prompted.

Consider, for example, the problem of change requests (see pages 99–105). The aggregated data on change requests—the count of outstanding requests and average number of days outstanding—was not of interest to Epsilon managers. They were focused on getting teams to articulate their problems, on creating a broader awareness across teams of those problems, and on developing better interactions within the Epsilon team. Senior management and other functional management, however, paid careful attention to the CR data. They used the reporting system to gain insight into the workload and progress of vehicle programs. It allowed them to compare various programs and make decisions about where to focus their own time and effort.

As different perceptions about how the Epsilon program was progressing were raised, it became clear that not only were the two groups of managers considering different sets of data, they viewed the same data differently. Epsilon managers used the CR system to communicate outstanding issues. They asked teams to use the CR system as soon as they knew of areas where problems were encountered and changes would have to be made. This let teams know what changes where being worked by different teams and increased the awareness across teams of possible implications for their subassemblies. To Epsilon program managers, the rising number of reported CRs represented a sign of success. It showed increased openness and better cross-team communication. To senior managers and managers from other functional areas, the escalating number of reported and open CRs were an indication of unsolved problems, outstanding work, and a serious problem with the program.

Company reporting mechanisms require a common understanding of what the numbers mean in order to effectively coordinate action. If one part of the company, like the Epsilon team, changes the way they use a system, the numbers that system produces will still be understood by others in the old context.

When Epsilon managers explained that the CR information was a result of their efforts to promote openness and better communication, it sounded like what all managers said they promoted. Since senior managers hadn't been part of the learning initiative, the concepts Epsilon managers talked about seemed consistent with what they themselves espoused in successfully managing programs. The understanding of quantitative CR information outside the Epsilon team could not jive with the unconventional qualitative use and understanding of the CR information within the team. Examined on the basis of different assumptions, the same information resulted in evaluations and actions which seemed incompatible.

As the reported CR measures decreased, indicating (to the executives' ways of interpreting the data) continued problems, the executives took unilateral action to improve the measures: They forced the team to reconcile their CRs by "fixing" them all within an extended weekend. The executives' demands were consistent with Model I theory-in-use, as was the response by Epsilon program manager: "Instead of calling them concerns from then on, we called them investigation issues or some other name so we could identify what the concerns were. That's better than nothing. But that's not what you really want" (page 105).

The challenge for those leading Epsilon's learning efforts was to respond to executives without resorting to the same approaches that characterized executives' behaviors. However, when program managers weren't able gain support from executives, they too took matters into their own hands by continuing with their efforts. Thus, their thinking and action were also consistent with Model I theory-in-use.

Faced with senior management's resistance and incredulity, Epsilon managers resorted to a commonly practiced form of engagement—trying to convince senior managers of the correctness of their approach.

UNDERSTANDING THE DIFFERENCE BETWEEN PREACHING AND TEACHING
Convincing another person of something is very different than learning something together. The word "convince" derives from the Latin vincere, meaning to conquer or vanquish. Rather than being open to alternative ideas, convincing involves a deliberate and persuasive effort to have one's own ideas, opinions, or decisions win out over others.

In a learning process, by contrast, people are interested in increasing their knowledge by understanding something from another person. Learning requires being open to test existing and gaining new skills, understanding, or knowledge.

Initially both senior and program managers had similar views of the way to successfully develop a vehicle, but Epsilon's managers' views were changed and enlarged through their learning process—a process which required engagement, involvement and the experience of learning together. It would be as difficult, or impossible, a task for them to change senior managers' understanding by convincing them as it would have been for Epsilon program managers to be "convinced" themselves.

Since Epsilon program managers were not in the position to create the conditions for a learning environment for senior managers, they "defaulted" to convincing. Argumentative processes and combative conditions were not new at AutoCo, however, and made it difficult for senior managers to learn or to understand what was different about the program managers' approach.

This situation illustrates a flaw in the logic of waiting until there are "results" before engaging senior managers in a learning process. For the new Epsilon team to learn more effectively, its leaders created boundaries between the team and the larger organization. Those boundaries allowed the behaviors, norms, and assumptions conducive to learning to take hold. But they also added to the conceptual boundaries between the team's "cultural island" and the larger organization.

When senior managers described what they saw in the Epsilon team as a "cult" (page 98) and the teams' performance as "out of control" (page 101), they were referring to language and behaviors that were not customary at AutoCo. The boundaries that allowed the Epsilon team to become more effective also isolated it in a way that, itself, spun out of control. As AutoCo executives undertook a major reorganization of the company, including its vehicle development organization, the accomplishments of Epsilon's learning effort, and their implications for approaches to organizing product development, were largely unnoticed.

Using AutoCo's example to design future learning initiatives

Epsilon teams, encouraged by initial learning efforts of the core team and inspired through managerial practice fields co-taught by program managers, achieved significant product development milestones. The achievements in developing the vehicle are measurable and significant and should not be understated. The "Noticeable Results" section (pages 9–11), for instance, documents a series of quality, financial, and behavioral changes which illustrate extraordinary results, expressed mostly in terms of milestone metrics in comparison with other vehicle programs.

Unfortunately, the product development achievements of the Epsilon program team appear less significant when other factors are taken into consideration. The vehicle's market performance was lackluster. The larger AutoCo organization was unwilling to recognize or embrace the learning approaches which Epsilon team leaders practiced and advocated. And many team members attributed their successes to program manager's personalities and behaviors, rather than to the learning efforts.

Ultimately, the Epsilon project was less influential at AutoCo than its organizers had hoped for. When the project ended, team members went "underground," not talking much about their time at Epsilon, working quietly at other automobile projects. Is this a situation where a team challenges the dominant norms of an organizational culture and years must go by before its influence gradually seeps into the larger system? Will the lessons from Epsilon ever have an influence? Are there ways to protect the innovators and the innovation ahead of time, by engaging with the larger system in a carefully designed, constructive manner, so that the innovators need not sacrifice their careers or positions?

To some onlookers at AutoCo, the Epsilon team had become a cult. Team members approached their work in an unconventional manner. They were guided by charismatic leaders, leaders whose behavior had visibly been transformed from an authoritarian to a more inclusive, participative style. They were part of a community of empathetic individuals and devoted to what outsiders saw as faddish principles. Elsewhere at AutoCo, opinions of the Epsilon team appeared to be influenced less by tangible results than by limited interactions and the informal myths floating around the organization about them.

In fact, the very thing which helped the Epsilon team members become effective with one another, breaking barriers to understanding which limited team effectiveness, distanced these managers and engineers from teams and executives elsewhere in AutoCo. This situation presents a typical unintended consequence of breakthroughs in organizational learning. While teams become more effective with each other, their new knowledge may make them less effective globally. This consequence highlights the need for a examining the basic assumptions around interactions that support learning and developing a diffusion strategy for that learning beyond the original team—at the start of any learning initiative.

◆ A KEY FOR LEARNING AT ALL ORGANIZATIONAL LEVELS: PROFESSING YOU DON'T KNOW

Learning, and developing the capability to be more effective, starts with a recognition of "not knowing" and the desire to overcome that inadequacy.

As the "boss" of a team, making a profession of ignorance is organizationally possible because you can claim your subordinates' support by virtue of your position. You can't rely on the same support when you're declaring your inadequacy to your supervisor. Professing what you want to learn is a strategy with subordinates that can also be used with superiors. If you don't know, your vulnerability creates a first step in developing an environment to engage others. The strategy is an overt effort to develop new skills and capabilities in individuals and teams.

Arguably, that shift becomes as critical for the efforts to bridge the boundaries with the larger system as it does for the work within the teams. For example, when program managers heard that executives "considered" the Epsilon team a "cult" (page 98) and the teams' performance as "out of control" (page 101), this would have been an opportunity for inquiry on their part. Program managers, in this situation, needed to find a setting to engage executives in understanding how they came to these assessments. They needed to accept rather than argue with executives about their perceptions and to ask how their actions contributed to those assessments, particularly when their view of what they were doing was very different. The culture at AutoCo is to have "nice" public conversations—not challenge, speak, or inquire openly. People held onto their beliefs and opinions about one another, never testing them, and acting as though they were valid.

The challenge for an organization is to get past the "nice" conversations. Helping organizational learning happen required, in the case of the program managers, leaving themselves vulnerable for not having answers. In their case it would have required creating opportunities to engage their superiors in evaluating whether or not their new approach was indeed leading to more effective ways to operate.

As the action science theory holds, if the learning efforts are to be sustained, the bosses too must engage in practicing Model II theory-in-use. The past actions of both the program managers and their bosses, however, are likely to have been inconsistent with Model II, and so they are required not only to be different with each other but also to lend support for others trying new behaviors, and thus being different. The bosses' authority, and their ability to wield it as a unilateral source of power, dissolves as they ascribe, like others, to testable propositions around the basis for their action, voluntary participation, internal commitment, and constant monitoring of their behavior. In Model II theory-in-use bosses and subordinates are equally accountable and responsible for the actions within their realm.

Power considerations play a crucial role in any organizational change, including organizational learning. A Model II approach is based upon people in positions of power freely and genuinely supporting their own and others' use of Model II in their organization. A person in the middle or at the bottom of an organization may find the Model II governing variables appealing, but may not have the power to create the physical and psychological safety people need to speak to what they hold as valid, make the choice to participate, and base participation on their own internal commitment.

Why, then, could the Epsilon managers not use the skills they had learned, the conversational tools for productive inquiry, to resolve problems with the larger system? Because these skills were taught with the assumption that they would be used in supportive conditions for inquiry. Program managers were in positions to relinquish their power for unilateral control with subordinates; however, they did not have this same ability in situations involving executives. Indeed, many organizational learning efforts fail to meaningfully address concerns about power and authority. This has been true since the T-Group era. When a senior manager espouses openness and trust in an effort to gain the same from others, his doing so serves his need for better information. The situation is different with his organizational superior, when his position no longer grants him the power to make assurances as to how the information will be used.

Model II is effective only if everyone who is affected by the improvement effort accepts and chooses to adhere to its principles. If someone doesn't accept Model II, they cannot be forced into it, nor can they be evaded. The challenge is that the way to move forward to engaging others to adopt Model II is by operating consistent with its premises and using learning tools to engage other people. The use of the learning tools requires sharing the approach and using it to help others become better at what they want. It does require an effort, and change from the status quo, to become effective with a Model II theory-in-use. The dilemma, however, in becoming better is that it requires insight and recognition about that improvement, which in most settings is interpreted as an admission of low effectiveness.

A conceptual understanding of action science ideas is needed to initiate, and later sustain, learning in organizations. These ideas are seemingly simple conceptually (easy at an espoused level) yet complex at an action level (difficult to consistently produce). Action science requires an interventionist[25] to help an organization learn by creating the conditions in which Model II theory-in-use is practiced. What the MIT researchers needed to do was act more as the interventionist, recognizing that their research project was that and would have implications for organizational change. They needed to not only think about Epsilon as located within an organizational system, paying attention to more than helping with Epsilon's team members, but to also help in working with AutoCo's senior managers.

What Epsilon program managers needed to do was not continue with their learning efforts without building some understanding for their efforts with AutoCo's vice presidents. The vice presidents would not, however, have understood these ideas without getting more involved. What Epsilon managers were saying was in some ways what everyone says, "What we are doing as a team is different." Yet, the distinction in their learning approach over team building wouldn't become evident unless there was some involvement in their efforts by the vice presidents. And, if the vice presidents weren't ready, or interested, in being involved then the challenge for Epsilon's program managers is to use the new tools they've learned to understand the vice presidents and their concerns, so as to more fully link their efforts to AutoCo's top management's needs and goals.

Applying learning approaches, creating supportive team conditions, and building better relationships with subordinates become seductive. It is all too easy to put off today those elusive challenges, like engaging the vice president, which provides limited, if ever any, satisfaction. Without clearly drawing a line that clarifies any learning effort as limited without examining and changing the deeper assumptions and actions of people at all levels in the organization, there will never be sustained improvement. Instead, disillusionment and cynicism are likely to develop as to the nature of corporations' abilities to improve, centered on the top management and their incomplete understanding of the changes a local team goes through. The outside architects and inside champions for those local changes need to be focused outwardly, designing their efforts from the start with an engagement strategy and diffusion approach which they follow through on to the larger organization.

DISCUSSION GUIDE

CHAPTER 11

A READER'S GUIDE FOR USING THE LEARNING HISTORY IN ORGANIZATIONS AND CLASSROOMS

This document was created to help individuals and teams learn from other people's experience. In fact, it was originally developed as a response to the dilemmas of traditional measurement, assessment, and evaluation approaches for capturing, reflecting upon and diffusing learning initiatives.[1] We knew that conventional assessments "killed" learning in at least three different ways.

First, when typical assessments are conducted, the results take the form of numbers (such as survey results); they're typically presented back as a set of "answers" that a sponsoring team will use to judge whether or not to continue investing in the initiative. Set up this way, there is an almost irresistible temptation for the project's advocates to push harder for their interpretation of the numbers and the project's detractors to argue even more strongly for their interpretation. The more that people get caught up in the need to lock in their positions, the more they forget about experimenting and gaining new knowledge through open-minded inquiry. After all, when you're struggling for tactical advantage, genuine learning can compromise your efforts because learning cannot take place unless you are willing to admit that your theories and methods might be incomplete or wrong.

Second, there's an irresistible pressure on the people being evaluated. As they become aware of being measured and judged, they "perform" for the evaluation. They try to intuit and satisfy assessment criteria instead of continuing to focus on improving their capabilities. The intrinsic aspiration which drives learning is supplanted by drive to look successful, the pressure for extrinsic rewards, and the fear of reprisal for not "measuring up."

Third, even when assessment experts recognize these problems, their analytical stance limits their abilities to inquire into the "softer" sort of changes which lead to "harder," more visible results. Performance gains brought by the innovation often dissipate as the assessment process diverts people's attention away from their original enthusiasm.

The learning history form was intended as a form of evaluation that people could use to consider the implications for their own projects. The form was developed, beginning in 1994, by a group of researchers at the MIT Sloan School Center for Organizational Learning. As co-leaders of the group, we (George Roth and Art Kleiner) had been asked to help "AutoCo," a large automobile company, assess the business value of their organizational learning effort. Other teams were interested in improving upon what Epsilon accomplished, but it was not clear exactly how to replicate or improve upon their approach. We wanted to find a way to capture and communicate the experience of this team so everyone could evaluate its success, without killing the environment of learning that Epsilon's leaders had so carefully crafted.

Borrowing concepts from social science research, theater, anthropology, oral history, process consultation, and journalism, we designed a "learning history" process and format that might tell a critical organizational story in the words of many of the people involved, each with his or her own perspective. The document was intended from the beginning as a "transitional object"—a device to spark reflective conversations throughout the rest of the organization. You do not need to have a learning history written about your own project to be able to use it. It can open the door to a deeper understanding of your own project—current, potential, or imagined—simply by comparing your experiences and thoughts to the experiences and thoughts of the members of the Epsilon team.

The learning history is deliberately phrased in the words of participants so that readers can feel some of the experience of living through the events—but from a variety of perspectives. The form is meant to call to mind a a group of people sitting around a campfire, each with his or her own piece of the narrative to offer. Nearby, there is commentary, written to help the reader see why these particular quotes were chosen and what they might mean. But instead of providing an answer, we design and edit the document to help people come up with their own answers.

Thus, as you read the document, pay attention to your own responses to it. What sounds familiar or different? What surprises you, excites you as a possibility, or causes anxiety? Each of these reactions, in turn, is a cue for thinking about your own experience in your own innovative endeavors. As you and colleagues within an organization inquire together into your reactions and perceptions of the AutoCo initiative, a common basis of inquiry will develop which can span your own organization.

In this reader's guide, we will offer some added material that may help groups of managers, and students of management, facilitate sessions with the document. This material includes several sections:

1. The context of AutoCo Epsilon

2. Putting reflection on the corporate agenda: a rationale for reflection

3. The learning history process

4. Learning theory and the learning history

5. Guidelines for learning history conversations

◆ THE CONTEXT OF AUTOCO EPSILON

Managers and students may reasonably wonder what happened before and after the events described in this document. Most specifically, they may wonder: What happened to the car when it reached the market? And what happened to the Program Manager, the Launch Manager, and other protagonists of this story?

The Epsilon team, in the end, was very successful at meeting AutoCo's vehicle development goals. Epsilon was launched on time, on budget, at record quality levels, and without the chaotic, frenetic activity typical of a vehicle launch. Most observers familiar with the Epsilon story agreed: The team was successful, at least in large part, because of its ability to apply a set of tools that improved communication and learning in the fulfillment of its tasks.

In a broader context, however, the vehicle has been a disappointment in the marketplace. Volume projections have been short of expectations, explained in part by a softening of demand in the luxury car market segment and the significant price increase that accompanied the introduction of the new Epsilon model. How relevant are these results to the Epsilon learning initiative? Although there are no clear answers to this question, there are several possible perspectives about the relationship between market results and the application of organizational learning approaches at AutoCo.

One reasonable perspective is that the financial and markets results are beyond the scope of the vehicle development program team and are therefore not relevant for evaluating the team's efforts and the application of learning techniques. Only the measures which a vehicle development program was responsible for, which pertain to their efforts, should be considered. The ability to evaluate design is important for automotive companies at large, but does not enter into a launch team's mandate—and the car design is almost completely determined by the time a launch team, like Epsilon, begins its work. At the other end of the time frame, warranty repair and customer satisfaction data may not be available for five to seven years after launch, by which time vehicle team members have long since been working on other programs. Automotive companies, including AutoCo, have thus developed detailed evaluation processes and quality measures that circumvent these long delays and provide them with data more quickly. Based on those measures, Epsilon is a very successful program, and perhaps no other data is needed.

An opposite perspective suggests that the marketing and financial results are critical. If the vehicle does not produce needed business results, all of the development of process is for naught. From this perspective, Epsilon's "learning orientation" should have incorporated the ability to raise questions about the car's design and position in the marketplace. In fact, a set of "undiscussable" issues influenced early decisions affecting the Epsilon program. Vehicle styling decisions involve AutoCo's most senior management. These decisions are critical to the vehicle's later success and are often controversial: there is little objective data when decisions are made to help predict which styling is right. There were two alternative styles considered early in Epsilon's program—a modern design intended to appeal to a new, younger, more sport-oriented luxury car buyer, and a more traditional design aimed at the older, more traditional luxury car buyer represented by Epsilon's current market segment.

Although the new engine, performance, features, and price of the new Epsilon model were intended to expand the market to younger buyers, the decision to appeal to the traditional buyer with the more conservative styling was made by a senior executive (shortly before retiring). This decision went against recommendations based on market research data.

During that the early part of the program development process, before the launch team was assembled, some executives voiced concerns that Epsilon's volume forecasts were unrealistic given its pricing and styling. There was a shared perception among executives that in some ways the program would inevitably fail, no matter how much "learning" was involved. The car style would not succeed at that price point.

There is an argument that this presumption created a Pygmalion effect which influenced senior AutoCo executives' interaction with the team and its leaders. Since they couldn't imagine the car succeeding in the marketplace, they wrote it off. This hypothesis is not included in the learning history because it could not be formally tested; it was too "undiscussable" to raise in interviews at the time. Nor is it guaranteed to be true; it represents the private theory of a couple of observers. There were also other explanations offered by observers for the distance between Epsilon program managers and the senior executives responsible for it. These ranged from entrenched personality conflicts to the pattern of managing programs by setting them in competition with one another and continually tearing down and roughing up program leaders. A more comprehensive learning history, on a future project, might well do AutoCo a service by bringing forth some of these dynamics.

But if any of these concerns were true, then word about them would naturally trickle down to Epsilon's managers, along with others in the company. If anyone had reason to doubt the car's ultimate viability, they should have had a way to raise those doubts and be heard. (In AutoCo's culture, however, that was not part of the job description, even for a program manager.) Since the program manager and other Epsilon team members failed to find a way to do this, they (according to this view) bear some of the responsibility for the car's failures.

According to an even harsher view, the car's marketplace failure should serve as a judgment on the learning initiative. If "learning" had such a great impact on the car's quality and performance, the car should have been compelling enough in its quality to rise above its market constraints and sell well anyway. Interestingly, a subsequent "update" of the vehicle, released in 1998, did sell much better than the original Epsilon. This suggests that the time to judge "success" or "failure" was much too limited; perhaps we should wait until the "next generation" of products before judging whether any particular launch succeeds or fails.

Another point of view suggests that Epsilon should be judged according to the influence of its process innovations, and their effects on the bottom line throughout AutoCo. An article in a prominent business periodical made this point about the team approach not long ago. "How we manage the program is as important as the vehicle we engineered" a senior AutoCo manager was quoted as saying. He went on to say that it is not enough to produce a "successful vehicle": development teams also had to develop the processes that allowed success to be consistently repeated.

In the Epsilon case, that success was determined by measures outside the team's ability to control, and reward and recognition depended, at least in part, upon those external measures. However, by that criteria, Epsilon was, at best, a mixed success. The influence that it has had on AutoCo was indirect. Many people at AutoCo still pooh-pooh the idea that Epsilon was influential; some argue that the team members did not live up to their reputation for openness. As the opening to the learning history notes, many of the learning initiative concepts were available elsewhere at AutoCo, and many other launch teams have pursued them—although none in as concerted and intensive a fashion. In all the AutoCo teams still working on learning initiatives, the tension between "hard" and "soft" results, between "improving the way we do things" and "not getting distracted from the task" still remains an issue. No other team at AutoCo seems to have resolved the dilemma that bedeviled the program manager and the launch manager: the simultaneous need to engage the larger system and inability to reach them.

This perspective has particular relevance for managers seeking a learning approach for other pilot groups. The program manager, launch manager, and top program team focused their efforts on the development of the learning process and the internal dynamics of the Epsilon teams. Their perception that they were operating in a "hostile" management environment made it much easier to focus on internal team activities. Theoretically, the learning and communication tools the Epsilon team learned are relevant and applicable in most business situations. Pragmatically, they are easier to apply in a team situation. Both team leaders and team members got immediate rewards and gratification in applying learning principles. Not surprisingly, their attention stayed focused on these activities, which kept them safely distanced and isolated from the more critical perceptions of outsiders. Could the intensive focus on learning within the team exist only at the expense of managing critical and important external relationships?

All of these considerations influenced the way the document was disseminated at AutoCo. To the credit of the internal learning historians, there was a deliberate effort to use the learning history to break through the time-honored isolation around senior executives. After all, the document clearly had serious implications for senior management. It raised issues around how their managerial style influenced their interactions with, and the cultures of, vehicle development teams. Taking a lesson from the Epsilon team's experience, one group of internal sponsors decided to present the learning history directly to AutoCo's top executives, before circulating it to lower-level managers within the organization. This would give executives the opportunity to decide what to do, rather than reacting to the implications which other teams drew from what happened.

The process of getting the Epsilon learning history on the agenda of senior management required extensive individual meetings with managers at AutoCo. They were first asked to review the materials, to make suggestions, and to get involved in bringing the issues to the next level of management. This process took over nine months, culminating in conversations with the AutoCo Senior Vice President of Product Development. The Vice President's support for the Epsilon learning history, its use in AutoCo, and its release as an MIT Center for Organizational Learning working paper is evident in the cover letter he wrote as a foreword to the document. Since its release, the Epsilon learning history has been extensively used within AutoCo and by companies associated with the MIT Center for Organizational Learning (now the Society for Organizational Learning).

◆ PUTTING REFLECTION ON THE CORPORATE AGENDA

Like the Epsilon learning project, the learning history itself has been a somewhat disturbing force at AutoCo. The creation and use of a learning history asks people in organizations to do something they typically wouldn't—reflect upon and assess what happened in a project. Many people and organizations do reflect on the past and draw lessons from it, but they don't do it systematically and collectively. Indeed, business organizations in particular recruit people who are inclined to take quick action, and they develop those capabilities for quick action even more strongly. Learning, by contrast, requires an additional step or thought process to occur between actions and automatic reactions. In learning, this step is reflection, the moment that mediates between action and reaction.

Reflection is the careful consideration of our thinking, feelings, and actions. At an individual level, reflection creates an awareness of our own thinking and feelings, and how they might be influencing our overt behaviors and actions. At a collective level, reflection makes it possible to understand the thinking and feelings that guide other people's actions, how those accumulated actions feed back into the collective system, and how to identify potential leverage points for change. Learning histories provide a way to look back at the past, learn from it, and become more effective in the future. Collective reflection integrates the past and the future by creating an opportunity for understanding and choice in the present.

Reflection, like trust, can be difficult to achieve. Talking about it doesn't make it happen. Reflection is a critical component in the process of building organizational environments conducive to learning. Techniques for inquiry—effectively surfacing, questioning and exploring assumptions and mental models which guide action—are important skills for reflection in groups. Developing the skills needed for reflection requires practice—and having data on thoughts and actions to work with. The data presented in learning histories provides a way for groups to practice and develop their own capabilities.

In the learning history process, reflection takes place at two levels. The first is individual, as members of the original team reflect on their own and others' efforts during the course of the learning history interviews. Using the materials drawn from the participants' assessments, the learning history document itself is created and used in conversational workshops. These workshops give participants an opportunity to reflect with each other and to learn about the thoughts, feelings, and potential actions of others in the organization—often for the first time.

Why do organizations need reflection? Precisely because they are so good at action that it dwarfs their capabilities for reflection. Action and reflection are not opposites. They are complementary concepts that support and reinforce one another in the process of improvement. The learning history process makes it possible to systematically build moments for reflection in to organizational settings. Although initial efforts may seem awkward, and the idea of scheduled reflection insuperable, creating opportunities for building skills and capabilities serves the organization and its members by putting reflection on the agenda—and not leaving it to chance.

◆ THE LEARNING HISTORY PROCESS

Not until there was extensive interest from other groups for building upon the Epsilon project accomplishments was it possible to initiate and sustain this kind of an investigative effort at AutoCo. This is one of the first principles for learning in organizations—the need for "pull" instead of "push" as a rationale for any new artifact of adult learning. People must be ready to learn, for their own reasons, with their own understanding of why the new material will be relevant. "Interest" is not something which can be legislated by top management. Where does "pull" come from in organizations? It could come from any source of curiosity or interest, but most often it emerges as groups try to develop their own new organizational practices. They soon see the value of building upon other groups' successes, rather than starting from the ground up on each new initiative.

To conduct the interviews and do field research for the learning history, we needed to spend hours of time with Epsilon team members, both past and present—as well as with key executives, suppliers, and customers. It was thus vitally important that the members of the Epsilon team were themselves interested in how they were doing in terms of their learning efforts, beyond traditional metrics. Their interest in learning in general, combined with their "learning labs" experiences, contributed to their interest in seeing their efforts captured by the learning history.

"Pull" also came from beyond the Epsilon team. Other groups at the Center for Organizational Learning (and since then at its successor, the Society for Organizational Learning) have been deeply interested in learning from the Epsilon experience. Thus it became increasingly important to be able to discern and present what was learned, and how it could be replicated and transferred to other interested groups. It was obvious that this "research" effort would require more people than the facilitators and researchers already working with the Epsilon team's learning labs. This meant we would have to introduce a new team of "learning historians" into the Epsilon environment, during the last few months while the project was coming to a close.

The possibility of adding new members, particularly those seen as "evaluators," created an ambivalent, at best, response from some members of the Epsilon team. It provoked questions like, "Are the additional researchers there to help us, or to help MIT?" Some Epsilon team members wondered how these efforts to document and assess their work would help them. Others worried that, even as they performed their tasks successfully, they would be remembered for the mistakes they made along the way.

It was also clear that the addition of new team members might alter the team dynamics. The learning project itself was going well, and there was little incentive to accept new members. If the project itself involved learning, why should the proposed research become the providence of "expert" learning historians? Why not just use traditional alternatives—observation, interviews, and the use of variable-based survey measures?

For a variety of reasons, the AutoCo and MIT researchers recognized that the conventional forms of assessment would be inadequate. They wanted a more ethnographic approach, aimed at capturing team members' experience. This raised epistemological challenges, however: Whose point of view, participants, or researchers, was more valued in considering how the Epsilon team was doing? Why, when MIT researchers had promoted learning and significant personal and organizational change, were the research approaches now proposed somehow discounting their personal experiences? How would traditional formative program evaluation methods truly capture and reflect the situated nature of their new knowledge? How would they, the participants and the organization, learn from the research as they had been learning throughout the project?

Every organizational change story is a messy, complex system in itself, and Epsilon was no exception. This meant, right from the beginning, that we gathered as many points of view as possible, including as the views of outsiders: consultants, suppliers, regulators, and bosses. If the learning history doesn't help individuals see events in a new light, then it hasn't served its purpose. It also meant that we worked closely with a team of sponsors and co-authors at AutoCo, several of whom joined us in conducting interviews and editing the final manuscript. For reasons of anonymity, we cannot include their names or titles, but they are as much authors of this document as Roth and Kleiner.

The steps of the learning history process are noteworthy because they illuminate concerns about crediblity and value of the document. First of all, to be credible and compelling organizational reflection must not only be relevant to but must follow from business results. Thus, we asked the learning history's champions at AutoCo to join us in compiling the list of "Noticeable Results" on page 9. These, in turn, served as the starting point for our interviews. Any knowledgeable observer would agree these results were significant, but people would probably disagree about their causes and meaning. Our job, as learning historians, was to draw forth a deeper understanding of the reasons why different people feel differently about it.

Interestingly, the inclusion of "Noticeable Results" made many people at AutoCo uncomfortable. They felt we were implicitly drawing a causal relationship between the learning initiative and these results—saying, in effect, that without the learning initiative, these results might not have existed. In fact, they believed that the learning initiative had directly produced many of those results—but they did not have any way to prove it, and they were reluctant to see the link mentioned as a fact.

We began all interviews by asking people to look at a list of the noticeable results, to pick the items that seem most relevant and pertinent to their own experience, and tell us about those. This let interviewees, not interviewers, select the focus of the conversation. (We also invited them to add noticeable results that we have missed.)

For nearly all the interviews, we used teams of two interviewers: one internal staff person (generally an "organizational effectiveness"-oriented internal consultant) and one external learning historian. Inside interviewers know how to ferret out critical details and nuances which make the document feel "real" and relevant. Outside interviewers feel freer to raise naive questions, ferreting out organizational blind spots and "undiscussable" issues that an inside interviewer might miss. In addition, as the insiders and outsiders educate each other, through the course of the interviewing, a much richer understanding of the company's issues is built up among the learning historian team.

We kept interviews down to earth. Conventional organizational survey interviews ask for analyses, evaluations, assessments, and judgments. We looked past those to ask simply for the story as people experienced it. "What happened next? What did you see?" We wanted interviewees to look past the surface myths of blame and contrariness and talk about their actual perceptions and observations. This helped them make new reflective connections and develop new insights, especially if they've never had an opportunity to talk thoughtfully about their experience to an interviewer before.

When the interviews were finished, the two outsider learning historians "distilled" the raw material into a coherent set of themes. Distilling interviews is a surprisingly intricate process. The team session requires considerable prework in closely reading and "coding" transcripts. Then themes must be chosen that are valid in terms of a "research imperative": They must rise out of the text, instead of being imposed on it by the learning historians. They must also be valid from a "mythic" standpoint—compelling enough that readers will feel emotionally involved. And they must be valid from a "pragmatic" orientation, as well: designed so that AutoCo's managers would not feel so challenged and confronted that they ignored it and set up so that they might make genuine use of the material in planning their own next steps.

To accomplish this, we adapted a little-used ethnographic format that fit the ambiguous nature of this document—told partly by outside learning historians, and partly by the participants themselves. In his book *Tales from the Field*, John van Maanen[2] describes a form of ethnographic storytelling called the "jointly told tale," in which anthropologists abandon their traditional stance as either "objective" observers of an alien culture or "subjective" converts that tell what it is like to be a native. Instead, researchers join as partners with the people they are studying to tell the story together, incorporating the "native's" experience and passion, along with the learning historians' broader perspective and objective training. This is a valuable model for any organizational research After all, the corporate "natives" are the same types of people who read the report. They can't be treated as subjects kept at a distance. Everyone gains when participants and researchers join together in telling the tale and presenting it to others.

The desire to have a voice in the presentation of the research inspired the use of a jointly told tale approach. Researchers and participants would "speak" for themselves, as much as was possible in the throws of a day-to-day business environment. Like the project's participants, researchers would have to make what they said, and why they said it, transparent to readers. The intent was to give readers a sense of what it was like to be one of the participants, to experience that from multiple perspectives, and to then consider what meaning the project might hold for them and their own teams.

To achieve this effect, we present the learning history in two side-by-side columns. The wider major column contains a "campfire narrative," always in participants' own words (and extensively quote-checked with them). The narrower minor column contains the researchers' evaluative comments, along with questions intended to spark reactions and reflection by the readers of the tale. The minor column also provides brief answers to the questions readers might have: Who chose these quotes? Why was it organized this way? Are these sentiments typical? Through this format, the reader has more information to develop his or her own conclusions about the major column story—while also taking advantage and testing them against the insights of the learning historians, contained in the minor column.

Other aspects of the format are designed to provide readers with a sense of context. Each segment begins with an introduction that sets the stage for events, and we try to draw readers' attention to seemingly unrelated forces that, in fact, have a deep systemic relationship to each other. Boxes provide detailed digressions about particular techniques used within the learning effort.

The credibility of the learning history also depends on our extensive validation process. When another learning history was released in the company that sponsored it, one of the senior executives in the company refused to endorse it at first. "Someone talks about being afraid of speaking out," he said, "but we don't have that kind of fear in this company." The learning historians replied that someone cared enough to make the comment in an interview, to approve it the first time the quote was checked, and then to approve it when the quote was checked a second time. Even if the company were free of fear, it was not free of the perception that fear existed.

Similarly, in the AutoCo learning history, you will see a great deal of "dangerous comment" about disagreements, misunderstandings, and frustrations. All of these provide a way for people to learn. In fact, without them, the document would give people a much less cogent "base" of data to learn from. These qualities are present in the document because of the twin aspects of validation: anonymity of voice and rigorous quote-checking.

Learning history participants are identified by position, not by name—even where the name of the person is obvious. This anonymity takes the pressure off any individual, allowing them to say things candidly without being "frozen" in association with a particular comment. It also allows the document to be more easily released outside the company. Our validation process, in short, provides the necessary protection for everyone involved, from the interviewees to the company as a whole; it creates a safe "space" in which dangerous topics may be discussed.

The validation process consists of three rounds of data checking. The first two take place by fax and email; participants, even though they are anonymous, have final approval over all of their quotes. Then we conduct a series of "validation" workshops with small groups of key interviewees, along with a few other people from elsewhere in the organization. This allows the original participants to relive their experience in the company of others—and to observe how it will be seen by the rest of the company. Participants find this invaluable, particularly as they move on to other roles in the company. Some may have already been branded as "missionaries," and the validation workshop shows them how their enthusiasm for a change effort comes across to others as proselytizing. Others may have felt timid about discussing the knowledge gained from their learning effort, and the validation workshop gives them confidence.

We do not hand out the learning history as a report for fear that it would just be read with the personal biases that are locked up in most people's minds. Instead, we take advantage of the gossip and buzz that have been building out of our interviews. We conduct "dissemination" workshops, somewhat like reading groups. People who are trying to undertake change efforts meet together for two or three hours in a reflective conversation, talking about the pitfalls and challenges that faced the group in the learning history. AutoCo, in fact, was one of the first places where such reading groups met, and they continue to meet to talk about this Epsilon learning history and several others that have been produced at AutoCo since.[3]

We believe that the document has its greatest potential for use among small groups in other organizations or in business schools.

By engaging each other in reflection, participants can help assess and evaluate each other's experience. The validation and credibility checks of the learning history process mean that the document is reliable as a coherent source of "data." But it is not complete. Some people were not interviewed; some interviewees did not say everything they had to say; and some of the most important material, perhaps, did not make it into the document.

Using a learning history to spark new conversations, which lead to richer shared understanding, serves the development of more effective collective action. As with researchers, management practitioners are encouraged to use the learning history as data to surface, test, and develop their own theories and practices for what defines effective action.

For researchers a learning history is a new form for presenting descriptions of change, a document which reports on changes primarily in the forms of stories. The data in a learning history can be used to develop and test theory. Are the descriptions of what happened consistent with the theories of learning and change? Do particular theories have the explanatory power to suggest what would or might have happened? The participants' stories in a learning history are a form of data which is particularly appropriate for complex dynamic personal and corporate change processes.

◆ LEARNING THEORY AND THE LEARNING HISTORY

Why is collective learning, particularly in the workplace, so difficult that special tools and techniques (like the learning history in this book) are needed? There are at least two reasons, which together reinforce each other's continued effects.

The first has to do with attitudes about the nature of learning itself. Learning is a natural phenomenon in individuals: Our existence and dominance as a species are attributed to our ability to develop new actionable knowledge: knowledge embedded in the form of new skills, capabilities, and innovations.

Yet many adults have grown accustomed to thinking of "learning" in a reductionist manner: simply as the acquisition of new information. Having gone to school, we possess educational and professional credentials that suggest that we now "possess" an adequate sum of knowledge. There is no need to learn more; we need merely put our learning to use.

This view of learning contradicts the way that collective learning works in real life. A more accurate view of learning is summarized in the ancient Chinese language, in which "learning" is represented by the symbols which follow.

The symbol on the left represents study. The figures that compose the symbol show accumulated knowledge; its components represent being "inside the door," and children. The symbol on the right connotes practice: The depiction of flying and youth are a reminder that young birds learn to fly through constant practice. These symbols of study and practice are inseparable.[4] In Chinese it is not possible to express the concept, "I know that." The idea of knowing can only be communicated by saying, "I am learning that."

In other words, learning is a never-ending process. You may know how to ski or paint, but there is always room to learn more, so that you can ski or paint more effectively. The same is true of business or professional knowledge. Every new situation represents an opportunity to apply an old "known" technique in an unknown "new" context. Hence, all learning is ongoing: "I am learning that."

The second difficulty with collective learning has to do with the nature of collective systems. Our instinctive individual abilities to learn, even if they survive a view of learning as possession, do not naturally translate into collective action. Organizations are essentially collections of people with individual skills and capabilities, and yet organizational members have a hard time bringing their capabilities to bear in being effective together. Even when everyone has the noblest possible intentions, people discount the value of each other's knowledge. They waste opportunities for following each other's progress and learning from each other. They unwittingly undermine each other's improvements. And they set up improvements of their own that operate at cross-purposes.

This difficulty also stems from a misunderstanding about knowledge: that there is one "best answer" to any problem or question, and that deliberate, reductionist analysis can eventually yield that answer. In reality, while analysis is necessary to solve complex problems, complex issues are too widespread and divergent for any single individual to "possess" all the necessary data for analysis. In practice, when people can learn to come together and pool their knowledge, analysis is only one tool they use. Inquiry, careful advocacy, experimentation, and in-depth reflection are all equally valuable.

Thus, overcoming the difficulties of collective learning requires new kinds of lifelong habits of behavior. These include the activity that theorist Donald Michael calls "error-embracing"—expecting even the best-prepared social or business policy to fail, and building in many opportunities for course-correction and reconsideration of goals.[5] This does not happen unless people can act with humility. A lifelong learner will routinely seek knowledge from others, even at the expense of looking foolish or impolitic. A lifelong learning will continually inquire, with both passion and skill, into the reasoning behind other people's views.

◆   THE THEORY UNDERNEATH THE LEARNING HISTORY

Describing the theoretical basis for learning history approach is intended to help readers apply and use a learning history. Designed to be compatible with an Action Science approach, learning histories are developed in projects which: 1) are conducted collaboratively with partner companies; 2) use a learning cycle for planning activities; 3) teach techniques for thinking and learning; 4) promote learning and development by building capabilities of organizational members; and 5) develop and test theories while seeking to improve management practices and positively influence business outcomes. In the process of documenting what others have learned in a form that facilitates broad communication to company and public audiences, a learning history process also encourages ongoing learning by managers and researchers involved in the learning history work.

What is this learning? Learning is the expansion of one's capability to produce behaviors that lead to desired results. Implicit in this definition is the idea that thoughts, and ways of thinking, determine what you seek to achieve and how you go about achieving it. One model of learning proposed by Chris Argyris and Donald Schön[6] suggests that knowledge is held by people in their private assumptions. This knowledge determines the strategies they use to govern their actions.

When the outcomes match expectations, the actions are reinforced and deemed "successful." When actions don't achieve expected outcomes, there is a mismatch, and individuals alter their actions in order to achieve

FIGURE 11-1 *Single- and double-loop learning*

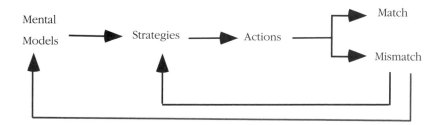

expected outcomes. This change in action is the basis of what Chris Argyris and Donald Schön call "single-loop learning."

Single-loop learning involves altering actions through the use of the same knowledge and strategies. For example, when people seek to overcome an obstacle by "trying harder," they are acting under the presumption that their original strategy was correct. They simply need to put more effort behind their actions. This approach is shown as progress around the inner loop, the loop leading to "strategies."

The alternative would be to look beyond the strategy upon which the "unsuccessful" outcomes were based. This alternative is depicted as the path around the outer (or "double") loop, through "mental models." Mental models are the deeply ingrained assumptions, generalizations, pictures, images, stories, or myths that influence how we understand the world and how we take action in it. In double-loop learning, people examine not just their actions, but their mental models: the tacit assumptions and habitual thoughts from which the strategies they employ arise.

The distinction between single- and double-loop learning is important in learning history work. This model illustrates that the study of learning involves going beyond what is directly observable: It requires engaging people at the level of articulating the thinking that accompanies actions. The study of learning itself requires reflection as a part of the process and as an outcome of the process. That reflection needs to rest upon description so that the strategies people attribute for their actions, and the matches or mismatches that they describe for their outcomes, can be examined.

The study of learning requires a description of action (what happened), awareness of the extent to which actions lead to successful outcomes (matches of mismatches of outcomes with expectations), the articulation of what one was trying to accomplish (strategies and motivations),

FIGURE 11-2 *Ladder of inference*

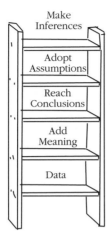

and an inquiry into what informed the strategies and motivations that guided action (mental models and basic assumptions). The ability to examine learning thus requires a process of examining the reasoning or inferential process which is part of how individuals see and interact with their complex worlds. A learning history document, in its two-column, noticeable result, jointly told tale format, is carefully designed and written to make people's reasoning processes visible to readers. The document, and the narrative that appears in it, is a visible record of what has been said, and is thus available to be pointed out by whomever looks at it.

An important concept and tool, developed by Chris Argyris, in examining learning is the "ladder of inference." (See page 24 for a description of this tool, and the way it was used in the Epsilon project.) Incorporating the "ladder" into everyday conversation, and inquiring into the observations and inferences associated with events, provides a conceptual guide for raising and checking varied interpretations of events.

The research of psychologists (Dewey, Piaget, Bruner)[7] and organizational theorists (Lewin, Lippitt, Argyris and Schön, Kolb)[8] proposes learning as a cyclical process involving action, here-and-now concrete experience, feedback on experience, and formation of abstract concepts that guide future action. Learning in organizations is inherently problematic, however, because people who take action and make decisions often do not get feedback, or what feedback they do get is limited and biased.[9]

Dewey's conception of learning is that it is a developmental process from which impulses are transformed into mature, higher-order, purposeful action. Building upon those ideas, Lewin proposed a model of experiential learning borrowing the concept of feedback from electrical engineering. He characterized social learning processes as those based on information that is generated through action and then used to assess deviations from desired goals.[10]

A basic problem with experiential learning models in business settings is that they don't describe what happens very well. Manager have limited opportunities for learning from "mistakes" or variances from expectations. When mistakes are made in business settings, there are psychological and social pressures to cover up the mistakes rather than to learn from them, what Argyris[11] calls "organizational defensive routines." Moreover, it is extremely difficult to learn from decisions whose consequences may unfold over years, and where those consequences may be distant from the original decision makers.

Secondly, there are dilemmas for collective learning in organizations which relate to the individual nature of experience. In any large and complex social system, individuals who belong to different parts of that organization may hold a wide variety of values, points of view, and opinions. The attributions which people hold for what happens is based on their mental models or theories for how things work in their organization. People's mental models not only select what information is important, but they are also the basis for past, present and potential future actions. The different perspectives which people have influence what they observe and learn.

Eliciting, and providing insight into, people's varied perspectives is an important objective for a learning history. Asking people to "tell their story" and assess themselves and others encourages people to speak from their perspective, which reveals what they consider important and relevant. Using the ladder of inference provides a helpful conceptual tool for grounding people's thought processes and personal narratives in common observable data.

The ladder of inference is also explicitly considered in the creation and presentation of written material in the learning history. This is illustrated by the horizontal ladder of inference between the two columns (see Figure 11-3), whereas participants' reasoning is illustrated by the ladder of inference in the right-hand column. Revealing the writers' reasoning

Figure 11-3 *Multiple ladders of inference in the learning history*

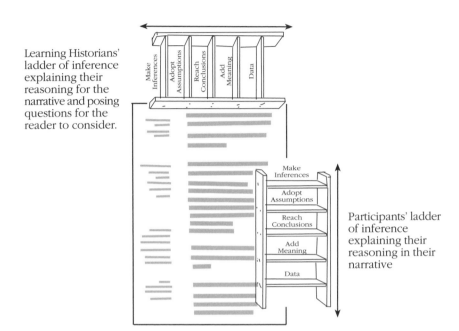

Learning Historians' ladder of inference explaining their reasoning for the narrative and posing questions for the reader to consider.

Participants' ladder of inference explaining their reasoning in their narrative

processes in the left-hand column encourages the reader's own reflection and models an integrity on the part of the authors for their responsibility and role in the document's production. It includes why particular materials were included, what might have been left out, how representative quotes were of others' thoughts, and what questions the quotes prompted. The team of learning history writers choose from a large volume of transcript data, and their reasoning for choices can help readers assess the material in the document more fully.

The ladder of inference concept is also important in dissemination and reading of the document. When people come together to discuss what they have read, they bring their own perspectives and reasoning processes, much of which they may not be aware of. The learning history acts as a common record on which to base collective inquiry, and for inquiring into participants' ladders of inference. The use of the learning history facilitates the process of creating shared understanding among the

Figure 11-4 *Multiple ladders of inference in learning history conversation*

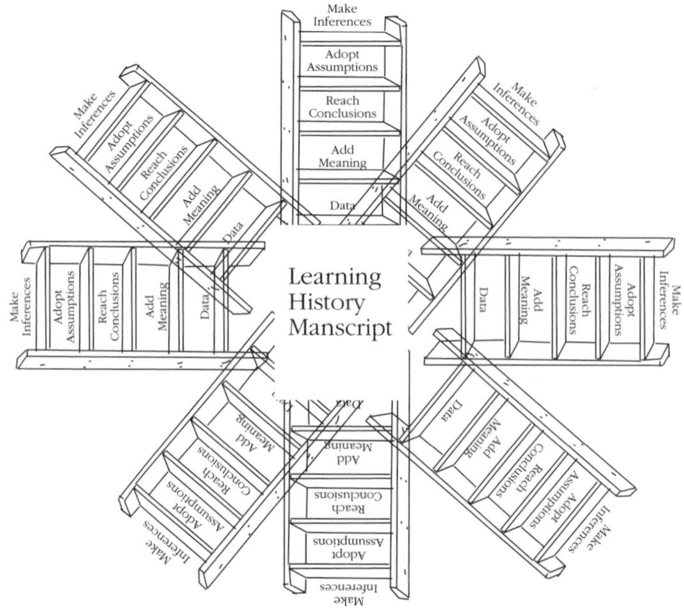

conversations' participants, and that shared meaning serves their coordination and commitment to future collective actions.

The conversation itself is an experiential learning experience for its participants. By inquiring collectively into another group's or organization's learning and change process—the new group can consider what happened and what meaning it has to them, assess success and failures along the way, test reasoning processes for why and how that happened, and apply the ideas to the group's own situations. It simulates a learning and change process, helping the new group develop their own capabilities for making collective sense of what happened and how, capabilities that the group will need as it goes through its own learning and change processes.

Why worry about this theory? Because the premise of learning histories, and the basis for their use in organizational learning, improvement, and change projects, rests upon a particular set of assumptions about

Figure 11-5 *Levels of culture*[12]

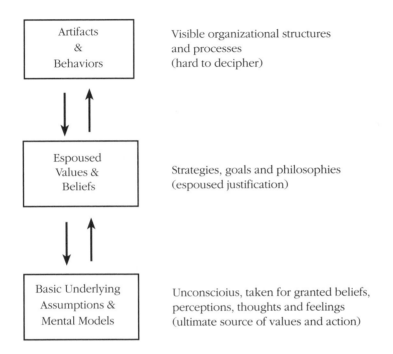

increasing individual and organizational effectiveness. Individuals within organizations will be more effective as they increase their awareness of, operate with an understanding of, and continually test the theories they hold and the underlying mental models which inform their own thinking and acting.

Most corporate change efforts emphasize behavioral changes at what is often called the micro-behavioral level (see Kanter commentary on page 137). They work with people—primarily through training programs —teaching new skills and instilling new routines and repertoires that help people communicate and act more effectively. Often, other more macro change efforts are targeted at the level of strategy and policies. The focus is at the espoused level, targeting beliefs and values that prescribe what is desired and appropriate for individual thought and behavior. Much like the process by which change efforts are instituted in organizations, these initiatives are often mechanistic, and thus have a mostly mechanistic impact. People learn to behave in new ways that are reinforced and deemed appropriate by those that hold the power to prescribe what is desired in organizations.

Using Schein's model of culture[13] (see Figure 11-5), we can see that traditional organizational change efforts emphasize the first two levels—artifacts and behaviors, and values and beliefs. The artifacts are what one sees and hears in an organization—tangible indications of the organization's functioning. It can be hard for outsiders to decipher their meaning because it is relative to the local context in which they take place. Values and beliefs are what people say they do, and why they do it. However, what people say does not always correspond to what they do. The third level—basic underlying assumptions and mental models—are the taken-for-granted ways in which people think and act. These have often become so ingrained that not only are they no longer noticed, but people would find it inconceivable to think and act in any other way. Basic assumptions guide people's behavior, thoughts, and feelings about things which have become so transparent that they are no longer consciously aware of them.

The culture model suggests that people's mental models are the ultimate source of values and actions. For example, when beliefs or values appear in conflict with one another, there is often a deeper underlying assumption which makes it acceptable to hold conflicting values, and thus reconciles the discord with a broader, subsuming basic assumption. Becoming aware of and understanding basic assumptions are hard for people in the organization precisely because they are so pervasive.

The challenge for organizations is that while the underlying assumptions and mental models are the ultimate source of value and action, they cannot be directly changed. Mental models change as a result of other changes—through people coping and making new sense of external changes or developing new internal mechanisms for integration. The idea of changing an organization's culture directly is similar to the notion of trying to change an individual's deepest attitudes by haranguing and preaching to him. Changes in thinking and assumptions about the world come from engaging people in considering alternatives and providing opportunities to experience new ways of thinking and acting.

A learning history engages people in the organization in its creation by asking people to "tell their story" of for change and learning. It also engages people in an organization in the suggested process by which it is used. The product and process of a learning history are inseparable—it is the process of engaging members of the organization in reflection that creates materials of a quality that support others' reflections.

◆ GUIDELINES FOR LEARNING HISTORY CONVERSATIONS

The objective of a learning history process is to produce better conversations in an organization so that it can move forward effectively. This objective might seem entirely unreasonable for managers, consultants, and researchers alike. How can a manager rely on a "research" document to be the basis of conversation? How can consultants work with a document that may not present past learning and change initiative with the "spin" they would want? How can a researcher be responsible for writing something which people actually read, never mind discuss? Each of these cautious considerations raises issues of an interdependence among researchers, consultants, and managers in the learning history process. They all need to work together, be included, and have a stake in the learning history if it is to engage an organization in a learning process.

What is the most appropriate way to evaluate a learning history project? We suggest that the most important criteria is the "ability of the organization to hear what the document (and the process around the document) says." The authors of the document are responsible for clearly and forcefully conveying the experience that participants have been through. They are also responsible for writing and presenting this material with full consideration for their audience's needs. The organization—particularly the champion, supporters, proponents, and internal members of the learning history team—is responsible for creating conditions where the learning history can be heard. These conditions include developing an interest in, and demand for, conversations about the learning history document. All of these, together, add up to the overall effectiveness of the learning history in achieving its core goals: To transfer and diffuse learning.

Specifically, these assessments should be made:

How much "pull" (demand) for the learning history has there been? How much perception is there that the learning history "story" is aligned with the organization's most important business objectives? How much of the practices described in the learning history are subsequently considered for adoption by other teams?

If the answer is, "Not much," then we would judge the learning history document and process have probably not been as effective as they should be.

Presenting the document to others

When a learning history is being used in organizations different than the one where it was created, it continues to be important to involve key managers in considering its messages and implications. Like any organizational intervention, the authority and power of senior managers needs to be aligned with, and supportive of, the intervention's objectives and process. A learning history, when used in group settings, is more than a report, but a set of experiences which may change people's awareness of their own situations, influence conversations, and unfold into possibilities for new actions.

The process of using a learning history to raise issues needs to be worked through an organization's existing power structure, providing the people in positions of authority opportunities to consider the questions it raises. If senior managers are not interested in learning and change, it will be difficult to have a significant effect on the way that organization functions while they continue to occupy their positions. Reluctant senior managers have the power to restrict the attention that issues are formally given and can influence the extent to which other people can openly talk about those issues. Developing a strategy which allows senior managers to consider the issues and become engaged in the questions that are raised is much more effective in promoting collective learning than trying to convince these managers that the learning history has the right answers for them. One strategy which has been effective has been to ask top managers to write cover letters indicating support for the learning process, use of the learning history by interested teams, and the desire for open consideration of the issues that are raised in the document and implied for the organization.

Once there is managerial support for the learning history process and the potential issues it raises for the organization to consider, the learning history can be made more widely available. This second stage of the dissemination process involves using it in conjunction with facilitated workshops where it is discussed. A learning history will provide limited benefit if it is read like a report. Individuals reading reports form their own judgments, and may even change their actions, based on what they read. However, the ability to develop shared understanding, and possibilities for new, more effective coordinated action, are not realized when a learning history is not collectively considered.

Dissemination Process

The learner learns what the learner wants to learn. Learning is a voluntary process. It is like leading a horse to water—you can get it there, but you can't make it drink. You can make people go to workshops, but you can't get them to learn something they don't want to learn.

What will draw people into a learning process? Our experience is that the desire to learn and improve is intrinsically driven and realized through conditions which an organization creates for its employees. These conditions include encouraging new ideas and actions, giving people the latitude to experiment, recognizing their accomplishments, and rewarding new behaviors.

Compelling stories of learning and change have a significant ability to influence people in trying something new. These stories are not the formal ones, those given at speeches, but the ones which are heard in corridors about how things really work "around here." They are also the stories upon which learning histories report. The learning history dissemination workshops are the opportunity for people in the organization to bring those mythical stories into in collective setting for open discussion. The power of a good learning history is to draw people into this discussion, whether it is about their own organization or another, and consider what value and meaning people in their environment give to what happened elsewhere and what might be possible here.

Our recommendation has been to distribute the learning history as part of voluntary workshops or meetings. Invite people to read it and then, a week or two later, meet in a gathering of a half dozen to a dozen people to talk through the learning history and the implications of it for themselves and other teams. The workshop is an opportunity for people to discuss what they have read, how they interpret it, and what lessons it holds for them. How people respond and the kind of conversation that emerges in this workshop is new data about the learning process.

Adults learn not so much by adding facts to their memory, but experientially. The dissemination workshop is an experience from which people can collectively learn. When the context and conversation of a dissemination workshop are based on a good learning history, they can help to create the experience from which people learn. As the poet David Whyte has commented, "Good poetry helps you remember an experience. Great poetry is an experience." In this same way, a well-designed and facilitated learning history workshop is the experience. In order to live up to this possibility, the learning history workshop must be understood in terms of the dilemmas of experiential learning and what can be done to create the conditions for collective experiential learning.

Preparing for dissemination

It is important to provide instructions for people reading a learning history (and later discussing it) to let themselves hear the stories people tell in these documents. By reading, listening to, empathizing with, and seeking understanding of other people's stories, we can accept perspectives and points of view other than our own.

We have developed the custom of placing a cover letter, or instructions, on learning histories as they are distributed. We cannot enforce their use in workshops, but we are obligated to inform people of the document's intended use, and how to gain the most value from the manuscript. We offer the following text as a boilerplate; others have taken this material and incorporated it their personalized cover letters that invite people to a scheduled workshop. Students in classrooms should also receive these instructions when the reading is assigned.

ATTENTION: THE LEARNING HISTORY OPPORTUNITY

You can read the following learning history the way you would read an ordinary report. However, if you read it that way, we do not believe that it will provide the intended value.

A learning history describes what happens in a learning and change process, in the voice of participants. It documents "hard" facts and events, and focuses on what people thought about events, how they perceived their own actions, and differences in people's perceptions. By recreating the experience of "being there," the learning history helps readers understand what happened in a way that helps them make more effective judgments.

Learning is not always an easy process. It involves taking on the mindset of a beginner, letting go of what you have worked hard to "know," and a willingness to examine situations which aren't turning out as intended. When people try new behaviors and do things differently they often make mistakes—in fact, mistakes are inevitable. In typical business settings, however, mistakes are covered up and undiscussable.

The people who tell their story in this learning history have made mistakes, and they have also had successes. Those experiences are communicated here. Thus, the learning history workshop seeks to create an opportunity to talk openly about what has been learned and to extend this discussion into its implications for current and future issues.

When you read this document as a learning history, in preparation for a meeting in which you can discuss its contents, we ask you to do two things.

First, consider it as a vehicle to better conversations. Read the document in parallel with other members of your team. Plan a couple of hours dedicated to coming together to talk about what you read and how it applies to your current efforts. As you read the learning history, notice what triggers your emotions —surprise, joy, anger, sadness, fear and so on —and mark those areas in the text so that you can go back to them later. Prepare yourself for how you might talk to your colleagues about your reactions and thoughts in reading this document.

Second, as you read, take on the mindset of a beginner. Listen to what people say, and wonder why they said what they did. Try to suspend your judgment; don't automatically condemn those who made mistakes or assume you know why mistakes occurred. Think about how a particular story is similar and different from issues you have encountered. Come to the workshop prepared to learn with one another the events which took place and their implications. Come with questions that might help you understand and empathize with the points of view that are very different than your own.

You may find yourself wanting to talk about the material in this learning history with others before the Dissemination Workshop. However, in doing so we ask you to consider that you are dissipating the personal energy you bring to the workshop that will combine with others in collectively making sense. You also may want to ask other people questions who have neither read the document nor have the opportunity to attend the workshop with you. We ask that you not talk to others about the learning history before the workshop, that you wait until after the workshop. Later, if you have found the learning history document and the conversation it generated helpful, then you might want to suggest that others form groups and have conversations after reading the learning history.

These are the general guidelines we suggest for discussing a learning history at the workshop itself. In general, the workshop will be successful if it helps to make visible previously unseen reasoning processes, particularly if they are different than expected. Discussing reasoning process, or how you think, is not a trivial matter. It requires safety as well as considerable skill and understanding on the part of all participants. A facilitator may help with this process, as well as some capability on the part of all participants with the concepts for working with mental models. We have generally recommended that people have some introduction to organizational learning concepts for participating in dissemination workshops (this can be done as part of a longer workshop, or developmental series of workshops that organizations conduct).

In starting the workshop, participants are asked what would be necessary for them to come together to openly and honestly discuss their reactions to the stories and what possible lessons the history holds for them. The cover memo that precedes the learning history manuscript and invites people to the workshop, emphasizes that as individuals they have a variety of prior experiences and different attitudes. It is important to remind people that the learning history workshop is a form of a "managerial practice field" where people come to develop shared understanding for learning and change processes.

To develop a shared understanding of a complex change process, the conversation in which team members react to the written document is carefully slowed down. Slowing down the conversation allows people to talk about their perceptions of what happened, the interpretations and attributions they made from events, and the generalizations they have for moving forward. Everyone attending the workshop, not just the facilitator, is asked to take responsibility for creating the conditions that promote learning for themselves and others.

We suggest the following process to facilitate the learning history workshop. This process is meant to provide general guidelines for the flow of conversation, not a rigid segmentation of what we talk about.

Phase One: "What happened?" and "Why?" The conversation is best initiated when people link their comments to what is written in the learning history. We generally ask people to describe what surprised them. Stick to key events and descriptions, noting issues that involved learning.

The question, "What surprised you in reading this document?" is often used to start this conversation. Another good opening question is to ask, "Where did you find yourself quickly making judgments, blaming people for mistakes, wanting to 'fix' things, wishing you could have provided expertise, or otherwise wanting to intervene in the situation?" In short, where do people find themselves reacting?

Another good question, in this phase, is to ask people to describe the things they expected that were not included. For example, in the AutoCo Epsilon story, there are no comments from other line leaders who were ready to learn from Epsilon's example. Were they intrigued? Skeptical? Disappointed? Encouraged? The document doesn't say. Allow yourselves to add notes about what you think might also have taken place "between the lines" of this document.

As people talk through these perceptions, they are adding their own interpretation and attribution to what is written. Often readers' comments may be very different from the commentary and questions written in the learning history's left-hand column. How is what was described similar or different from what you experienced? Where do you have very alternate interpretations from what participants (in the right-hand column) or learning historians (in the left hand column) say? How do notes that people made in left hand columns compare?

If the session is facilitated, then the facilitator should continually ask where it was in the text that people found themselves reacting in different ways. He or she should ask exactly what words led to their interpretations. If there is no facilitator, then participants should continually do this for themselves. By going back to that text, participants can clarify the perceptions and judgments people bring in their reactions from those that are found in the learning history.

The point is to accumulate a shared understanding of "what happened" in the story. When participants agree on "what happened," there are two results. First, differences of perspective have come to the surface. Second, there is a shared base of "data" (or "ground truth," as the U.S. Army calls it), from which significant questions can be raised.

That means it is time to move on to phase two.

Phase Two: "So what?" and "What next?" Can generalizations and implications be drawn from this learning history? What are the implications of the experiences portrayed in the learning history for present initiatives? How typical and significant are the alternative interpretations that came up in this workshop? In this phase we link the past with the present and future. What are the important questions for people to think about as they leave the workshop? What are the responsibilities of people in the workshop in causing the conditions described? Can we identify in ourselves, or help others see, the implications of our behavior patterns that limit our options? What will help us all move forward?

The reading group should consider how their comments link to their responsibilities. What might be the causes of the behavior patterns the group wishes would change, and what responsibility do people have, or could they take, in bringing about desired improvements?

The particular use of learning history dissemination workshops depends upon how it fits into an organization's overall developmental process. For example, what are the organization's objectives in initiating learning processes, and how can they evolve given the particular cultural peculiarities of the organization? The workshop itself and the depth of inquiry it is able to obtain depends upon facilitator skills as well as participants' familiarity, skill, and comfort with mental model and learning concepts.

In several projects where learning histories have been written and used, people's response is not as unanimously positive to the document as was their reception to the reflective interviews. Some people in the organization are enthusiastic about the portrayal of the learning process, others, particularly managers promoting learning efforts and their consultants, have been "disturbed" by what the learning history says. Two major causes for this reaction have been identified. First is the consideration that the learning history puts the problems of the past and present in stark contrast with the ideals for a future. The second cause for dissatisfaction relates to managers' desire for prescriptive histories. They don't just want to be told what happened and how people think about it; they want to know what to do. More theoretical lenses, such as causal loop diagrams which map the forces at play, have been requested from the researchers. People want researchers to move from documenting events to include more synthesis, analysis and recommendations.

It is not clear what the implications of these reactions are for learning histories. In a number of cases there is evidence that managers expected the learning history to provide only the highlights—in essence, the "great achievements" that people in the learning initiative wanted to tell the rest of the organization about. Was the learning history expected to be a recording of success—creating a legacy for the managers and consultants that led the change efforts? What is the tolerance of organizations to read about their own mis-steps and false starts along the road of learning and development? Does the age-old adage, "history is written by the victor," have an implication in these situations?

The response to a learning history may in itself indicate the openness and responsiveness of an organization. Consider, for instance, what happens when you strike a large bell. It may be struck by a variety of objects. The force from those objects reveals the character of the bell in that it rings only at a frequency inherent to its own internal, physical characteristics. Different objects and the force with which they strike the bell affect the sound volume produced, but not the character or frequency of the sound. In a similar way, a learning intervention reveals the character of an organization. Perhaps the learning intervention has been particularly effective, producing a loud tone which more clearly reveals an organization's important characteristics. Once those characteristics are revealed, they can be understood and the organization has gained a new awareness and an opportunity to change more effectively.

Is the resistance to the message of the learning history like the phenomena of holding up a mirror to one's face? When most people look in a brightly lit mirror the initial impression is not one of approval. We notice blemishes and imperfections that we don't normally see. Not only don't we care to see them, often we forget we have them, and that damn mirror is a sharp reminder of reality.

Perhaps learning histories represent that kind of organizational mirror. If so, then people have a pragmatic responsibility to consider the document ever more closely in the context of the vision they are pursuing.

ENDNOTES

◆ PREFACE

1   Mary Walton, *Car: A Drama of the American Workplace*, 1997, New York: W. W. Norton.

2   For more information on the skills, techniques and process of change organizations have used to develop their learning capabilities see Senge, et al. *The Fifth Discipline Fieldbook*, 1995, and *The Dance of Change*, 1999.

3   The term "reflectionable knowledge" was first used, to our knowledge, by organizational studies researcher Otto Scharmer.

4   Argyris and Schön have written many collaborative books, but we recommend Argyris' *Overcoming Organizational Defenses* (1990, New York: Prentice-Hall) as the most accessible for the individual and organizational skills that promote learning.

5   James P. Carse, *Finite and Infinite Games*, 1986, New York: Ballantine Books.

◆ CHAPTER ONE

1   For a list of these achievements and events, see Noticeable Results on page 9. For a chronology of the three-year project, see the project timeline on page 11.

2   The learning history team used a grounded theory, qualitative data analysis methodology to discern key concepts and patterns. See Strauss, 1987, *Qualitative*

Analysis for Social Scientists; Corbin and Strauss, 1990, *Basics of Qualitative Research*; Miles and Humberman, 1994, *Qualitative Data Analysis*, and Glaser and Strauss, 1967, The Discovery of Grounded Theory. In analyzing large quantities of qualitative data with a team of inside and outside learning historian, we have found it helpful to think in terms of meeting three "imperatives"—research (loyalty to the "data"), mythic (loyalty to the "story"), and pragmatic (loyalty to the audience's needs. Each imperative represents a set of "pure" priorities—all important, and all in contention with each other. They can't be approached simultaneously. They are attended to in sequence, but there must be deliberate, balanced consideration of all three, in every phase of a learning history effort.

3   "Collocation" means that people from diverse engineering functions developing the car (i.e. chassis design, air conditioning, suspension, alternator, sound systems, dashboard subsystems, etc.) work from offices in the same location. Team members are physically place together during the time it takes to design the car, instead of coming together only for formally scheduled meetings.

4   Dr. W. Edwards Deming, "Foundation for Management of Quality in the Western World," paper delivered at the Institute of Management Science in Osaka, July 24, 1989, quoted in William J. Latzko and David M. Saunders, *Four Days with Dr. Deming: A Strategy for Modern Methods of Management*, 1995, Reading, MA: Addison-Wesley, p. 35.

5   Russell Ackoff, *Creating the Corporate Future*, 1981, New York: John Wiley and Sons; Peter Senge, *The Fifth Discipline*, 1990, New York: Doubleday; Peter Senge, Art Kleiner, Charlotte Roberts, Rick Ross, Bryan Smith, *The Fifth Discipline FIeldbook*, 1994, New York: Doubleday. Generic structures (also called "system archetypes") are covered in *The Fifth Discipline*, p. 93ff; and *The Fifth Discipline Fieldbook*, p. 12ff.

6   Peter Senge, "Moving Forward: Thinking Strategically About Building Learning Organizations," *The Fifth Discipline Fieldbook*, p. 15; material about guiding ideas on p. 24.

◆ CHAPTER TWO

1   See Peter Senge, *The Fifth Discipline* (1990; New York: Doubleday), p. 93–113 and 378–390; Daniel H. Kim, Systems Archetypes: Diagnosing Systemic Issues and Designing High-Leverage Interventions (1993, Pegasus Communications); and

Senge et al, *The Fifth Discipline Fieldbook* (1994, New York: Doubleday), pages 121–150.

2   The ladder of inference is described in Chris Argyris, *Overcoming Organizational Defenses*, (1990, Englewood Cliffs, NJ: Prentice Hall, p. 88–89); Argyris, Putnam, and Diana McLain Smith, *Action Science*, (1985, San Francisco: Jossey-Bass, pp. 57–58). Also see *The Fifth Discipline Fieldbook*, page 242.

3   The "left-hand column" exercise is based upon the two-column method developed by Chris Argyris and Donald A. Schön. The research method was first presented in their book *Theory in Practice* (1974, San Francisco: Jossey-Bass). Also see T*he Fifth Discipline*, page 195, and *The Fifth Discipline Fieldbook*, page 246.

4   March and Olsen, "A Garbage Can Model of Organizational Choice," in *Administrative Sciences Quarterly*, 1972 and "Garbage Can Models of Decision Making in Organizations" in *Ambiguity and Command*, Pitman Publishing, Inc. 1986).

5   For more information on the "problem solving treadmill" concepts see Daniel Kim's articles, "Using 'Fixes that Fail' to get off the problem-solving treadmill" and "Fixes that Fail: Oiling the Squeaky Wheel—Again and Again . . ." in the November 1990 and September 1992 editions of *The Systems Thinker*, Pegasus Communications, Cambridge, MA)

6   Adapted from "A Framework and Methodology for Linking Individual and Organizational Learning Applications in TQM and Product Development," by Daniel H. Kim, 1993, MIT Ph.D. dissertation, p. 282–296).

7   "Colocation" means that people from the diverse engineering functions developing the car (i.e. chassis design, air conditioning, suspension, alternator, sound systems, dashboard subsystems, etc.) work from offices in the same location. Team members are physically placed together, during the time it takes to design the car, instead of coming together only for formally scheduled meetings.

◆ CHAPTER FOUR

1   For more about the learning labs at Epsilon, see p. 51. For theoretical information on designing managerial practice fields and learning labs see Daniel Kim and Peter Senge, "Putting Systems Thinking into Practice" in *System Dynamics Review*, 1994, Vol. 10, Nos. 2-3, pp. 277-290.

2   The dissertation research of Bent Bakken (Learning and Transfer of Understanding in Dynamic Decision Environments, unpublished doctoral dissertation, Sloan School of Management, Massachusetts Institute of Technology, 1993) reports the difficulty of subjects transferring their learning from one simulation environment to another, similar, simulation environment.

3   For an explanation of playing "the beer distribution game" see Chapter 3, "Prisoners of the system, or prisoners of our own thinking?" in Senge, *The Fifth Discipline*, 1990, New York: Doubleday/Currency, pgs. 27-54.

◆ CHAPTER SEVEN

1   This learning history is focused on the Epsilon project, its learning initiative, and the issues Epsilon's efforts raises within AutoCo. In reading this document a number of people have surfaced questions regarding the relationship of the Epsilon team with senior level managers and the structure and support of the MIT research effort in engaging executives. The Epsilon managers were unable to get top management involved in learning project issues. The team requested, several times, that the OLC help them design a process of engaging the larger system. Involving busy executives and engaging them was the focus of a related research project—the Executive Champions Workshop. This other research project did not meet the immediate needs of the Epsilon managers.

2   The project engagement clinic occurs as part of the process of starting a research project. A set of interviews were conducted with managers on the team to surface known issues. A document with a summary of these interviews was then read by the MIT researchers and Epsilon managers before attending the clinic. The clinic provided an opportunity to test the ability and willingness of managers to engage with challenging issues of the kind that surface through learning initiatives. An important issue raised in the clinic was the implications of conducting research while trying to accomplish business objectives. For more details and list of questions on clinic, see page 15)

3   "Collocation" means that people from the diverse engineering functions developing the car (i.e. chassis design, air conditioning, suspension, alternator, sound systems, dashboard subsystems, etc.) work from offices in the same location. Team members are physically placed together, during the time it takes to design the car, instead of coming together only for formally scheduled meetings.

◆ CHAPTER TEN

1   As it happens, Chris Argyris, one of the critical founders of action science, advised some of the project leaders early in the Epsilon project and continued to observe the evolution of the project from a distance. Many characteristics of action science were employed by the Epsilon team leaders, which makes the action science theory a particularly appropriate framework for examining the ramifications of the learning effort at Epsilon. This essay includes comments made by Chris Argyris during informal discussions of the learning history document.

2   The term "action science" is identified with a book by that name: *Action Science* by Chris Argyris, Robert Putnam, and Diana McLain Smith (1987, San Francisco: Jossey-Bass). This book builds upon the precepts of Kurt Lewin's approach to action research and John Dewey's approach to experiential learning, with specific implications for research and research methods. Other books by Chris Argyris and Donald Schön cover the theory, methods and applications of these concepts in organizational settings. The books which have been often mentioned by the MIT team which undertook the learning project at AutoCo include: *The Reflective Practitioner, How Professionals Think in Action* by Donald Schön, 1983, Basic Books; *Organizational Learning: A Theory of Action Perspective* by Chris Argyris and Donald Schön, 1978, Reading, MA: Addison-Wesley; *Overcoming Organizational Defenses, Facilitating Organizational Learning* by Chris Argyris, 1990, Englewood Cliffs, NJ: Prentice Hall; *Experiential Learning, Experience as the Source of Learning and Development* by David Kolb, 1984, Englewood Cliffs, NJ: Prentice Hall.

    The doctoral thesis of Daniel Kim ("A Framework and Methodology for Linking Individual and Organizational Learning: Applications in TQM and Product Development" unpublished doctoral dissertation, Sloan School of Management, Cambridge, MA, 1993, Chapter 6) provides the ideas and insights of a researcher applying organizational learning and system dynamic approaches in working with a product development team.

3   Ibid. Argyris et al., 1987: page 4.

4   Op. cit., Argyris and Schön, 1978.

5   In Model I, behaviors are governed by (1) achieving the purpose as an individual has defined it, (2) winning and not losing, (3) suppressing negative feelings and (4) emphasizing rationality. These governing variables lead to actions that emphasize unilateral control of environment and tasks as well as unilateral pro-

tection of oneself and others. The consequence of Model I is escalating errors and decreased effectiveness in problem solving. Model I suggests that there are limits to the boundaries of what is acceptable. There is low freedom of choice and difficulty in producing valid information, resulting in defensive interactions and relationships. Learning is inhibited because there is little public information and testing to determine if strategies are effective in achieving desired results.

In working with organizations and confronting individuals with predictions based on these assumptions, Argyris and Schön have found that people espouse an approach which is opposite Model I. The governing variables proposed in opposite Model I are (1) broad participation in defining purpose, (2) everyone wins and no one loses, (3) expressing feelings and (4) suppress cognitive expressions of rationalizing action. In opposite Model I, protection of self and unilateral control are present but hidden, and conditions for learning are the similar to the overt use of Model I.

In developing a system which produces conditions and behaviors consistent with learning, Argyris and Schön develop what they call Model II theory-in-use. The governing variables are (1) valid information, (2) free and informed choice, and (3) internal commitment. While these governing variables are often espoused in organizations, they are not often practiced. The role of the action scientist is to behave consistent with these variables, produce actions consistent with them in the organization, and thereby interrupt the counterproductive characteristics of Model I.

Model II behaviors involve sharing control with participants who are competent and have a role in designing and implementing their actions. The unilateral advocacy of Model I, or concealing one's views in opposite Model I, is superseded by behaviors and thinking which combine advocating for what is desired and inquiring into what others want. In a Model II approach people's inferences and evaluations are illustrated by the data that led to them, the surfacing conflicting views is encouraged, and thoughtful consideration is given to creating conditions for public testing. As its proponents themselves recognize (Argyris et al., 1990, page 102), "at an espoused level Model II . . . sounds like motherhood and apple pie . . . the trick is to produce them in the real world."

6   The recent update to Argyris and Schön's original organizational learning book (*Organizational Learning II, Theory, Method and Practice, 1996,* Reading, MA: Addison-Wesley,) explicitly expresses their concerns about the literature on organizational learning. They examine two sets of studies—research on naturally occurring innovations (medical field innovation and strategic decision making

about DRAM markets) and intervention research (decentralization, activity-based costing, total quality management, reengineering, and strategic human resource management)—to find limited learning as the consistent outcomes (see pages 200–242).

In examining cases of organizational learning and change, Argyris and Schön point to mixed results around learning as coming from gaps of explanation (how organization kept undiscussable the issues raised by knowledge privately held by members) and gaps of implementation (interventions that provide only partial or temporary improvement).

7   From Argyris and Schön, op cit., 1978. Model I theory-in-use table from pages 62 and 63; Model II theory-in-use table from page 137. The tables as presented by Argyris and Schön include additional concepts of "consequences for behavioral world," "consequences for learning" and "effectiveness."

8   Ibid. "A Comprehensive Model II Intervention," pages 150 to 176. Also see Argyris, op cit. 1990, and Argyris, *Knowledge for Action: A Guide to Overcoming Barriers to Organizational Change*, 1993, San Francisco: Jossey-Bass.

9   Ibid. page 250.

10 The emphasis is on producing actions consistent with these theories. While people may espouse Model II ideas as their behaviors, or the desired behaviors of others, they frequently take actions which are consistent with Model I. Or, they often espouse opposite Model I, which are then themselves embedded in a Model I view of the world, and when expected changes don't happen, frequently revert to overt behaviors consistent with Model I theory-in-use (Argyris et al., op cit., 1985, page 92).

11 Argyris and Schön (ibid., page 250) suggest that researchers interested in (limited) organizational learning "attend to the directly observable data of organizational inquiry which must, in turn, be linked to higher levels of aggregation." They propose that researchers work in collaboration with practitioners who seek to build capability for enhancing the "rare events of productive organizational learning."

12 Ibid. pages 246–249.

13 Organizational defensive routines are akin to the defensive behaviors associated with individuals. When confronted with difficult or embarrassing information, individuals react "defensively." Defensive reactions include continuously protect-

ing oneself from criticism, exposure of one's shortcomings, or other real or perceived threats to one's self-image. Defensive behaviors limit what one hears, thus keeping oneself ignorant to the consequences of one's own behaviors, and are often accompanied by aggressive counter-behaviors. Defensive behaviors in individuals and organizations are antilearning, overprotective and self-sealing.

At an organizational level, defensive routines are "actions or policies that prevent individuals or segments of the organization from experiencing embarrassment or threat. Simultaneously, they prevent people from identifying and getting rid of the causes of the potential embarrassment or threat" (Argyris, 1990, page 25).

14　While Senge's approach to organizational learning is known for emphasizing a systems thinking component, it should be noted that Model I and Model II, particularly at the organizational level of aggregation, are themselves systems concepts. Each are a set of governing variables and action strategies which are compatible, coherent, and consistent with one another. A shift from Model I to Model II is not accomplished by changing one governing variable at a time, but requires that one set of values, strategies and assumptions supplant another set of values, strategies, and assumptions. Systems thinking concepts inform and are embedded in action science approaches.

15　For a description of the project process used by the MIT Center for Organizational Learning, including a "project engagement clinic," see George Roth and Peter Senge, "From Theory to Practice: Research Territory, Processes and Structure at an Organizational Learning Center," *Journal of Change Management*, Vol. 9, Iss. 1, 1996.

16　The example of Model I includes the use of an espoused theory that is opposite Model I. A distinction is made (Argyris, Putnam, and Smith, 1987, page 92) between Model I and opposite Model I. Opposite Model I, which is a mirror image of Model I, is based on governing variables of (1) participation in defining purposes; (2) everyone wins, no one loses; (3) express feelings; and (4) suppress cognitive intellective aspects of action. However, the elements of opposite Model I are embedded in an underlying Model I theory-in-use in which unilateral protection and control are present but camouflaged. People try to work some elements of opposite Model I, and when they don't work, revert to Model I. The behavioral consequences for learning and effectiveness are thus the same as Model I.

17　See Schein, "Three Cultures of Management: The Key to Organizational Learning," *Sloan Management Review*, Vol. 36, No.1, Fall 1996.

18　Ibid.

19 Op. cit., Argyris and Schön, 1978 and 1996.

20 See Schein, "How Can Organizations Learn Faster: The Challenge of Entering the Green Room," *Sloan Management Review*, Vol. 34, No. 2, Winter 1993 and "Can Learning Cultures Evolve," *The Systems Thinker*, Pegasus Communications, Cambridge, MA, August 1996. Typical approaches to change in organizations have been based on increasing survival anxiety—creating crisis and using fear to propel change. An important consideration in promoting learning and change is the relationship between the fear of not learning (Survival Anxiety) relative to the fear of entering into unpredictable and unknown situations (Learning Anxiety).

21 Op. cit., Argyris, 1990, page xiii.

22 Op. cit., Argyris, 1990.

23 Joseph Campbell describes this situation as the archetypal story of the hero's journey. A foundation of a culture are the myths that provide for, and shape, the understanding people have of their social world and how it functions (see Joseph Campbell, *Myths to Live By*, 1972, New York: Bantam Books).

24 The story of the Ford Taurus team is told in Mary Walton, *Car*, 1997, New York: W.W. Norton & Company.

25 This principle extends back to the early research and writing by Chris Argyris (*Intervention Theory and Method*, 1970, Reading, MA: Addison-Wesley) wherein he proposes that creating the conditions in which these appropriate values are realized in the organization is the primary work of the interventionist. Thus, action science holds a normative position in terms of its desire to change the status quo and create conditions governed by Model II values as the legitimate basis for action science research.

◆ **CHAPTER ELEVEN**

1 Roth, George, "Learning Histories: Using a new form of documentation to assess and facilitate organizational Learning," 1996, MIT Sloan School of Management working paper 3968.

2 Van Maanen, J. (1988), *Tales of the Field,* University of Chicago Press: Chicago.

3 The Learning Initiative at the AutoCo Delta Assembly Plant, 1996, by Ann Thomas

(see http://www.sol-ne.org/res/wp/AutoCoDeltaLH.html).

4   From Professor Showing Young, National Sun Yat-sen University, Taiwan, ROC letter to Peter Senge, January 25, 1992.

5   Michael, Donald, On Learning to Plan—and Planning to Learn, 1993, 1997, Alexandria, VA: Miles River Press.

6   Argyris, C. and Schön, D., *Organizational Learning: A Theory of Action Perspective*, 1978, Reading, MA: Addison Wesley.

7   Dewey, John, *Experience and Education*, 1938, Kappa Delta Pi; Piaget, Jean, *Psychology and Epistemology*, 1971, Middlesex, England: Penguin Books; Burner, Jerome (1964) "The Course of Cognitive Growth," *American Psychologist*, 19: 1-5.

8   Lewin, Kurt, *Field Theory in Social Science*, 1951, New York: Harper & Row; Lippitt, Ronald, *Training in Community Relations*, 1949, New York: Harper & Row; Argyris, C. and D. Schön, *Organizational Learning: A Theory of Action Perspective*, 1978, Reading, MA: Addison Wesley; Kolb, Deborah, *Experiential Learning: Experience as the Source of Learning and Development*, 1984, Englewood Cliffs, NJ: Prentice Hall.

9   Argyris, C., *Overcoming Organizational Defenses: Facilitating Organizational Learning*, 1990, Englewood Cliffs, NJ: Prentice Hall.

10   Kolb, Deborah, 1984, op cit. page 21.

11   Argyris, C. (1990) O*vercoming Organizational Defenses: Facilitating Organizational Learning*, Englewood Cliffs, NJ: Prentice Hall.

12   Schein, Edgar, *Organizational Culture and Leadership*, 1985, San Francisco: Jossey Bass; Schein, Edgar, *Organizational Culture and Leadership*, 2nd Edition, 1992, San Francsico: Jossey Bass.

13   Schein, Edgar, 1985, page 17.